electronic trading masters

electronic

SECRETS
FROM THE
PROS!

trading
masters

ALLEN JAN BAIRD

John Wiley & Sons, Inc.

New York • Chichester • Weinheim • Brisbane • Singapore • Toronto

DISCLAIMER

Library of Congress Cataloging-in-Publication Data:

Electronic trading masters : secrets from the pros / edited by Allen Jan Baird.
    p.   cm. — (Wiley online trading for a living)
    Includes bibliographical references.
    ISBN 0-471-40193-5 (cloth : alk. paper)
    1. Electronic trading of securities.   I. Baird, Allen Jan.   II. Series.
HG4515.95 .E44 2000
332.64'0285'4678—dc21   00-049612

Printed in the United States of America.

10 9 8 7 6 5 4 3 2 1

For Kira, with love.

preface

Electronic stock trading has recently become one of the most notable and potentially lucrative professions on Wall Street. Public interest in this topic is reflected in the constant stream of stories appearing in print and television, as well as the dozen or so books that have been published in the last year alone.

This book of interviews enters the world of short-term securities day trading in a way that is different from self-help guides or other books. It delves into the real trading experiences and strategies of successful traders in detail and with a much deeper understanding as a background. In many cases, actual trades are given thorough examination over many pages to accurately capture how successful traders trade. How are some of the most successful traders earning $10,000 or more on their good weeks? For the traders interviewed in this book, there is hardly a month in the last two years when they have not been profitable, a remarkable record of both success and consistency.

Rather than provide another get-rich-quick format of interview questions, the interviews range very broadly over the previous trading history of the participants so that their evolution as a trader can be seen. Individuals have tried first one form of trading and then another before they discovered success in electronic direct access trading.

The people interviewed emerge as real people with life histories and memorable personalities who have emotionally struggled and often continue to struggle with trading. Rather than reading an interview with another Bob, Dick, or Harry, whose names are forgotten by the end of the interview, the traders interviewed here appear in full portrait as someone you have gotten to know as a complete person.

When I started this book, my criteria for inclusion was that a trader be actively trading on a direct access electronic system for at least two years, demonstrate a profit record as self-reported over that time of at least $500,000 per year, and experience few if any monthly losses. I found a number of traders who made much more than this, but were not as consistent month after month, and they were not included. I also included a few traders who made somewhat less than this, but whose experience or style of trading was notable in some regard. I believe consistency is as, if not more important, than the total amount of profitability as a sign of success.

I intended to interview only traders who traded NASDAQ with Level II, since this is the arena where electronic trading has had the most dramatic impact. However, several traders who met my criteria otherwise but tended to predominantly trade listed stocks are also included. These traders had very unique styles of trading and, in one case, provided the most detailed method of "tape reading" listed stocks I have ever seen in print.

I have also included an interview with Matthew Andresen, the president of Island ECN. His perspective on electronic trading is extremely important for those who wish to understand how the current issues of the electronic marketplace will affect trading in the near future.

In no sense are the traders interviewed here an exhaustive list of successful day traders. There are certainly very many successful traders who could have been included had I known about them or if they had consented to be included. I found some successful traders who did not wish to be interviewed, either because they did not want any personal publicity in an age when success may bring scrutiny or scorn, or perhaps because they did not wish the methods of their success to be widely known. Most of the traders interviewed in this book were forthright with their strategies and techniques, and only once did a trader balk at revealing the details of his strategy.

As the book neared completion, I became acutely aware that all the traders interviewed were men, and I called three firms to locate at least one woman trader who met my criteria. I was told that there were definitely women traders who met my criteria of success although they were much fewer in number. A manager at one firm who had closely observed successful woman traders made the tantalizing observation that woman were far more likely than men to accept the principles and techniques of sound trading at face value, were more likely to implement them without troubling issues of maintaining discipline, and were more likely than men to ask for help when they needed it. If this observation is true, then it would suggest that women may have some abilities that men find particularly difficult to acquire. Unfortunately, I was not able to locate and interview a successful woman trader in time for the completion of this book, and so this topic remains unexplored.

I did not wish to restrict my interviewees to the traders at any one firm exclusively, but to search out traders from different firms who might have different perspectives and trading styles. Although I was not able to include traders from all the different trading firms, of which there are scores, I was able to find a number of traders from a diverse group of firms. In no sense, however, should the traders included in this book be taken as a valid sample of all successful traders, when I speak of "all successful traders" I am referring only to those interviewed here. When I began this book, I was worried that successful traders were trading in similar styles which would result in a somewhat repetitive series of interviews. I was delightfully surprised to find, however, that although all successful traders interviewed agree on the core sound principles of trading, the implementation of these principals in practical strategies can be quite diverse. This makes sense when you realize that markets are always composed of participants who have different market perspectives and trading styles. That, after all, is just what makes a market.

Although this book largely consists of interviews with individual traders, I have included three other chapters that may be of general interest. Some may wonder about my own trading experience and qualifications for dong this book, so I have included a Prologue which is an autobiographical account of my own trading experience up to and including my attempts to learn electronic trading. While I do not include myself among the group of "Master Traders," I have had a broad professional background in trading and have found some success trading electronically.

I have also included a chapter dealing with several interrelated issues about trading and the securities industry. These topics consider whether day trading is a new or old profession, how profitable day traders are as a group and why, a short history of how and why NASDAQ has emerged as the foremost interactive electronic marketplace, and how regulatory and economic issues are likely to shape trading in the near future.

The final chapter in the book draws together the common experience and knowledge of the traders interviewed, to discover if there are any general principles all successful traders agree on, but also noting areas of difference.

acknowledgments

I owe a debt of gratitude to many people for helping me finish this book. No small part of the success of this book is due to the interviewees themselves who generously made time available for interviews and ensured that the interviews were enjoyable to me as well as being informative. I owe particular thanks to Brad Luce who without complaint sat for a second interview on short notice when our first interview was lost because of a recording malfunction.

Peter Kearns and Johan Carlson at Lexit Financial Group were particularly generous in allowing me a sabbatical to finish this book just as we were in the critical early stages of establishing our proprietary trading group. Jeffrey DiCicco, my associate in this project, is due great thanks for taking over my responsibilities at this stage and offering his constant friendship and support at all times.

Many others supplied critical help or support in doing this book, including Andrew Goldman, of Island, ECN; Michael Lieber, Lieber and Weissmand Securities; Jay McEntire and Clint Case, Protrader.com; Robert Kanter, ETG; Paula Delaurentis and Gabrielle Santicchia, Carlin Equities; Keith Drymond, Momentum Securities; Gary Roth, Equity Trading; Martie Flores, Milan Kojic, and Tony Oz.

Claudio Campuzano, my editor at John Wiley & Sons, actively believed in this book from its proposal stage and was constantly supportive thereafter. Jennifer MacDonald was helpful in preparing the manuscript at John Wiley & Sons. My copyeditor,

Charlotte Saikia, deserves much thanks for her many good suggestions and improvements.

My wife Kathleen, who has patiently endured more than one book I have written, proofread chapters and offered many useful suggestions. Our daughter Kira has always been a source of relaxation during my breaks in writing, and I'm sure has helped me input a keystroke or two. To both of them, I owe special thanks.

contents

electronic trading masters

prologue

Some may wonder about my own trading experiences and qualifications for undertaking this book. Although I do not consider myself a Master Trader, I have had some experience as both a financial author and a professional trader. You may find my experiences either interesting, informative, or amusing, depending on your own success in the markets.

I'm surprised that I didn't discover direct access electronic trading in stocks earlier than I did. I first became aware of the stock market as a young boy, when in May 1963, the stock market suffered its worst monthly decline since 1929. *Life* magazine showed pictures of older people with tears in their eyes, sick with worry. Becoming interested in the topic, I discovered in my local business library a copy of Robert Edwards and John Magee's *Technical Analysis of Stock Trends,* which I read with fascination. Although I had no money to invest myself, I naively wondered why other people didn't apply these techniques and make a lot of money.

When I entered college, the cultural landscape was considerably different than it is today. Business students on most campuses had the lowest grade point averages of any major, and their social status was not much higher. I opted for a career as an academic, but I sometimes dabbled in stocks, without giving it much attention, and without too much success. I bought wheat futures once using a simple moving average system just before the biggest bull market in grains in a decade and tripled my modest account in several months. My broker was astonished when I asked him to close the account because I needed the money for graduate school.

A chance encounter with a fellow graduate student at the University of Pennsylvania in the summer of 1982 was to be a decisive turning point in my professional life. He remarked that Stan Weinstein, a stock market forecaster, had just issued a call that the a new bull market in stocks was to begin. I knew enough about the stock market to know that it led the turning points in the business cycle, and that the average post-World War II recession lasted between one and two years—just about where the economy was in the summer of 1982. Deciding that Weinstein was probably right although not necessarily for the right reason, I bought six-month call options on IBM, GM, and other blue chip stocks.

My timing was perfect. This was two weeks before the exact bottom of the 1980–1982 bear market in stocks. Within two months, my account had tripled in value. Naturally, I believed I would soon be rich. Unfortunately, I was also soon to prove the truth of two proverbs about speculating: (1) It's bad luck to make money when you start, and (2) one shouldn't confuse making money in a bull market with having brains.

After my initial success, I felt without any particular justification, that the rise in stocks had been too rapid. I decided to sell my calls and then to sell more calls short in the expectation that stocks would sell off temporarily. Perhaps they did for a few days, but they quickly resumed their strong advance, and I was starting to lose back what I had made. I was fortunate for a beginning trader to have enough common sense not to continue to sit on losing positions. But I did lose money, with some ups and downs, for the next three years trading part-time.

During these early years of part-time trading I had finished a Ph.D. dissertation in developing a multivariate regression model for forecasting international time series fertility rates, which later won an academic prize and was published as a book. Although I had been losing money slowly for three years trading part-time, I felt that my statistical training, if only applied correctly to the stock market, should prove rewarding. After all, if I could predict the future course of birth rates, why not the stock market? So in 1985, I decided to quit my academic posts and trade full time as a retail client.

Rather than concentrate on trading individual stocks, which sometimes moved with the general market and sometimes against it, I traded OEX stock index options and tried to predict the short-term moves of the general market. My first year of trading full time was not a success. I had developed some short-term statistical models based on volume and momentum that I believe in retrospect were quite accurate, I used these models to try to pick the tops and sell short in generally rising markets. Although I was often correct and the market would sell off, the market never seemed to sell off that much, and would resume its advance leaving me scrambling to cover my short calls. I seemed to be correct temporarily but the market would quickly reverse. I can see now that I did not have a problem in predicting the market, but I did have a problem of psychological perception, which lead me to try persistently to trade against the trend.

At that time, I perceived that my problem was that I was trying to trade the market short term, without having full and immediate control of my order execution and also its cost. I had been among the first to use a Quotrek device—a hand-held receiver of live trading data via satellite. But I noticed that the prices I received on my data feed were at variance with the prices I could expect to receive on my executed orders. There was considerable "slippage" in these two prices, which was usually to my disadvantage.

I determined that there were several causes for this slippage. When I noticed a change in market trend, I still had to call my broker, relay my order verbally, have him reconfirm verbally to me, then have him send my order to their trading desk where it was then relayed to the floor of the exchange, where finally a floor broker executed my order. This took time, and very valuable time it was. As I later realized when I became a floor trader myself, this time delay could be as much as five to ten minutes.

I also realized that even once my order was received on the floor, it had to be exercised against the bid/offer spread of traders on the floor, and that in fast-moving markets this bid/offer spread could be wide. Again, as I learned later when I became a floor trader myself, that bid/offer spread was often very inefficient (especially in options) depending on how good or honest your broker was, and how busy the market was. Finally, I realized I was paying a relatively large percentage of my expected profit in commissions, despite the fact that I had negotiated relatively low rates as an active trader.

By the end of my first year trading full time as a retail client, I had lost about $30,000. The cost of my learning curve, like many new traders, was high. I was emotionally devastated and realized I could not continue trading the way I was. I decided, however, that my problems could be overcome if I became a member of an exchange myself. I would have immediate knowledge of prices, total control of my order, and I would pay just a fraction of what I was paying in retail commission rates. I am certain that if my experiences had taken place in 1996 and not 1986, I would have become an electronic trader. Without that choice at the time, however, I discovered where the cheapest membership of any stock or stock index futures exchange was in the United States. In March of 1986, I paid $100 for a membership on the New York Futures Exchange.

The validity of my reasons for becoming a floor trader were initially confirmed. With the ability to immediately execute my own orders and paying only dollar commissions, my trend of losses ceased. It has been a source of wonder to me ever since that more large retail clients didn't do what I did. Many of them are paying in yearly commissions many times over what it would cost them to lease a membership on many smaller stock and option exchanges.

Despite my floor membership advantage, however, for the next year I did not make a profit. I did not employ any one method of trading consistently enough to benefit from its success but was exploring different styles of trading available to floor traders. After about a year, I started to make money consistently, if only modestly, by selling puts and calls and collecting the premium and then using futures to hedge my positions when the market went against me. It was a simple strategy, but one that seemed to be working.

I started to employ my option strategy about eight months before the stock market crash of 1987, and only a kind fate let me be modestly successful with this strategy before then. If I had used this strategy longer and made more money, I'm certain now that I would have been bankrupted by the crash. My position going into Monday, October 19, had been short 10 out-of-the-money New York Stock Exchange Index (NYSEI) calls and short 10 out-of-the-money NYSEI puts. I was also short about four NYSEI futures contracts to partially hedge the short put leg of the position. This position was actually slightly bullish, since I did not believe the market was going to crash but would probably rally.

On the day of the crash, the market came in lower and continued to drop as my short puts went in-the-money. As a defensive tactic, I continued to sell futures until my short futures were equal in number to my short in-the-money puts. This is a classically fully hedged option position, and while I lost money, I presumed that the money lost would be limited. What I did not count on, was the behavior of options prices which under rare and extremely exceptional circumstances may move counter to general prices, if the extrinsic value of an option is priced in terms of extreme volatility. This is exactly what happened for the first time in traded options in October 1987.

To see this, consider that the short out-of-the-money calls I had sold *before* the crash for $400, were worth $2,500 *after* the crash even though they were even more out-of-the-money by 500 Dow Jones points! This is paradoxical and seems to defy common sense. Yet, it is theoretically justified if the market is expected to move up or down 200 percent in the next month. Another factor in the perversity of option prices at this time was that market makers could no longer freely "make a market" in options because of their own restricted financial circumstances. The options market had become illiquid and inefficient and I found that I could not cover my short options because there was no one able to sell them back to me. I and a partner lost a considerable amount in the crash, and I decided to take a break in trading for almost a year.

When I came back to the New York Futures Exchange in 1988, the volume on the exchange had dried up. Daily option volume, which before the crash had traded many thousands a day, then traded only several hundred contracts. Nevertheless, I decided to resume trading as a market maker in options, and applied new strategies that would later be published in my book, *Option Market Making.* I was successful with these strategies over the next 10 years that I was a floor trader. The exemplary proof of properly conceived market maker positions was shown in the mini-crash of October 1989, when I made $150,000 in one day. In 1990, I used this money to buy a seat on the New York Cotton Exchange, after which I did not trade a stock for the next nine years.

It wasn't until March of 1999, that I became involved in electronic stock trading, when I visited the branch office of some novice electronic stock traders who were consistently losing money. Why they were losing money became apparent to me very quickly: They had little understanding of loss control or money management. Traders routinely took 400 or 500 shares in positions, when it was clear that they had no track record of consistent success or sufficient capital to justify this size position. Their apparent attitude was that if you believed enough to buy a stock, then you should buy as much as possible!

In addition, most novice traders had little conception of taking small losses. Having taken large positions, they felt determined to show a profit, even as the stock moved against them two, three, five, or more dollar points per share. Taking large positions without taking controlled losses is a prescription for financial disaster as many regretfully learned.

This fortuitous encounter with stocks, however, made me realize how momentous the changes in stock trading had become. It was quickly apparent to me that "Level II" NASDAQ direct access is directly equivalent to floor trading, albeit a new kind of electronic floor trading. The immediate electronic control and execution of orders is exactly the floor trader's advantage. Also, the three cents a share commission for execution I was paying at the time, was close to professional floor trader's commission advantage. I therefore started trading stocks myself on direct access systems.

I went through several stages in my first six months of trading before I began to show some consistency in my own profitability. Although I had been trading for many years, trading stocks on NASDAQ Level II requires some adjustment and learning. Although I had been warned that speed of execution is a critical factor, most successful floor traders routinely make trading decisions within about a tenth or quarter of a second and this was not a problem for me.

A more expensive lesson concerned mastering Level II execution systems and experiencing a shut down of the system while I had a stock position open. I mastered trading on three different execution systems. The glitches and peculiarities of each of these systems cost me money in the process of learning. One system in particular cost me several thousand dollars before I realized that it was treating my attempt to sell an existing long position as a short sale, even though I had not requested short sale status. A short sale can only be executed on an up-tick according to the up-tick rule, but since I was attempting to exit a long position in the face of some market decline, there were not many up-ticks to allow me to exit my long position. Eventually, I learned that this particular execution system would only act in this way when I had placed a limit order to sell my existing long position above the market even though this order had not been executed. I had to cancel all limit orders in this stock before I could exit an existing long position without it being treated as a new short sale. This peculiar feature was not on the other execution systems I had used, and I bear full responsibility for not learning about it before hand, but nevertheless it was a costly mistake. Learning about execution systems probably cost me a total of about $4,000.

Some early advice I received to trade only NYSE stocks was well-intentioned but less than helpful. I do not prefer to trade NYSE stocks for short-term trading profits and do not do well when I try. While Supper-DOT access does save time and represents a gain in control over the retail order, trading listed stocks short-term requires specialized techniques and experience about interpreting the publicly unseen context of specialist intention, what is on the specialist's book, and the floor brokers and traders in the "crowd" around the specialist's booth. Yet there are certainly successful traders who are able to "read the tape" and make good estimated guesses about what is going on the NYSE floor just by examining the record of time and sales of each individual transaction as it is reported.

Trading on NASDAQ, however, I found to be is a totally different matter. The existing orders and participants are much more easily distinguished. There is still considerable nondisclosure of orders on broker order books, but the marketplace has a much more transparent character. Indeed, the NASDAQ market resembles the situation of floor traders exactly. No one knows each order book for each broker and trader, but each trader is able to trade directly and immediately with any other trader or broker. The game is to discover whether there are major buyers or sellers in the market, who are usually trying to disguise what they are doing, and then trade accordingly. I decided, therefore, after losing several thousands of dollars on listed stocks, only to trade NASDAQ stocks where I thought there would be greater flow of information advantage. For me, at least, this proved eventually to be the correct response.

It took me several more months and several more thousands of dollars of losses, however, to begin to understand the trading character of the different groups of NASDAQ stocks. One group of stocks tended to trade in relatively narrow ranges of only several dollar points per share during the day but were highly liquid in having many market makers and traders trading on both sides of the market at each price level. Microsoft, Intel, and other stocks with this high level of interest and volume were part of this group. Generally, I recommend people who are beginning trading using Level II to start with these stocks until they feel comfortable reading a Level II screen and mastering their execution system. You probably won't make too much money, but you probably won't lose too much either. Another group of stocks, such as Amazon and Yahoo [in 1999], were much more volatile and could move several dollars in as many seconds. They also had fewer market makers and traders on each price level, which sometimes made it tricky to get in or out of the stock where you intended.

I also learned that the much heralded immediate execution on NASDAQ Level II was strictly speaking not correct. I discovered that in fact it took about 2 or 3 seconds from the time I would enter a buy or sell order for it to reach the counterparty I wished to trade with. Apparently this was at least some function of the speed of the Internet connections and relays I was using. Although these few seconds may seem trivial, in fast-moving stocks, this time delay can prove critical, if not disasterous. Through experience, for example, I learned that the bids and offers on stocks such as Amazon or Yahoo frequently do not remain displayed for much longer than 2 or 3 seconds. The net result is that if you are trading these stocks with a communication system that is slow by 2 or 3 seconds, you will find that you are not able to buy or sell to other participants before their bid or offer disappears or is taken by someone else who may have a faster system than you. There is nothing more frustrating than trying to take a profit by hitting someone's bid at $95, not being executed and then trying to hit every bid displayed down to $92 before being executed just as the market now rallies all the way back to $95. So much for "immediate" execution, and I realized after several more thousands of dollars of losses, not to try to trade this second group of stocks unless I was trying to hold for a very large gain or was able to improve the speed of my Internet connections.

During these early months of trading on NASDAQ, I attempted to discover a pattern in the participation of the other market makers and ECNs, but without quick success. Although the number of ECNs is relatively small, there are literally hundreds of different market makers who can trade a stock. Who is important and who is not? Although I had learned enough to pay attention to large institutional market makers, there were still many of these and I did not seem to be able to easily discover recognizable patterns about whether they were buying or selling as a concerted strategy.

I had been advised by one experienced trader that it would take me six months to a year of watching market action before I would be able to see what the major players were doing in a NASDAQ stock. I did not feel I wanted to wait quite this long for my education to be complete. So I bought a computer screen capture program that records everything happening on a computer screen in a file that can be played back. On my computer screen, I set up Level II screens, price charts, general market indices, and so forth and recorded what happened all day. When I played these files back, and then replayed them, I was astonished to discover after only several days of study that I could now "read" what was going on in the market rather discernibly. Market player moves and trades, which lasted only several seconds and had slipped by my attention while normally watching the market, I could now observe closely and study by repetitive playing of my tape files.

I discovered that there were at least a dozen market configurations that were very important in predicting where prices were likely to go next, both in the short run and in the next major move. Not all of this was straightforward signaling, and there was considerable deception in market activity by major players, but even these deceptions had repetitive patterns that could be recognized.

When I started to trade NASDAQ stocks again after this discovery, I found that I was now grossing sufficient profits to cover my commissions and had reached the level of trading where I could trade and expect not to lose money. Part of my difficulty in making a profit, however, was that although I could see where prices were likely headed over the short term, the slowness of my execution system and Internet connection still prevented me from fully capturing the profit potential of what I saw. While I waited to improve the speed of that connection, I realized I must find some other key to trading to be successful.

What I found was that there was a broad third group of NASDAQ stocks that I had not been trading, but it was probably where the most profit potential actually lay. Why it took me so long to discover this group of stocks I do not know, but it happened when I was talking to a new trader who showed highly erratic patterns of profits and losses day after day. On this particular day, however, he was up about $2,500 by early afternoon trading just two hundred shares per trade. I noticed the two stocks he had been trading, which I had never heard of, and put them on my screen.

It was immediately apparent to me why he was successful trading that day: There was major buying or accumulation going on in these two stocks. The stocks would go up several points and then back off to levels where major market makers began buying again, pushing the stock up several more points. This had been going on almost all day with no major pull backs.

My problems with slowness of Internet communication and execution system were not likely to be a problem in these stocks since the players routinely left their bids and offers up for 10 or 20 seconds. I started to trade these two stocks for the rest of that day and noticed quickly that I was starting to make money. It happened that the price pattern of these stocks continued the next day, and I continued to make profits.

I realized that the missing piece of the puzzle to profitable trading for me had been finding the right stocks to trade. I had previously been spending most of my time trying to trade the stocks in groups one and two, and somehow neglected to discover this third group. In some cases, these stocks were stocks in the news for some reason or another, or would soon be in the news. But as I later learned more fully, many of these stocks had no reportable news stories and, indeed, seemed to have few other traders, as evidenced by ECN activity, trading them. But how could I discover which stocks were trading like these stocks?

A key part in solving this problem of early identification was that I subscribed to a commercially available "filter" program which would identify stocks according to user criteria. Stocks, for example, that were making new 20-day highs on higher than normal volume, or whatever the user wished to input as a criteria. This was the answer to my problem, although it took me a month or so to master how to effectively use this kind of program. At first I was seduced by the almost magic quality of having stocks being signaled to me that were meeting my criteria and I tried to jump in and join the emerging trend. However, after one particularly frustrating day in which I lost money in every single one of the stocks I was trading by this method, I realized I was doing something wrong. If I could consistently lose money by any method of trading stocks, I realized I had the key to a successful strategy and that was simply to reverse what I was doing. I started to short the "filtered" stocks if it were apparent by market action and Level II that the upward trend in these stocks was weak or overextended. And, indeed, I did start to make money using this method.

I now use my filter program more generally to generate stock leads that I may or may not trade from either the long or short side, but these stocks may be displaying important trend potential. I do not use the filter as a mechanical trading tool but as a preliminary selection list that I will follow for the day or days to follow, continually adding and dropping stocks to this list. Among the 30 or 40 stocks I am following, I may find 5 or 10 that I will trade during the day for periods of time, or sometimes all day. I was not only watching my selective group of stocks exclusively, but I was continuing to watch the market as a whole for signs of overall market strength or weakness, and trying to align my trading in any one stock with this overall market direction.

I also gradually became very skilled in short-term scalping tactics. While still trading only 200 share positions, I began to experience first $500 and then $1,000 gross profit days. Because I was making a large number of trades per day, commissions often ate up much or all of my gross profit, but I had little doubt that my skill was greatly improving. Unfortunately, I was still using an execution system that was particularly cumbersome for this kind of fast trading, did not have a direct link to trading with INCA (the most liquid ECN), and did not have a dedicated communications line which probably doubled my time to complete an execution. Nevertheless, when I made my first $1,000 net profit after commissions one day, I realized I had mastered this trading technique and my subsequent trading has only confirmed that this was my turning point.

At the time I had started to trade electronically, there were few books available about the topic and no formal training. However, I had traded successfully for many years as a futures and options floor trader, so I was not exactly inexperienced. Was it possible that a new trader could follow in my footsteps and learning trading with proper instruction?

About this time I was approached by an online electronic brokerage, with a proposal to start a proprietary trading desk in stocks. I was familiar with the famous bet made between Richard Dennis and William Eckhardt about whether a completely inexperienced group of people could be trained to become successful commodity traders. Dennis won the bet and that group of traders went on to gain some public recognition as the "Turtles." Could the same result apply to stock traders?

I accepted the position of Director of Equity Trading and with a colleague, we began to build and train such a group. Although nominally successful in proving that traders could be trained, the Turtles group was not based on a random selection of people who happened to walk through the door. Dennis and Eckhardt had carefully screened those finally selected into the training program with extensive interviews, with the result that most people who applied for the job might have found it easier to get accepted into Harvard Law School than be hired as a Turtle. Nevertheless, I believed that this approach was a good one. But by what criteria should such potential traders be chosen?

We did not particularly look for people with trading experience, although this was not held against anyone either. Rather we sought to look for those personal qualities that would make a good trader. There were two particular areas in which we focused much attention.

I devised a series of mathematical or analytical reasoning questions that potential trainees were asked to solve in their heads without the aid of calculators or paper. These questions were designed to discover people's natural quickness and aptitude with numbers in about five or six different dimensions. We believed that good traders are completely comfortable with numbers and doing quick reasoning and logical calculations on a routine basis in their head. This method seemed the only method that we could use to discover this about someone in a short period of time.

For those who are curious, a sample question might be something like the following: "Would you rather own a stock that went up 80 percent the first year and down 40 percent the second year, or a stock that went up 4 percent each year for two years?" Although interviewees were asked to answer this question in their head, if the answer seems obvious to you, I advise you to take a calculator and calculate the right answer. In fact, less than half the people asked this question got the right answer.

Another most important aspect of a successful trader is how he or she can deal with the emotions and discipline of trading. But how are these qualities to be determined in advance when interviewing someone who has never even traded? Short of giving every potential interviewee an elaborate battery of sophisticated psychological tests, which still may not prove discriminating enough, there is no easy answer to how to proceed in this complex area of personality. We did look for certain life experiences that might give clues about how people might react under stress, uncertainty, and adversity, and what motivations they had for seeking to become traders. To guard against our own subjective perceptions, final candidates were interviewed by at least two and sometimes three people and only if all agreed was the candidate considered a potential hire.

There is no doubt in our minds that the final group hired is an exceptional group of people who show outstanding numerical and analytical abilities coupled with sturdily developed and mature personalities. Following their hire, trainees went through a rigorous two-month training program in all aspects of trading, including obtaining necessary securities licenses, group discussions and market calls, individual statistical analysis of paper trading results, along with tradition classroom instruction and exposure to successful traders trading during the day. It is too early to tell whether this group will succeed in becoming successful traders, but we have every expectation that they will.

chapter 1

the emergence of electronic trading

When Thomas Alva Edison telegraphed the real-time prices of gold trading on the floor of the New York Gold Room during the gold panic of 1869, he ushered financial markets into the modern world of technological communication. Since then, financial markets have embraced technological change in various ways to improve the public price reporting of transactions on the floor of the stock exchange and the speed and ease of long-distance communication between brokers themselves and brokers and their customers. The electronic ticker tape, the telephone, and more recently the computer and the Internet, have all had their role in shaping the modern financial marketplace.

But it has only been in the past decade that a truly interactive electronic marketplace has emerged in the United States. Interactive electronic trading is a matching system that allows multiple participants to trade electronically with one another with direct access to automatic execution. It is a very powerful transformation in the way securities are traded on markets, perhaps the most powerful ever, and the issues it raises for public investors and traders, financial institutions and brokers, and regulators are complex and rapidly changing as we begin the twenty-first century.

The most far-reaching transformations have been occurring in the NASDAQ market with the implementation of a truly interactive electronic market. This significantly broadens the market to ordinary investors with online and direct access Internet capabilities. The changes in NASDAQ have largely been the direct result of major changes in securities regulation and the technological advances in small computers and Internet communication.

Following the introduction of the special Order Handling Rules in 1997, the bid-offer spreads and brokerage commissions for trading stocks on NASDAQ fell sharply. This represents a saving of potentially billions of dollars for public investors in costs of stock market transactions.

Against this backdrop of change, day trading has seized the public eye as many new and existing traders rushed into the new electronic marketplace swelling the volume and activity of trading. From being a market where the only direct professional traders were market makers and large institutions, NASDAQ now trades more than 20 percent of its trades on non-Instinet Electronic Communication Networks or the Small Order Execution System (SOES), which are the trading execution systems of the new day traders. This represents literally hundreds of millions of share volume daily.

Where there is this much activity, there is bound to be an opportunity to make money. Who are these new electronic traders and how are they doing? These are the topics of the interviews in this book.

To put these individual traders' experience in context with some important issues, this chapter attempts to answer the following questions: Exactly how and why did electronic trading evolve over the past several decades in securities markets? Is day trading a new phenomenon or is it only a new form of the older Wall Street profession of exchange member floor trader? Although the traders interviewed in this book are highly profitable, are day traders as a group profitable and what might account for the differences in success among day traders? Finally, what is the future of electronic direct access trading and how are regulatory issues and economic forces being resolved to bring about further change?

The Story of NASDAQ

The recent story of NASDAQ is largely about the emergence of electronic securities trading. Trading of stocks in the United States has been conducted in one of two forms for over a hundred years. Trading was done on either a "listed" stock exchange, where trading was face-to-face between member brokers in an ongoing auction market (e.g., the New York Stock Exchange), or on the over the counter (OTC) market, where dealers traded all other stocks not listed on any other stock exchange. Trading in the OTC market was largely done by telephone in what is called a *negotiated market.*

Historically, the public price reporting on listed stock exchanges has been very good via a ticker tape which widely disseminates with only a slight delay, the actual time and sales of transactions occurring on the floor of the stock exchange. The reporting of closing or last trade prices of stocks on listed stock exchanges has also been very good and widely disseminated in newspapers or other media. This is rightfully seen to be in the public interest, since an informed investor is the cornerstone of public confidence in the securities markets.

The price reporting of OTC stocks, however, has not been very good, since neither intraday nor closing trade prices were centrally reported or disseminated to the public. The only knowledge the public had of trading and prices on the OTC market was the bid and offer quotes of OTC dealers at the end of the day reported in what were known as the "pink sheets." The pink sheet quotes, however, were neither real trade prices nor prices that a dealer would necessarily trade at. They were indications only. This lack of public information about the transactions and prices traded on the OTC markets led to a Securities and Exchange Commission (SEC) study and proposal in 1963 to implement an electronically automated market in OTC traded stocks.

Before the National Association of Securities Dealers (NASD), which is the OTC self-regulatory organization, could implement such a market, however, the first interactive electronic system was introduced privately by Instinet in 1969. The Instinet achievement was notable because it allowed the updated display of bids and offers by anyone on the system, and also the direct electronic execution against bids or offers by anyone else on the network. Instinet was the first fully electronic interactive marketplace in securities. The enduring success of Instinet is reflected in the fact that it still trades today the largest percentage volume of NASDAQ stocks of any market participant. Instinet, however, was designed to trade large blocks only and has remained restricted to large institutional clients and brokers.

In response to the SEC proposals, the NASD introduced in 1971 the NASD Automated Quotation (NASDAQ) system to automate the OTC markets. An electronic system would display the bids or offers of hundreds of market makers in several thousand of the better known and better capitalized stocks on the OTC market. Stocks not traded on NASDAQ would be relegated to the Bulletin Board, which would not be automated. NASDAQ, unlike Instinet however, did not allow the automatic direct execution against displayed bids or offers. For an order to be executed, telephone communication was still necessary. NASDAQ was an electronic display market but not an interactive execution system. It took another 25 years for NASDAQ to catch up to Instinet's early achievement.

In 1984, NASDAQ took its first small step in the direction of interactive execution markets with the introduction of the Small Order Execution System (SOES) that gave small retail customers the ability to trade against NASDAQ market maker bids and offers. Although the technology existed after 1984 for an electronic interactive market, traders, NASDAQ, and market makers largely choose to ignore SOES and did not widely advertise its availability. The result was that trading on NASDAQ continued to be exclusively between dealers on telephone as before.

The stock market crash in October 1987, however, finally led to major changes in the way the NASDAQ and SOES worked. It was discovered by regulators and congressional investigators that during the crash many market makers would not honor their electronically posted bids and offers, and frequently did not even answer the telephone, causing many customer marketable orders to remain unexecuted. To restore and bolster investor confidence in NASDAQ and to ensure that market maker prices were honored, NASD required mandatory participation in SOES for all market makers in 1988 and further introduced an SOES execution platform that was now to be electronically direct. Small traders could now be guaranteed electronic trades through SOES for the first time.

Not only did SOES achieve a technological breakthrough, but it introduced for the first time on NASDAQ professional traders who could compete with market makers in price discovery. Nevertheless, it took a number of years for SOES traders to become established and accepted in the marketplace. For many years, NASD and dealers attempted to limit SOES trading through various rules designed to keep public participation at a minimum. Public SOES traders initially were not allowed to trade more than 500 shares in a trade, nor could they conclude more than two trades a day. Also, new firms were sometimes prevented from getting access to SOES execution platforms. Over time, many of these limitations have been eliminated or modified. SOES now requires market makers to honor all bids and offers with an obligation to trade at least the number of shares displayed on their bid or offer at least for one trade. SOES traders remain restricted in not being able to trade in the same direction in the same stock more than once every five minutes although they are allowed to trade up to 1,000 shares in any one trade if the market maker displays that large a size.

A controversy surrounded the role and activity of SOES traders that revolved around the idea of whether SOES traders were taking unfair advantage of market maker pricing. Market makers sometimes would post bid or offer prices that were poorly priced and SOES traders would trade with them at these mandatory prices often resulting in a SOES trader profit and a market maker loss. Some market makers complained that it just took too long for them to update accurate electronic quotes, and that SOES traders were making a profit on this slowness. This was probably the only time in Wall Street history where professionals complained that retail customers were making money at their expense. Some NASDAQ market makers held the view that SOES traders were really bandits, and the term "SOES Bandit" was introduced in the press in the early 1990s.

SOES traders did not dispute that they were making money, but argued that a profit existed because at least some market makers were inefficient. The free market has always accepted the principle that inefficient businesses are allowed to suffer in the light of open competition. Many traders would accept or find interesting Harry Houtkin's account in *Secrets of the SOES Bandit,* where he describes the struggle that was fought for the success of SOES against entrenched market maker oligopolies who stood to lose millions in lost revenue by making markets more efficient and open to the public.

In 1990, NASDAQ took a further step in direct access trading by introducing SelectNet. SelectNet allowed market makers to trade with each other at each other's displayed bids or offers through direct electronic execution called *preferencing.* This system, however, was initially restricted in use to broker-dealers exclusively although now it is available to all traders.

While technologically sophisticated, SOES and Selectnet did not affect the quoted bid/offer spreads on stocks as much as might be expected through a more open competition. Generally, they remained very wide. An investigation into this phenomena on NASDAQ initiated in 1993 by the U.S. Justice Department, concluded in 1996 that many market makers were colluding to keep bid/offer spreads at artificially wide levels. This spread manipulation was a result of either voluntary action by the group of market makers in a stock, or coercion of unwilling market makers through harassment. Although NASDAQ and market makers initially denied that collusion was taking place, market maker reliance on recorded telephone lines, long the market maker's primary means of communication, supplied the evidence of just such activity.

This investigation led in 1996 to antitrust actions against NASDAQ broker/dealers that resulted in a billion dollar fine against NASD, the owner and regulatory arm of NASDAQ. Although this fine was the largest of its kind, it may not be so large when it is considered that even a ⅛ artificially widening of the bid-offer spread on a billion share volume represents $125 million of potential profits *a day*.

Recognizing the need for NASDAQ market reform, the SEC under Arthur Levitt took the initiative and mandated that NASD reform NASDAQ into a truly functioning electronic marketplace that would bring together in one place all electronic systems, including Selectnet, SOES, and Instinet, as well as introducing new types of public execution systems. The result were the special Order Handling Rules introduced in January 1997, which had a profound and positive effect on NASDAQ. The new rules required that market makers honor all displayed limit orders of the public that were placed inside the bid/offer spread. This led to a narrowing of spreads and execution of public trades at the best prices available. Another rule forbid market makers to display bids and offers on SelectNet or SOES if they gave better bids and offers in private markets such as Instinet. For the first time, NASDAQ was required to have one centralized electronic marketplace that was accessible to all traders and dealers alike.

The most important change in 1997, however, was the introduction of electronic communications networks (ECNs) into the NASDAQ system. ECNs are posting and execution systems on NASDAQ that can be entered by any market participant. Any ECN can trade against any other ECN, market maker, or Instinet trader on the NASDAQ market. There are now about 10 ECNs on NASDAQ, including the most active ones, Instinet (INCA), Island (ISLD), and REDI. The total listing of market makers and ECNs making bids and offers in a stock is now openly shown on a Level II screen.

The introduction of ECNs into NASDAQ had a lasting and powerful effect on improving the fairness of pricing on this market and has far-reaching financial ramifications. A notable success of ECNs was evident very early in the sudden narrowing of spreads between bids and offers of most NASDAQ stocks. This spread, which is an implicit measure of the public cost of doing a trade, fell by almost half. Stocks such as Microsoft or Intel, which had traded with a spread of a quarter or three-eighths, now routinely trade at spreads of one-sixteenth. Given an exchange volume of a billion shares a day, this saving to the public of one-sixteenth could be $60 million a day.

Not surprisingly under these circumstances, there has also been an explosion in volume traded and traders using the new system. Along with the electronic revolution in telecommunications and computers, these regulatory reforms have also led to the expansion of electronic floor trading, as the historical advantages that floor traders have always enjoyed become available to the retail trader also (see the next section).

The reforms on NASDAQ are continuing and there are discussions about what the marketplace of the future is to look like as all markets become more interconnected including listed stocks being traded on the New York Stock Exchange and other smaller or regional exchanges. These issues will be discussed further in the last section of this chapter.

Growth of the Electronic Floor Trader

Historically, all stock exchanges have required the participation of three types of participants. A retail investor or customer, who initiates the buy or sell order for a stock based on his or her belief that the stock has good or poor value. A professional broker who takes this customer order and executes or *fills* it on the stock exchange. And finally, a third party is necessary who completes this transaction and takes the opposite side of the customer order that the broker must execute. Most customers believe that their order is filled on the exchange by trading with another broker for another customer, who just happens to want to do the opposite transaction in the stock. Sometimes this does happen. But more commonly, when a broker takes a customer order to the floor of a stock exchange, there is no other broker with another customer order that is waiting to be filled that is the exact opposite in price and quantity of the first customer's order. If you had to wait for this to happen, this kind of market would be *illiquid,* and *inefficient.* How then can this customer have his order filled immediately and at a fair price?

The third or counterparty to the public are most frequently professional traders, who are willing to assume the risk, for the right price, to take the risk of the opposite side of a retail customer order. These professional traders are variously known as *market makers, listed specialists, dealers, floor traders,* or *speculators,* depending on exactly how and what type of stock exchange they trade. If there were no professional traders, then brokers with customer orders would frequently not have anyone to trade with and would not be able to fill their customers' orders. All traders work by supplying the liquidity of exchange in the search for fair and more efficient price discovery. For providing this liquidity function, professional traders are paid for their services. Indeed, the control and filling of the customer order is a billion dollar business and the heart of much of Wall Street's profits.

Brokers earn their money by charging a commission to the customer for executing an order. How then do the professional traders earn their money for providing liquidity services to the broker and customer?

Market makers "make a market" by providing a two-sided quote, a bid and offer for specific size, to any broker who requests it. The market maker profit in this transaction is some function of the difference between the bid and offer, since market makers buy on the bid or low price, and sell on the asking or high price. This is known as the *bid-offer spread,* and might be compared to a willingness to buy at a wholesale price and sell at a retail price, and in this sense, is no different from any other kind of merchant. If prices had no trend and were evenly divided by supply and demand, then the bid-offer spread should exactly equal market maker gross profits in the long run. If prices trend, as they surely do, then market makers must be professionally adept at providing a two-sided market but still manage the risk of uncertainty during the time it takes them to complete both sides of earning this spread. Good market making becomes a skill of short-term anticipation of the market and risk management. There are various rules regulating how market makers must function on an exchange. On NASDAQ, there are many market makers, sometimes also known as dealers, competing against one another in the same stock, to provide the highest bid or the lowest offer, so that brokers may receive the best prices for an executed order. On listed stocks, there is only one market maker by the rules of the exchange, and he is known as the *specialist.*

Market makers and specialists, however, are not the only ones competing to take the opposite side of a broker's customer order. Almost every exchange also has any number of floor traders, who are also willing to trade against customer orders. Floor traders differ from dealers by being unwilling to make a two-sided market that is narrow or immediate, but usually are ready to trade at some price and risk level. Floor traders often have stronger views about trend direction than a market maker and really want to trade, if they are willing to trade at all, only on one side. Floor traders are speculators and not investors or market makers, but they do compete at times against market makers for filling customer orders at the best price, and it is this competition that helps keep market makers' prices fair and liquid.

Floor traders have always enjoyed two important advantages over retail investors and even off-floor professional speculators, which has helped their profitability. First, floor traders by virtue of being members of exchanges, were able to instantaneously execute their orders at current prices. This immediacy advantage allows floor traders to transact their trades at prices that the retail customer does not see until after a small time delay when they are publicly reported. Customers ordinarily face a time gap in knowledge of pricing that although small, is highly advantageous to the floor trader or market maker who are often working for very small margins of profit.

A second advantage to both market makers and floor traders compared with the public customer is the generally low commission costs of executing an order on an exchange as an exchange member. Professionals pay only cents per share of the volume size of their trade. A professional trader can trade a hundred shares for a dollar or less, whereas the retail customer usually pays ten dollars or much more in commissions. It should not be difficult to determine who has the better advantage trading.

Although not as widely appreciated, market makers and floor traders also have considerable margin or leverage advantages by being members of exchanges. The public customer is regulated by the Federal Reserve Bank's margin requirement, which currently is 50 percent; that is, customers must deposit in cash at least half the value of the stock transaction they do. Stock exchange members have margin requirements set by the exchange, which are much lower than this. This increased leverage allows exchange members to make an absolute profit with a much higher percentage rate of return on capital, than available to public investors.

Who are floor traders? Most people probably have never heard of this profession. Historically, floor trading has always been limited to a small group of people. The number of floor traders in the United States by the 1980s was only a few thousand and most of these were found on commodity or futures exchanges and not stock exchanges. Floor trading on stock exchanges was more common in the nineteenth and early twentieth centuries, but after World War II has gradually shrunk. The chief disadvantage or obstacle to becoming a floor trader has been the cost of a stock exchange membership, and the need to be located geographically in either New York or one of a few other major cities.

Without the recent revolution in electronic trading, it is possible that floor trading in securities would have completely died out as large institutions grew to dominate the marketplace. However, as more fully outlined in the previous section, the recent technological revolution in computers and electronic communication, and the regulatory reforms largely spearheaded by the SEC, have given a new life to the profession of floor trader.

Floor trading has always had the following features: the ability to directly trade with brokers and market makers on an exchange, the ability to immediately execute any trade and know the result and other current prices without a time-reporting delay, low cost of commissions or fees as a business expense, and availability of lower margin and higher leverage.

The recent regulatory and electronic transformation on NAS-DAQ has now allowed public traders using Electronic Communications Networks on a Level II execution system to achieve the same advantages that floor traders have had in the past. On Level II, an electronic trader, without using an intermediary broker, can now trade directly with any trader, broker, or market maker who is listing bids or offers in a stock. The execution of the trades of Level II traders is virtually instantaneous and the knowledge of the result is immediate. Electronic trader commissions have fallen to levels equal to or approaching levels of professional floor traders. For high volume traders, fees are negotiable. Finally, although retail electronic traders are still governed by Federal Reserve Bank margin requirements, an electronic trader can alternatively join a stock exchange firm that allows its traders increased leverage more characteristic of floor traders.

Finally, the new electronic trader has one other advantage that floor traders never had. Geographically, there is now no longer any restriction on the location of trading, since it is all done through electronic telecommunication. NASDAQ is not a physical exchange located in New York, Boston, or anywhere else except in electronic space. So electronic traders can live and trade from any location.

The new electronic marketplace on NASDAQ allows anyone who is a member of the system to obtain the historical advantages of floor traders. Fueled by these changes, a new group of *electronic floor traders* has emerged. While a new profession has not been created, an older one has been greatly enlarged. Anyone with a relatively small amount of capital can become an electronic floor trader. It is no longer necessary to electronically communicate with your broker to place or confirm a trade, let alone use archaic telephonic communication. A professional securities trader may trade directly, immediately, and with low cost, on an open electronic marketplace with market makers or brokers, and even with other traders.

While individuals can access securities markets directly, however, it is still necessary to do so through a large firm that has registered as a broker-dealer or member of an exchange, and has the capital commitment to provide state-of-the-art electronic trading facilities. Facilitating the emergence of the new class of electronic traders has been NASD brokerages offering services in this area and private proprietary trading firms. These dealers and firms have suitable office space, capital, and the sophisticated equipment to trade electronically. Although an electronic trader technically has an account with a brokerage firm, the brokerage no longer has any brokers.

While most electronic traders trade at offices where the complex and sophisticated electronic equipment for trading can be set up, remote or home site trading will become more accessible and less expensive. Centralized office trading, however, is likely to remain the significant forum of trading, since many traders may prefer to work away from home, and benefit from a common trading room with other traders.

For traders opening up accounts at NASD broker dealers, accounts and trading are governed by NASD and SEC rules. At firms that are members of listed stock exchanges, traders more typically become member-owners of the firm and must pass SEC Series 7 licensing requirements. There are advantages and disadvantages of each type of trading account. Under NASD rules, traders at NASD brokers have account insurance and strong regulatory protection; advantages that are lost to traders who are member-owners of their firms, who face general business risk if their firm should default. On the other hand, trader-owners enjoy special exchange membership advantages, chiefly lower margin requirements. This allows traders at private firms much greater leverage in their trading. Although this introduces greater risk in trading, it implies that this greater risk is rewarded with greater potential profits.

One type of trader, however, is not an electronic trader, although he or she may believe that she is. Online investors and traders are not electronic traders because although they use a computer Internet connection to their broker, their order is not directly or immediately filled with market makers and other traders on the exchange. Rather, after sending their order to their broker, the broker must still fill the order in the traditional way of relaying it to an exchange, and then reporting back to the customer the result. These features are not characteristics of electronic floor traders, but of traditional retail brokerage customers.

Are Day Traders Profitable?

The changes in NASDAQ have led to the creation of a new profession of direct access traders, or electronic floor traders. How well is this group doing? There is much controversy over this question, yet few statistics are available to resolve this controversy. As this book will attest, there are certainly some people who are making a great deal of money trading electronically. But how representative of all traders is this group? That we do not know.

The facts of trader profitability as a group are few. Brokerage firms that have many day trading accounts have not published the results. The only published empirical study has been the Ronald Johnson Report commissioned by the National Association of Securities Administrators Association (NASAA) and released in August 1999.

The Johnson Report analyzed the statistics of traders' profits and losses for 1997 for a representative sample at one New England electronic brokerage firm. The Johnson Report found that 69 percent of traders lost money at the firm examined during that year, with 31 percent making some kind of profit. Moreover, the Johnson Report noted that those traders who made money were often making money on positions held for periods longer than one day, and concluded that day trading proper, was an unprofitable strategy for most. The high percentage of losing traders is a sobering statistic. Electronic trading, like floor trading, is a rough business. The results of the Johnson Report have entered the public domain in press reports that frequently note that 70 percent of day traders lose money. However, the Johnson Report has never been critiqued or reanalyzed following its publication, and it might be fruitful to review its findings more carefully.

The year of the results studied by the Johnson Report was 1997, just after the Order Handling Rules were first introduced. This was, in other words, exactly the time that many new traders entered trading for the first time because of the availability of ECNs on the NASDAQ marketplace. Indeed, the Johnson Report sample is heavily composed of new traders with less than six months trading experience, or precisely that group of traders especially likely to experience losses while they are learning. The Johnson Report does not take this sample selection bias into account in drawing its conclusions.

Moreover, the Johnson Report does not indicate that these new traders received any special or thorough training. As most successful traders in this book will agree, new traders who do not receive training are especially prone to experience large losses and are less likely to become successful. Although the Johnson Report does not try to explain why these new traders were largely unsuccessful other than by offering the blanket statement that day trading is an unsuccessful strategy in general. However, the Johnson Report does supply the data that suggests why these traders in particular were unsuccessful.

The Johnson Report sample were paying about $25 in commissions per trade and were also trading in 1,000 share sizes for the most part. This last fact is probably determinant in explaining why these new traders were unsuccessful, since it is virtually unanimous among the successful traders interviewed in this book, that new traders should begin by trading small size accounts until they become profitable. For the most part, this has to do with the fact that new traders are especially prone to not take losses quickly or small enough. A five-point loss on a hundred shares is $500, but $5,000 if you are trading a thousand shares. Most experienced traders never take a five-point loss, but this is not uncommon among new traders until they learn the rules of trading or discipline.

We do not know why these new traders were trading such large size trades when beginning, but some good inferences are possible. New traders without training tend to trade large size under the mistaken principle that if you believe you are going to make money on a trade, you should trade as large as possible. This certainly does not represent sound money or risk management principles for most experienced traders, but it is a principle even more dangerous to violate where a new trader has not established that he or she has any consistent probability of success in making the trade in the first place.

Probably another reason why these new traders were trading too large a size trade was the commission cost of $25 per trade, which is relatively high by current standards. These traders may have wished to capitalize on an economy of scale where $25 on a 1000 lot trade represents only 2.5 cents per share, instead of 25 cents per share on a hundred share trade. Yet until a trader has become successful, this is a false economy of scale.

A preliminary re-analysis of the Johnson Report suggests that it was not so much day trading per se as a strategy that led to the large losses experienced, but that the sample of traders was highly inexperienced. The sample examined contained a high percentage of new untrained traders, who violated many of the most elementary and prudent loss protection and money management rules involved in any kind of trading.

Upon secondary analysis, the Johnson Report data show that the longer a trader has been trading, the more successful he or she becomes and the lower the risk of ruin. There were 27 percent of traders who had at least six months or more trading experience in the sample, who may be called the experienced traders. The experienced traders were much more likely to be profitable, with 42 percent making money compared to only 26 percent of those trading less than six months (see Table 1.1). The success odds for a trader goes up significantly if the trader is able to last just six

Table 1.1   Profitability of inexperienced versus experienced traders

	Traded Five Months or Less ($n=19$)	Traded Six Months or More ($n=7$)
Profitable	26.3%	42.8%
Unprofitable	73.7%	57.2%
Total	100%	100%

Source: Johnson Report, Exhibits C-1, D-1.

months. The experienced successful traders do very well indeed, according to the Johnson Report data, earning about $8,500 on average per month.

The risk of ruin statistic also drops sharply for these experienced profitable traders, from 34 percent for novices compared to 10 percent for experienced (see Table 1.2). If you were able to show a profit trading and had traded at least six months, there was only a one in ten chance you would lose all your money if you continued to trade.

What the Johnson Report data more realistically show is that following the introduction of ECNs on NASDAQ in 1997, an especially large group of new inexperienced traders began trading and showed a high failure rate. However, this pattern of failure may be largely inferred to be a result not of day trading strategies per se, but the lack of proper training that led many of these new uneducated traders to violate the sound and long established rules of any kind of trading. Even at that time, the Johnson Report data show that if a trader is able to survive for even as short as six months, the risk of failure drops sharply, and the potential average profitability for remaining experienced and successful traders is high. In effect, new traders without training are undergoing a steep "learning curve," and must learn to be successful or close their accounts. The traders interviewed in this book have made this successful transition.

It should finally be observed that the Johnson Report does not evaluate the risks of failure against the potential rewards of success. Many new traders may be willing to risk even a high failure rate where the potential rewards are so high. The economics

Table 1.2 Average risk of ruin percentages by trader experience

	Less < 6 Months	6 Months > More
Profitable	34%	10%
Unprofitable	100%	100%

Source: Johnson Report, Exhibits C-1, D-1.

of expected value theory suggest that it is still a good bet to wager $5,000 on each role of the dice, even when you may expect to lose nine times out of ten, but if you win, you will win an income of $100,000 a year for life. In this sense, trading is much like the risks of any other small business formation. Most newly formed small businesses in the United States have a high failure rate, restaurants often being used as an example. Yet a successful restaurant can be very successful and make the odds worth taking. Many traders interviewed in this book state that they treat trading as a business, and from this perspective, the decision of a new trader to try trading may represent the best entrepreneurial spirit that has developed and enriched the United States.

The final piece of evidence that confirms the success of day trading strategies, comes from the author's personal experience and knowledge concerning the unwillingness of traditional brokerage firms to fill professional day traders' orders with what is called "auto-execution." Auto-execution is the immediate filling of a retail customer's order by the brokerage itself acting as counterparty, rather than send the order to an exchange to be filled. The customer suffers no disadvantage when a brokerage does this, since the price received is based on the best bid or offer then available on the exchange for that stock. Indeed, the customer receives some slight advantage because the order is filled quicker than having the order sent to the exchange.

Brokerages are willing to fill customer orders with auto-execution because it allows them to act as a market maker and attempt to earn the bid-offer spread on the order they have taken. In other words, in addition to earning a commission, they now have a chance to earn an additional income by selling on the offer and trying to buy on the bid, or vice versa. This extra source of income is so valuable, that some brokerage firms are willing to pay other brokerages for the right to auto-execute retail customer orders in what is called payment for order flow, which will be discussed further in a following section.

Why is this practice suggestive that day traders are profitable? Because no brokerage is willing to accept professional day trader firm accounts for auto-execution.

If day traders as a group were unprofitable, then broker-ages would be expected to be very willing and eager to auto-execute these traders' orders as an extra source of their own profit. However, brokerages consistently refuse this business. In fact, if they discover that a professional day trader has gained access to an auto-executed account, they will terminate this feature promptly. Brokerages are quite willing to trade against retail customers who presumably do not show any short-term market savvy, but are very unwilling to do so against professional day traders.

It is self-evident to the traders interviewed in this book that day trading can be profitable. They also believe that the skills of successful direct access trading can be taught, at least to some degree. Many think, however, that without proper training or in-struction, the odds of success are much lower and the costs of learning are going to be very high. This belief might be summed up in the statement, that if you think education is expensive, try trading without it. All of the traders interviewed did learn to trade successfully on their own, usually with little formal in-struction or mentoring, and often with remarkably low or inex-pensive losses as part of the cost of learning. What distinguished this group from many other traders who have not become suc-cessful? This question will be considered again in the concluding chapter of this book.

But when asked why it was that traders might be taught the skills of successful trading yet still not be successful, several an-swers emerged. One factor that is important is the amount of capitalization that a trader begins with. A five or ten thousand dollar account is probably too little to become successful. There has to be some comfortable margin of capital available to with-stand some early losses that most agree is usually necessary to become a successful trader. Losing five or ten thousand dollars probably should be expected as the cost of learning even with training. Starting with too small an account may mean that by the time you are skilled, you may be too poor to profit from it. Several traders believe that starting with too small an account will adversely affect a new trader emotionally when he or she experiences losses. The old adage that scared money never makes money is still probably true.

How much should a new trader start with? Some recent books on trading recommend that a new trader start with at least $100,000. Probably this high a figure is recommended because many traders who became successful lost as much as $50,000 or more before becoming successful, so this size initial capital is seen as necessary. One trader interviewed believed this high a figure was necessary to take advantage of the diversification effects within his style of trading.

I believe that it is possible for new traders to start with less than $100,000, but good formal training is an absolute must for anyone interested in entering this profession. One of the benefits of this training will be the reduced amount of money lost while gaining experience.

Another reason a smaller amount of money is appropriate comes from psychological studies that have shown that people evaluate value or money in terms of percentages rather than in absolute dollar amounts. For example, studies have shown that people are more willing to travel a long distance to save 20 percent ($10) on a $50 item they are buying, but are not as willing to travel as far to save $10 (1%) on a $500 item they may want to buy. In principle, the same person should be willing to travel equally far to save the same $10, but they generally aren't. For psychological reasons, people tend to treat absolute dollar figures differently depending on the context. For the same reason, a new trader may be more careful in losing $5,000 if his or her account size is $25,000, but less careful about losing $5,000 if the account size is $100,000. In this first situation, this loss represents a 25 percent reduction in capital, while in the second situation, it represents only a 5 percent reduction. There is $95,000 left after all, isn't there?

Psychological characteristics are probably the key to why most of the traders interviewed in this book believe that successful trading skills can be taught, without that implying that most people can become successful. As one trader bluntly put it, "You can teach people the rules of trading, you just can't teach them to follow the rules." Every trader interviewed agreed that having discipline was the single most important psychological attribute of a successful trader, and many traders attributed new trader failure to this lack of discipline. This important topic will be further discussed in the concluding chapter of this book, but suggests that the variability in trader success may have much to do with the psychological differences among people.

The Future of the Electronic Stock Market

The final chapter on the changes in the electronic marketplace has not yet been written. There are broad trends that appear irreversible at this time, and point to a new, completely liquid and open marketplace in securities where private and public markets merge. Exactly what form this will take or when it will happen, however, remain uncertain.

Electronic trading continues to be a focus of regulatory scrutiny. The early empirical results following the NASDAQ Order Handling Rules introduced in January 1997, showed that bid-offer spreads, the most sensitive measure of cost of business to the public, showed sharp declines on average. Most other measures of reform showed positive success, most notably the greater liquidity in the market. If success is measured in terms of how much was saved by retail investors in the narrowing of the market maker spread, then there was potentially literally billions of dollars saved by this regulatory reform promoting competition and open markets.

Recently, regulators have shown more concern about the standards and practices at firms that offer direct access systems to retail investors. The SEC has consistently taken the position that there is nothing illegal or unethical about day trading as a speculative investment. However, the SEC has been concerned that the risks associated with day trading are not entirely understood by many new speculative investors, especially where misleading advertising has been involved. The SEC has also been concerned about questionable lending practices at some firms.

Recommendations from regulatory reports have generally suggested that existing standards and rules are sufficient to maintain fair and orderly markets, but that existing rules must be enforced. Regulatory bodies have found great cooperation in firms in meeting these existing standards once deficiencies were pointed out. Two major reports of the SEC, the Unger Report and the Examination Report of the SEC Staff in 2000 did not find any pattern of gross abuses or any threat to fair and orderly public markets.

The NASD has proposed a possible "appropriateness" standard to be applied to customers of retail securities firms: Customers would have to meet strict standards of appropriateness to be allowed to trade actively electronically. Provided that adequate disclosure of risk were made, however, there is not a broad consensus to impose new restrictions on the private choice of investing strategies. Restricting choice may be seen as an infringement on legitimate investor decisions, long accepted as the cornerstone of free markets.

A proposal that has more support is to change the margin and capital requirements of what would be described as "pattern day traders." Minimum account capital size of $25,000 would be required of traders who fit this definition, but the daily allowable margin would be lowered to 25 percent from 50 percent for trades opened and closed during the day. There are many, however, who challenge the need for these new requirements, seeing them as an attempt by the well-capitalized segment of the securities industry that has been losing money to the electronic marketplace to place restrictions on short-term securities traders.

For the most part, these and other regulatory initiatives are not expected to change or alter the fundamental significance or activity of electronic traders although they may supply some added protection or restriction for small investors depending on one's point of view.

Another issue confronting regulators is the practice of *payment for order flow*. Payment for order flow is where a market maker or broker is willing to pay a fee to another broker who holds an executable order from a customer, so that the executing broker will trade that order with the paying broker rather than with one of his competitors. Payment for order flow has been practiced legally for many years and is a very large source of Wall Street income and profits. A broker with an executable customer order, not only receives a commission from the customer for executing the order, he also receives another fee from the broker he trades with. This fee is not directly rebated to the customer in a commission reduction and the customer usually does not even know that his order has been sold in this manner.

The reason dealers and market makers are willing to pay for order flow is fairly obvious since market makers are trying to earn the spread between the bid and offer on a large volume of transactions. Paying for this additional order flow increases their chances that they will be able to complete a transaction on both sides, thus earning the spread. If they are able to earn $125 on an eighth-point bid-offer spread on a completed round turn transaction on one thousand shares, for example, they may be more than willing to pay $20 to an executing broker to get that order for themselves.

So long as the executed price to the customer is no worse than the best available in the marketplace, the defenders of payment for order flow believe that the customer has not been manifestly harmed and therefore the practice should not be regulated or restricted. While this argument carries an initial plausibility, it does not readily answer the objection of opponents of payment for order flow that the practice can cumulatively erode the competitive price of stocks in a marketplace. Consider a case where two market makers, A and B, compete and each offer identical best bid and offer prices. If B is able to capture a large portion of trades through payment for order flow, the public will not immediately be harmed since they continue to receive the best available prices. But over time market maker A will likely be forced out of business through lack of orders, and once A has left the marketplace, B can raise prices accordingly resulting in higher prices to the public customer.

Defenders of order flow payment may respond by noting that it has long been accepted in the free market that businesses that are unable to compete effectively should go out of business. As a general principle, this is undoubtedly true. However, it has also been a long accepted specific principle of securities market regulation and law that the public should be afforded some protection in how stock markets work. In this case, payment for order flow carries absolutely no real or potential benefit to the public customer, but in fact, has some real disadvantage as order flow payment may thin the ranks of competing market makers. A situation that can carry no benefit but only a serious disadvantage to the public in receiving the best prices in stock transactions, therefore, is not in the public interest in the opinion of many people. At this time, however, restrictions of payment for order flow are not likely to be enacted by regulators.

There are, however, several other important areas of the electronic marketplace that may soon be undergoing more significant change, as the interview in this book with Matthew Andresen, president of the Island ECN, indicates. The issues here are somewhat complex and interrelated, so a look at the possible future is not easy.

One issue that looms very large is the eventual shape of how the listed stock exchanges will work, especially the New York Stock Exchange (NYSE), and other smaller or regional exchanges. The NYSE has experienced some electronic transformation in how business has been conducted over the past decade or so, notably the introduction of the "consolidated quote" system which allows the best bid and offer on a NYSE listed stock that is also traded on a regional exchange, to be widely broadcast electronically. The Intermarket Trading System (ITS) allows members of any listed stock exchange to electronically send orders to be filled at prices indicated on any of the other related listed exchanges. Although an electronic system, in practice, it remains slow and executions are not guaranteed. More importantly, it is only available to exchange members and is not accessible by the public.

Over a decade ago, the NYSE also introduced Super-Dot, standing for "direct order transmission," which is the electronic routing of broker orders directly to the specialist's booth on the floor of the exchange, eliminating the need for a floor broker to execute this type of order. There is a size limitation on orders transmitted through Super-Dot, and large block trades are still executed by floor brokers on the NYSE. However, during the 1990s the Super-Dot system became available to retail traders at some firms known as "Dot shops." Using Super-Dot directly was only a partially automated electronic execution system, however, because although it did eliminate the need for a broker, an order transmitted to the specialist's booth directly, still need not be filled by the specialist before two minutes. During this two-minute delay in execution, a marketable order would not be guaranteed a price necessarily even close to that shown when the order was sent. Moreover, limit orders may not be executed at all even though bids and offers shown when the order was sent would have suggested a fill.

If a member of the NYSE from 1880 returned to the exchange floor today, he would likely feel remarkably comfortable doing business now as he had over 120 before since most large and important orders are still executed in face-to-face communication. The NYSE is the last major stock exchange in the world that still conducts its business in this manner, despite some minor electronic innovations. For anyone looking at the future, the key question is how long will the NYSE continue in this manner?

No doubt one of the problems of reform on the NYSE has been that it is a member-owned institution, and significant electronic reform of the exchange would likely result in the loss of income for many of the firms that act as specialists or floor brokers, as has happened in every other electronic transformation of a traditional stock exchange. It may be reasonably inferred that these stock exchange members are not so willing to reform themselves out of business. How then can change take place in this context?

There are probably two areas in which change may come about on the NYSE and the related listed exchanges. Over a year ago, the NYSE proposed that it was going to change its ownership structure by becoming a public company with shareholders, who would not be members of the exchange. If such a proposal were carried out, it would likely remove the membership opposition to the transformation of the NYSE both by allowing existing members to receive a considerable cash value for their memberships, and also eliminating them as a controlling voice in the future of the exchange itself. Moreover, it would give the NYSE a large capital influx that would allow the exchange the economic means to compete with electronic competitors either through outright acquisitions or development of a new electronic marketplace. However, the proposed transformation of the NYSE into a publicly owned shareholder corporation that was scheduled for late in 1999 was postponed and, at this time, the NYSE has not publicly announced any new date when this change might occur.

On another front, however, the NYSE might be vulnerable to change brought about by its competitors. Island and other ECNs have recently initiated the regulatory process to become recognized as exchanges themselves. As this book's interview with Island's president Matt Andresen makes clear, one reason for this initiative is to be better able to compete in the trading of listed stocks. It is probably not widely known that Island's customers are already able to trade listed stocks on Island. However, the current trading of listed stocks on Island or other ECNs is not linked to the consolidated quote system of listed exchanges nor is there any direct routing of orders possible between the two loci of trading. The trading in listed stocks between listed exchanges and ECNs remains fragmented. However, if Island is able to achieve exchange status, this would open the door for Island and other ECNs to enter the consolidated quote system for listed stocks and compete directly with listed exchanges for stock orders. Exactly how this new system would work, and even whether it will meet with regulatory approval, however, remains unclear at this time.

Recently, the NYSE has responded to these competitive pressures by announcing the soon to be introduced electronic automatic execution of small lot orders on the NYSE called Network NYSE, in effect, an ECN of its own. How this new system will operate, exactly when it will be introduced, and whether it is too late to head off the competition for listed stocks from existing ECNs, are questions that currently remain unanswered.

The other area of looming change is on the NASDAQ marketplace itself. While ECNs have been applying for exchange status, NASDAQ has proposed through its owner and governing body the NASD, becoming an exchange ECN itself. In what is being called "Super Montage," NASDAQ would change from being a meeting place where market makers and ECNs trade between themselves into its own super ECN, where orders could be displayed and traded on one central and open book. Exactly how this will change the trading on NASDAQ itself remains unclear, however. Would the NASDAQ-ECN simply become another ECN competing with other ECNs and market makers for market share, or would the new NASDAQ-ECN become the envisioned central order book for all orders eliminating the need for ECNs, and separate and distinct market maker quotes? No one is sure of the outcome of these changes.

The changes impending for listed stock trading and the new NASDAQ marketplace mean that electronic direct access trading is likely to change significantly in the near future. Level II montages may allow the direct electronic execution of listed stocks that is not possible now, as the specialist system is replaced or loses its competitive advantage. Yet Level II screens of the future may also look quite different as NASDAQ becomes a central order book ECN. Whatever happens, however, it probably would be a serious mistake for regulators to curtail the freedom of individual traders to choose the routing systems for their orders, or the open competition among ECNs and market makers to receive or trade against those routed public orders. It is this freedom to compete that has made the NASDAQ marketplace the most vibrant and innovative place for securities investment and trading in the modern world.

chapter 2

Joseph Dedona

Joseph Dedona is one of the most successful traders interviewed having earned close to $2 million for himself last year without ever keeping more than $50,000 in his account. He is 33 years old and grew up in Brooklyn where his parents own small stores and restaurants. His high school had just established a computer science room where Joe became interested in computers, especially his first computer, an Apple. When he went on to attend St. John's University, Joe majored in computer science with a minor in business. Following college graduation, Joe held several jobs as a programmer in Fortran and Cobol but realized to stay in the field he would have to learn the newer languages such as C++ and Visual Basic. Deciding not to do this, Joe became a manager at a new car dealership for five years. It was here that Joe first became interested in the stock market.

How did you first become interested in stocks?

While employed at the new car dealership, I met a customer who was a broker at a New Jersey brokerage firm and he got me interested in stocks.

Did you start trading then?

I opened an account with this small firm which did a lot of IPOs. I put about $40,000 into my account. Unfortunately, this firm, the name of which I will not mention, was what I later learned was known as a "chop shop." That means, for one thing, you could buy, but they wouldn't let you sell. One of the first trades I made was to buy 1,000 shares of an IPO stock that they were promoting which came out at six dollars. This was okay, but I wanted to also buy some AOL (America Online). My broker didn't think this was a good idea, so he talked me out of it. Meanwhile the IPO stock I had bought had gone up to nine dollars and my broker convinced me to buy another 5,000 shares. Like an idiot, I did. Well, with shear luck this stock quickly traded up to 18. At that point I told my broker to sell, but he wouldn't execute the order. I didn't understand this. And then the stock started to drop, going from 18 to 17 to 16. At one point the stock was $15, and I called my broker to sell at that price. He told me if I sold I would only get $12. This didn't make any sense to me, but really what it meant was that my broker just wouldn't sell my stock. Meanwhile the stock had come down to about ten dollars. I didn't know what to do.

So what did you do?

Finally I opened an account at a large Wall Street broker and had the stock transferred there. Fortunately, the stock bounced back to 15 and I sold it immediately. That was my first, worst, and best experience. I had a stock that could have given me a $50,000 profit, watched it all disappear, and then still made some money on the stock. This experience stuck in my mind—you can make money trading stocks. I realized I could make a year's salary in just about one month. The stock was Alcohol Sensors. It's now trading at about two cents.

So what happened next?

At this point I had accumulated about $90,000 and realized that this was much easier than owning your own business or franchise. So it occurred to me that maybe I should see how I could do trading stocks for a living. And that's what I tried at a more reputable brokerage house than my first one.

Did that go as well as your first speculation?

It was a total disaster. My account went from about $90,000 to $32,000 in six months. At that point, I generally did not make independent stock picks but followed the stock recommendations of my broker. It was a prestigious brokerage house, so I relied on their reputation, especially after my experience with my first broker. What I didn't understand initially was that their stock recommendations were expected to be held for longer term appreciation, at least a year. They didn't expect you to buy a stock in the morning and then sell it in the afternoon. One of their picks was Informix. I bought 1,000 shares for about twenty dollars. Several days later it was up to twenty-two. When I wanted to sell, my broker disagreed with me and urged me to hold. I didn't understand this. I made 10 percent in two days. I wanted to take my profit. But my broker convinced me to hold, which I did. Well, the stock pulled back to 20 and my broker urged me to buy more. Then the stock dropped even further so I bought more. My broker then recommended selling puts (the obligation to buy the stock if it drops in price) to take in some cash premium to offset some of my losses. So I did this. Well, the stock continued to drop and then one day it opened on a large gap down to nine dollars. With having bought more stock on the way down and then selling puts obligating me to buy even more stock if the price drops, I got completely clobbered. With some of the other stocks my broker recommended having also lost money, my $90,000 account was down to about $32,000 at this point. So I said the hell with this, and I transferred my remaining money to a Schwab brokerage account.

Did you consider just giving up trading at this point?

No. While I had been trading through my reputable broker, I also had learned the game the other less reputable brokers were playing. I would open up small accounts at these other brokerages and buy their IPOs. When they went up in price I would transfer the account to my reputable broker and then sell the stock. I also began to watch more actively traded stocks on NASDAQ that my reputable broker would never recommend, such as US Robotics. I felt I had some very nice picks during this time if only I would have bought them.

So you still weren't actively trading stocks at this time?

No. But early in 1996 I decided to do trading the right way and make my own decisions. I opened up an account at Schwab. Someone about this time had told me about NASDAQ Level II and how important this was. So I subscribed to "PC Quote," which supplied this kind of data for $300 a month. I then set up my computer with a high-speed Internet connection, Level II quotes, and an online brokerage account for executions.

How did you trade with this setup?

With NASDAQ Level II I could see the bid growing and the offer shrinking, which was an advantage when entering orders.

Didn't this still take too much time for a profitable trade considering that your order had to be relayed first to Schwab and then to the market maker on NASDAQ for execution?

No, because Schwab would guarantee for their own customers the inside market (the best bid or offer displayed on NASDAQ) at the time the order was received. This actually worked to my advantage because if the market maker on NASDAQ was displaying one hundred shares, Schwab would fill their customer's order at this price for up to a thousand shares for most stocks. So I would place my order, check on my computer to see if my order had been filled, wait until the price went up an eighth or a quarter, and then send a sell order to Schwab. If I traded a thousand share lot, after commissions I could make $200 on the trade. This was incredible to me. When I started, I was making $700 or $800 on a good day, which to me was a week's salary. Of course, some days I would lose money or just scratch (neither make nor lose money). I was still very naive at that point because I would just buy on offers or sell to bids, and never even considered putting my orders on the bids or offers to be taken by someone else.

How many trades did you do then?

Some days I would do four trades. Other days I would do twenty. It all depended. I was strictly trading momentum. You could see the bids building up when the stock was getting ready to explode. I started getting a feel for this. You could see Instinet (a large institutional ECN) putting in a bid for 80,000 shares and this would move the market on the upside. Of course, Instinet would also sometimes hide the quantity they wanted by displaying a bid for only 1,000 shares when what they really wanted was 90,000 shares. I was trading stocks such as 3Com and Ascend.

Were you profitable trading this way?

Some weeks I was up a $1,000, some weeks I was down a $1,000. I probably built up my account by $20,000 over a couple of months. Of course, if I had just bought 1,000 shares of one of these stocks and held it I might have made just about as much money at the time. But trading started to become exciting. I enjoyed it. I realized I could do this and make money. Also I had no overnight risk since I did not carry positions after the close most of the time. I remember I did take some overnight positions in Ascend at the time and got killed. Killed for me then was taking 1,000 share position and having the stock open the next morning down two points (two dollars).

Did you prepare yourself for actively trading by learning from someone else or reading any books?

I didn't do much reading about trading. I did read one book on how to invest in IPOs but that didn't really pertain to me because I had stopped buying IPOs at that time. I did read some information on Web pages but I don't remember now what sites those were. I do remember that I was becoming aware of how market makers made their money by buying on the bid and selling on the offer. I was also becoming aware that market makers were being deceptive so that when they were bidding, they were actually selling. They would artificially make it look like a buy while they were selling stock on the offer. I was catching on to this. For example, there might be one market maker on the offer and ten on the bid, and then when you go to buy, the stock doesn't move and just craps out. I couldn't understand why and I started reading about this on day trading Web sites. Typically they would have some tidbit of information from their top trader or whatever.

Did you talk to or learn from anyone else about trading?

No. People thought I was crazy. There was nobody to talk to. Also, I was trading at home so I had no one to talk to there either.

Could you describe your day at that time?

It was like a business. I got up in the morning and put on CNBC. I would start my computer at 9:00 and watch the market build up on the pre-opening. From 9:30 to 4:00 I would not leave the screen. That was it. Some days it was worth it, some days it wasn't worth it.

Did you continue to make money?

No. I had made about $20,000 during my first few months, which brought my account up to about $50,000. But then I proceeded to lose about $30,000, which brought me down to about $19,000.

Why did that happen?

I started to take overnight positions, which did not work out. I remember I took a position in Applied Materials right before the stock split. At this point I was also starting to trade options, so I decided that if I was going to take an overnight position I should sell calls and buy puts which I did. Well, the stock opened down 10 points, but because I had sold calls, which were now worthless, and bought puts, which had increased in value, I ended up making a small amount of money on this drop. The problem was that I took my profit in the puts by selling them but kept my position in the stock. And of course, the stock just crapped out even more, so I did lose a lot of money on this trade. As I said, my account now had fallen to below $20,000.

So you were learning what didn't work.

Right. I was also learning from the Web sites what the different ECNs were; what Island was; what INCA (Instinet) was. It was at this time that I understood what ECNs were. I remember e-mailing Schwab asking them if they were going to allow traders to trade through ECNs. Of course, they said no. Well, I was ready to give up on Schwab. I was already having problems with their Internet connections. I remember one day in 1997 when the Dow dropped a huge amount and it took me an hour to get a connection to Schwab to place an order. It was horrible. I remember seeing Dell go from 70 to 85 in half an hour and I couldn't get a connection to Schwab. I saw that the ability to make money was there, but before I gave up and said this was not for me, I decided to try a professional brokerage that had superior services. Schwab was good but it just was not top of the line.

So how did you decide where to go next?

I checked some Web sites and saw some ads in the *New York Times* for SOES (Small Order Execution System) traders and I went to one of those firms. I did trade SOES there but I didn't stay long. There were several things I didn't like about them including the fact that I had a long commute. Also, there seemed to be a lack of managers present to help you if you had a problem and there were some other problems with their execution system. So after about a month I left this firm having neither made nor lost much money.

And this is when you found your present firm?

Yes. I checked the *New York Times* ads and found one that said they were opening up a new office with superior trading services. I was a little bit apprehensive about contacting them because many firms that I called did not want day traders. As soon as I said I had traded SOES, they would hang up on me. So I called this other firm and I was surprised that they actually talked to me. They were very nice and told me to stop by. I did, saw the office and said this was for me. This was at the end of 1997 and I've been here ever since. This was the firm of Lieber and Weissman Securities.

What is this firm like?

Well, when I first came here it was virtually deserted. There were only a few people here. But they were very helpful and I liked the setup. I should mention that Lieber and Weissman Securities (LWS) is a proprietary trading firm, which at the time was a member of the American stock exchange. What this meant was that I could no longer trade with SOES, which is available only to retail brokerage houses, which LWS was not. They are considered a professional trading firm but because they were members of the stock exchange there were other benefits to traders. For example, they are exempt from retail client margin requirements and governed by exchange margin requirements instead, which are more attractive to professionals. For this reason, I only put $10,000 in my account, but could trade just about as much stock as I was trading before.

Did you need to take the industry professional broker licensing exam, the Series 7?

No. At the time, traders with LWS were considered part of the stock exchange, which did not require a Series 7 license. The American Exchange changed this rule about a year ago, so LWS became a member of the Philadelphia Stock Exchange, which did not require a Series 7. However, the Philadelphia exchange now also requires a Series 7 for all traders after February 2000, and so I will have to take this exam.

So how did trading go at LWS at first?

I opened the account with $10,000 and said to myself, that if I lose $5,000, I'm out. I was still a momentum trader and I would buy by taking the offer and sell by hitting the best available bid. Well, my account dropped to $7,000 when I finally got smart and changed how I was trading. Most people in the office at the time were trying to make at least a point or more on their trades and this was what I was trying to do also. I would typically have a stock in my favor for a quarter but I wouldn't take the profit. It would drop and I might buy some more. But it was evident that this strategy was not working out. I was momentum trading but I was never taking a profit. What I had learned to do at Schwab, for some reason I had forgotten and was not doing at LWS. So I finally decided to take profits no matter what it was, whether an eighth or sixteenth. This was after about three months at LWS. And from that point on I had a big turn around.

Did you track your progress or set yourself any goals?

I kept a daily chart of my profits. At first I was only making several hundred dollars a day and I set myself a goal of $300 a day on average which would be $75,000 a year. To me that would be tremendous. I did get to this goal and then I set myself a slightly higher goal at $500 profit on average per day. I met that target and then moved up the goal again.

How many shares were you trading at this time?

I was trading several hundred shares when I first came to LWS but when I noticed I was consistently earning on average at least an eighth point profit, I quickly moved up to 500 share lots. Not only was I likely to be profitable on my trade, I had more stock to sell out at higher prices if I was right. That's because I would only sell out my position in several hundred shares at a time.

So you were a scaled out seller on the upside?

Right. After I made the trade I would offer several hundred shares at an eighth higher, and then another several hundred shares an eighth higher than that. I've been following this strategy now (summer, 1999) for a year and a half.

What execution system were you using or do you use?

I started out using Rox which allowed me to route NASDAQ orders to Island, Instinet, and three separate NASDAQ market makers. For listed, I could route to Dot, Pacific Coast, Boston, and Chicago. I also have Redi-Plus, but I'm so used to using Rox that I don't use Redi as much. Some days I will trade on both systems. I also have an Instinet terminal.

Can you tell me more about how you are interpreting the momentum using bids and offers on NASDAQ Level II?

Probably my most valuable tool is an Instinet machine, which allows me to see all the bids and offers on INCA (Instinet ECN) that may not be displayed on NASDAQ Level II. I also use INCA to trade on. This provides extremely valuable information.

Can you give me an example?

There may be an Instinet bid for a large quantity, say 20,000 or 40,000 shares, and this would not be displayed on NASDAQ Level II. So I would buy the stock and offer it out for a quick profit.

How often does this happen?

Very often. Maybe a dozen times a day. It probably happens more than this, of course, if you take all stocks into account. I can only watch one stock at a time on an Instinet machine.

Would you still make money if you didn't have an Instinet machine?

Oh yes. I've been trading without an Instinet machine for most of the time I've been trading. I only got an Instinet machine a few months ago. But it is an added benefit. You must realize that some of these situations only last a very short time, so you have to be quick. Many people are looking at the same thing. Maybe only 10 percent of my trades are done on Instinet.

Are there any other ways you use Instinet?

I'll use Instinet as an alternative to Island. If I am trying to sell stock on the offer and there is already 4,000 shares offered on Island, I won't want to use Island because the shares I offer for sale are at the end of the Island queue and will only be taken after the first 4,000 shares are taken. In that case, I may offer my shares on INCA. Another time Instinet is valuable is trading IPOs. Instinet is also an ECN which means the fills are instantaneous if you are buying or selling, whereas if you go to a market maker through SelectNet you may have to wait or not get filled at all.

Why is that?

Market maker XYZZ may be offering a 1,000 shares, but if you try to buy from them they may not do anything with you. Under NASD (National Association of Securities Dealers) rules, market makers on NASDAQ do not need to give you an instantaneous fill but can wait to fill your order or even reject to fill you at all. Market makers will give you the stock when they are certain the stock is ready to drop. I think this is horrible, but these are the rules. Market makers have all the cards in their favor. This is why I prefer to trade with Instinet or Island even if I have to pay up an eighth above the market maker offer. I do this because at least I know I'm getting done, whereas I won't know that if I trade with a market maker.

Don't market makers have to fill your order if you use SOES?

Yes, if you are a retail customer. Remember, LWS is considered a professional trading firm as a member of the stock exchange, so I can't trade SOES. Not that it would help me that much anyway. The rules for SOES are very restrictive. SOES won't help me most of the time.

So how do you trade with market makers?

Market makers have all the cards in their favor. None of them will sell to you when it's going up and none of them will buy from you when it's going down. They only have to do whatever they are showing for size on one trade, but after that they have 17 seconds or whatever to decide whether they're going to do any other orders. You have to be ahead of the game to trade with them.

Can you tell me any more things about how you identify momentum?

Joe Kernan (stock commentator on CNBC). He's good for a pop in a stock. He'll mention a stock and you know it's good for a point. Sometimes he'll tease you. He say, "I have news on this stock, it's up 22 percent right now and there's further news coming out." So I check my stock lists for a stock that is up 22 percent for the day and I would just buy it.

Can you tell me more about other techniques of trading?

It really is just identifying momentum, or sometimes a change in momentum at certain support and resistance levels. For example, I might look at a chart of Intel which is coming up to a previous high at 80. I might offer a short at $79^{15}\!/_{16}$. If the momentum reaches resistance at the 80 dollar level, it may reverse and drop. Or conversely, a stock may be dropping down to a new low. I would put in a bid to catch the bounce back up, especially if it's nearing a round dollar number.

Do you find that these major dollar numbers, such as 80, 75, or 70 have any special significance?

Often they do. I don't know why because $71^{5}\!/_{16}$ should have the same significance as 70 but the market often treats these two numbers differently. When a stock comes to these round figure levels you often will find a lot of market makers on the bid or offer. So if there are ten or so market makers bidding 70, I'll bid $70^{1}\!/_{16}$. More often than not, I'll get filled that price. The beauty of it is, that if the stock does not bounce but looks like it's going lower, then I can sell out at 70. My risk is $^{1}\!/_{16}$ but my upside potential may be a quarter.

Do you have special times of day that you prefer to trade?

Usually in the morning. Whatever money I'm going to make during the day I will try to make in the first fifteen minutes or half-hour. Often I'll make about 70 percent of what I am going to make on the day by 10 o'clock. Of course, if I'm down by 10, I'll spend the rest of the day trying to make it back. There's tremendous momentum in the morning.

How do you identify this momentum in the morning?

I've had a year and a half of just gut feeling and experience. I do watch specific market makers and even have some of them highlighted on my screen. I watch specifically what they are doing. If they were buyers the previous day, then they may be sellers today. I'll see where they are on the open to see what they are doing. Things like that. A lot of this is gut feeling that is hard to explain.

Do you have techniques that you don't want revealed in a book?

Well, I don't have anyone calling me up with inside information if that's what you mean. But no, I don't have anything available to me that's not available to anyone else. However, I have a few techniques which I will keep to myself.

What makes you different from unsuccessful traders?

The most important thing I know that most people who lose money don't know is how to take a profit. At the end of the day, I will talk to a number of the other traders. They'll ask me questions and it's a pleasure for me to help them. So someone will say they've lost $300 today. I'll look at his trades and ask him why he lost a point on some trade. Well, he'll say he was up a quarter point but expected to make a dollar. Well, if he's trading 500 shares then he's being pigheaded. He could have made $100 and ended up losing $500. Another trader lost about four points on Lycos yesterday. He went short at 273 and the stock dropped to 270 and then rapidly reversed to about 277. He hadn't placed any orders to cover after he made his short, which would have given him a profit, and then he had trouble covering. He was trying to buy from market makers after the reversal but nobody was selling to him. He lost four points on what should have been a profitable trade. When I get into a stock either long or short, I immediately offer or bid the stock out. I don't wait for the stock to trade to my price level of profit and then try to place an order. I do it immediately before the stock has gotten to that price target. If you try to sell after the stock has reversed, you're finished. Nobody's going to buy stock from you.

How do you choose which profit level to set as a target?

It depends on the stock. Internet or volatile stocks I will try to make more than an ⅛ or ¼ point of course. If I buy eBay for example at 270, then I am immediately offering 200 shares at 271 or $270^{15}\!/_{16}$. This stock trades in whole points the way other stocks trade "teenies" ($\frac{1}{16}$). CMGI also trades like this. Yesterday I bought CMGI at 179 and offered it at 180. When I saw that the price was not moving up, I immediately hit a bid for 179$\frac{1}{8}$. So I only made an eighth on it. Some people may say "big deal." But right after I sold out, the stock immediately crapped out for (dropped) two dollars. Dell trades differently and much more narrowly. So if I get in, I'll be offering some out at $\frac{1}{8}$ higher and maybe some more at seven teenies higher. Maybe I won't get any of this and I'll just sell out where I bought it.

So you're not greedy.

I'll usually leave something on the table in profit potential. The funny thing is that some guys are much slower typers than I am, so while I've already bought and sold a stock, they're still typing their orders to sell and sometimes they will even make more money on a trade than I will if there is a really strong move. Of course, sometimes they'll get burnt because they're just slower than I am in getting out.

How many stocks do you trade at a time?

Just one. I treat each trade individually. I have to concentrate on it, because there's only a small window of opportunity to make money in the kind of trading I do. I can't concentrate on anything else. Occasionally, if another stock starts to pop and I still haven't closed out my other position, I'll do two stocks, but I'm more prone to make mistakes. I know some successful traders can hold five stocks at the same time, but they're more position traders. I'm not a position trader.

And how do you handle your losses?

On fast-moving Internet stocks, I get out immediately if the stock moves against me. Stocks like Microsoft, Cisco, or Dell, you're not going to lose five points on, so I may hold on if it goes against me.

How much will you hold these stocks if they go against you?

It's hard to answer that, since it would mean I've made some kind of commitment to it. But probably half a dollar and I'm out. It's stupid to even let it go against you that much unless you are building a position in it. But generally I'm not a position trader. The only time I might hold on to a loss temporarily is if I think it's a fake out. That they are dropping their bids for no reason. There are no major offers on Instinet or heavy selling apparent.

Do you ever average down on a losing position?

No, never. I've seen too many guys wipe doing that. I'm also not in positions that long on average. I'm usually in a trade less than a minute. Thirty seconds. Ten seconds. Five seconds. I'm just trying to catch short-term volatility of the market and then get out.

Do you prefer to buy on the bid, or buy on the offer?

I would say that I'm buying on the bid about 50 percent of the time.

What do you see just before the momentum gets under way?

I might see a stock dropping for no reason. For example, today during the first half hour, eBay dropped about twenty-five points for no apparent reason as everyone seemed to be pulling their bids. I put on a short, but then noticed that nobody was leaving their bids. The short-term tick chart seemed also to be indicating a bottoming out. So I just took a shot and covered my short and went long. I had to buy on the offer.

So you were watching a short term tick chart of prices?

Not the trades. Just bids. I keep charts showing just the highest bids. A chart of trades can be a little deceptive, since some of these trades are off the market or reported late. They are not always showing an accurate picture of the market.

So you're looking at a tick bid chart. Why not a chart of the offers?

Because bids show where the support is in a stock. Where are the buyers? This is the most important information to me.

Do you use moving averages or indicators like that?

No. The most important chart I watch in addition to the stock I'm watching, is the S&P 500 futures chart. That is like God on my screen. It is very accurate in signaling the direction of the market. Whether it's a buy or sell program, it is going to affect the market one way or the other. If I'm long a stock and I see the S&P start to drop, I may just get out of the stock. Or if I'm long a large cap stock such as Microsoft and I've sold out 200 shares of my 500 share position and I see the stock starting to drop, if I see the futures starting to tick up, I'll hold back getting out of the rest of my position. Nine times out of ten, at least in large cap stocks, this will prove the correct action to take. For smaller NASDAQ stocks, this does not work as well. These stocks respond to whatever reason they are in play that day.

Do you look at the basis, or the difference in spread between the S&P futures and the cash index?

No. Perhaps I should, but the futures chart seems sufficient for me. It seems simple, but it works.

Do you look at anything else in addition to the stocks you are watching?

One thing I sometimes watch is the 30-year bond yield quote. On my system the symbol for this is TYX. Sometimes the move in yields will have an effect on the market, with yields moving inversely to the direction of stocks. I have found that if the bonds are having an effect on the market, then the opposite will happen after 3 o'clock, after the bonds stop trading.

Do you ever try any arbitrage between two closely related stocks?

The only arb I've been trading lately, is to trade Netscape depending upon what America Online is doing. AOL seems to lead Netscape, at least lately.

You've said that you don't trade listed stocks. Why is that?

I strongly dislike the New York Stock Exchange. To me it's like trading a NASDAQ stock with one market maker. It's impossible. When Island is able to trade listed stocks, I will give it a shot. (Note: Island does trade listed stocks, but not on the consolidated quote system, see interview with Matthew Andresen.)

What was your worst trade?

The worst trade in my entire experience was the trade I mentioned earlier when I was using a retail broker. The worst trade I've had since trading with direct access was $750. This was on a couple of hundred shares for about three points. This was EntreMed. I bought it, put out my offer, and in two seconds there were no bids. I tried to hit every bid, but there was nothing.

What was your best trade?

I was short 500 shares of an Internet stock and made about $13,000. It just collapsed in about four minutes. I shorted it because it had a huge gain in the morning, about 20 points, for no reason. I shorted it about $128 and then covered 100 shares 10 points lower, another 100 shares at 105, and the rest under 100. My best day was when I made $108,000.

In the past year, how consistently successful have you been?

In the past year, I haven't had a losing month. My longest losing stretch in that time was maybe three days when I lost about a total of $1,000.

How do you account for such consistency of success?

When I see my days going negative, I just stop trading. If there's nothing I'm doing that's right and maybe I'm down $500, then I just quit for the day. I'm just going to be miserable. Actually, that's not quite true. There are days when I may be down $1,000 within the first few minutes of trading. Sometimes this is because I've made a mistake entering the order or for some other reason, and on these days I've come back. There's no greater feeling than being down a $1,000 and then bring your account back to flat. I shouldn't really generalize about this since it doesn't happen that often. So I have a rule to stop trading when I reach a loss for the day of $500 and maybe half the time I do.

The successful day traders are those who act like market makers, buying on the bid and selling on the offer. In essence, they provide liquidity to the market. Those trading this way have consistent profits year after year. Traders using different techniques wind up having big winning days followed by losing days. In the end they have nothing because they cannot be consistent.

Do you consider yourself a disciplined trader?

Yes. Definitely. I also consider myself superstitious. I never talk about how much I made for the day.

Have you ever stopped trading for any length of time?

Well, that's a problem. I don't know when to stop. If you get to the point of consistently making money, then when you take a vacation you're actually losing money. So how do you take a vacation? I did take off one week last year and it happened to be a tremendous week in the market. People sometimes tell me December is the best month to take off, but last year December was my best month. The day after Thanksgiving last year was also a great day. I and maybe one other trader were the only people in the office trading. My happiest days are when the market closes for a holiday, but other than that I will not take a vacation.

Do you enjoy trading?

Definitely. I can't wait to get into the office in the morning. I love it. Even if I had a bad day the day before. People sometimes say you can get burnt out trading, but that hasn't happened to me yet.

When you make money, do you increase the amount of size you are trading or just take your profits out and invest them somewhere else?

I don't increase the size of my trades but just take it out and put it in a Schwab money market account. I suppose if I had invested my money in the stocks I trade during the day I would have made some money, but not as much as I made trading. I suppose I'm also a bit scared of investing since I've had such bad experiences with overnight trades. I would worry that half my portfolio could be wiped out overnight. There's no better feeling than going home at the end of the day without holding stocks, since nothing is going to hurt me, such as wars, political events, earnings warnings, and so on.

Why is it that you don't do more shares if you make more money?

I will only trade up to a 1,000 shares. Many of the stocks I trade have maybe a ten or fifteen second window before they reverse. With a 1,000 shares, you have time to get out, by offering stock out. If you try to trade more than that, you may still be holding stock when the stock runs out of steam.

How many trades do you make in a day?

I don't keep track of that. In terms of the number of shares I trade, maybe on the low side I'll trade 8,000 and the high side maybe 60,000 in a day. On average I will trade 30,000 shares a day.

How many stocks are you watching to select from to make a trade?

Maybe six. I'll have a Level II screen up for each one. I can link any of these stocks to the tick bid chart I watch.

Is the time of day important to your trading?

The most active trading is between the open and about 10:30. After that things just move around. Between 11:00 and 2:30 trading can be pretty horrible. I do try to trade during that time, but you have to be very picky. There's no volume. After 2:30 it gets better again.

Where would you like to be in 10 years?

One of my main goals is to be able to save enough money to be able to live off the interest with a six-figure income. I would like to retire from trading, but I wouldn't retire and not do anything. I would still be involved in the stock market, maybe open some businesses in my community, and give something to charity, things like that.

chapter 3

Michael McMahon

Michael McMahon had a varied career before he became an independently successful trader and later one of the most popular instructors for the Online Trading Academy. Fifty-one years old, Mike was born in Philadelphia into a family with grandparents who had come from Cork and Limerick, Ireland. His father worked as a tool and dye maker and his mother was a fashion buyer for clothing stores. When he was a child, his family moved to southern California where he attended Catholic schools through high school. He ran track and tried out for the Olympics in Mexico in 1968. He graduated from UCLA in political science in 1971. Following college, he was drafted into the Army 82nd Airborne Rangers where he became an assistant drill instructor. After leaving the army, he worked for the U.S. Divers Corp. where he was technical instructor and liaison to the United States and other navies around the world. Having learned to dive at age 9 and later becoming a surfer, he started his own business in 1974 teaching scuba diving and selling diving equipment. This business was very successful and expanded to a second shop before he broke his back in 1980. Because of his health and related financial reasons, he sold his shops and spent a year in rehabilitation learning to walk again. He is also a passionate cook.

How did you first become interested in stocks?

When I was about 10 years old, my best friend's father was a stockbroker, and whenever he was around I would ask him questions about the market. I bought some Sperry Rand in the early

1960s. By the time I was 15, those shares had gained enough that I could buy an old clunker with my profits. I thought this was terrific. I was a teenager with hormones and a car, all made on the back of a stock!

I continued to buy and sell equities in college and considered myself a fundamental investor. I studied the true valuations of the companies in which I invested, their products and the likely demand for them, the company's management team, and issues such as those. Mostly, I invested in blue chips such as General Motors, Sperry, and General Dynamics.

I later owned a deep-sea diving business, and in 1980, I broke my back. Naturally, I could no longer teach diving, and my doctors weren't sure I would walk again. Then and there, I made a mental commitment that if I could not make my living picking up a hundred-pound dive tank, then I would have to work with what's between my ears. This became the backbone of my discipline. Although I was fortunate in that I did walk again, it was during this time I developed my passion for markets.

Because of the Hunt brothers' attempt to corner the silver market, and because of all the mergers and acquisitions going on in the early 1980s, I was looking for leverage in my investments. At this time, a commodity broker called me and urged me to invest in live cattle. I said I wasn't interested because steers were too often on my plate. Then I hung up! I did check the cattle market several weeks later, though, and realized that if I had invested $10,000, I would have made about $125,000. That did it—I was hooked.

I opened a commodity account and for my first trade I bought sugar at one and half cents a pound. It went up to about five or six cents and I made a killing. I placed another trade in wheat and did well in that. Of course, I immediately thought I could walk on water. I thought trading was terrific. I started with about $50,000, and took home between $125,000 and $140,000 for a few years, mostly trading precious metals and wheat.

What was your trading strategy?

I used news feeds, technical analysis, and chart. Also, when I traded wheat, I kept my eye on meteorology.

How long did you continue to trade commodities?

In 1982, I got long in silver just before it went limit down for three days in a row. I couldn't get out. I lost $227,000 in those three days, which blew out my entire account.

That must have been pretty depressing.

It was depressing. And my wife wasn't real happy either.

So what did you do then?

That's when I decided that the only person who made sure money in commodities was the broker. So I took my Series 3 license to become a commodity broker, which is what I did for the next few years. I developed a book of about 50 to 80 accounts. I didn't like being a broker. People had their own ideas about how to trade an account. They would give me instructions to do the opposite of what I truly thought was right. They would lose money and then blame me. The firm I was with closed, so I went to another firm where I continued as a broker and started to trade my own account again. But when that firm started to move into some very gray areas in addition to precious metals, I realized it was time for me to leave. I moved to Hawaii believing if I could trade, I could trade from anywhere—which isn't true. Nobody wants to trade at a brokerage at 3 A.M. I came back from Hawaii after six months and then held a series of corporate managerial jobs for the next six years.

Were you trading during this time?

I still had an account at Merrill Lynch but I didn't do trading per se. I still held positions in stocks, wrote covered calls, and tried my hand at dividend capture strategies. There were a lot of different ways to make money in stocks, and if you can pile a couple on top of each other, you can do very well without having to take a lot of risk. When I left the corporate world in 1993, I decided to trade stocks full time.

How did it go?

Terribly. I was trading up to a thousand shares at Merrill Lynch, but every time I did a trade I had to overcome a commission of $200 in and $200 out. I was making a living out of it, but that was about it. On a $50,000 account, I would make another $50,000 by the end of the year. This wasn't bad, except that I was eating my profits to live.

I used technical analysis, buying on major support lines, and selling just before major resistance lines. Because of my earlier success with stocks, I was still paying a lot of attention to fundamentals. I didn't trade stocks I didn't know, and the stocks I did trade were mostly blue chips.

I wasn't making a lot of money, so once again, I went back to the idea of leverage. I knew there was horsepower in options, which I had some experience with earlier writing covered calls and buying puts. So in 1995, I started to trade stock options at Paine Webber. I would buy calls or sell naked puts. I had very mixed results. I would be up $50,000 one month, and then down $30,000 the next, then I would be up $20,000, and then down $40,000. I looked at this and said to myself, "Either I don't know what I'm doing or there's something wrong with me." It turned out there was something wrong with me. It was pure, simple greed. I was taking more and more risk, and realized that trading options wasn't my element in the first place. So, I gravitated back to trading stocks.

How did you actually hear about direct access trading?

I had never opened an online account with a broker.com, but had always used a traditional brokerage with whom I had established a relationship. But in the middle of 1997, I heard an advertisement on CNBC about direct access trading. Although they didn't call it direct access back then, I learned I could place my order right on the NASDAQ with Level II. That was the hook that got me. I didn't have to talk to Chip or Bob or Harry any more. The transparency of the market on Level II was just wonderful. I was led to believe, initially, that I could pick up the spread whenever I wanted, although later, I found out differently. So I opened an account with Block Trading, which is no longer in business.

What was that like?

I hate to admit it, but I was not very computer literate. They had some classes there, but they weren't very good. People talked to us about the different routing methods, discipline, risk management, the psychology of trading, and that sort of thing. It was great for a beginner, but for me, it fell on deaf ears. After all, I had been in the market for decades and, therefore, I knew it all. They had a paper trading demonstration system as part of the training. It was incredible; I pushed a button and green "play" money showed up on the screen. Demo is good training for execution but it is not very helpful in the reality of trading department. In fact, I was quoted in the *Los Angeles Times* as saying "It's too good to be true, there has to be something wrong," which did not endear me to this firm.

What execution system were you using at the time?

CyberTrader 1.5. They used Island, which was the only ECN they had a subscription to.

How did your trading go?

My first problem was that I was an old, slow trader. I'm used to technical analysis and something that's going to develop over days or even possibly weeks. Level II at first lured me into overtrading. I started to see momentum in the stocks, and I was just not as quick and adroit as some of the other people, thus, I was pulling the trigger too late or jumping out too early. I could see the roller coaster and I knew what that meant from a charting standpoint but when it was scrolling in front of me, I would get caught up in it. I was only trading one or two hundred share positions, but in the first couple months I was down around $20,000.

How did you respond to this early loss?

I decided, at that point, to take a month off. When I crunched the numbers, I found out that I had lost maybe one or two thousand dollars on the trade points, but burned another $18,000 in commissions. They were charging a ticket of $20 plus fees on each side of a trade no matter what size. I looked at "me" and wondered why I was overtrading. I've always had an innate belief in myself so I said to myself, "You're letting yourself down. You know how to do this or you can figure it out." So I reinstituted my discipline after I came back, and I've been successful ever since.

So tell me about your trading after this point.

Because I'm a little bit anal at times, I've analyzed a lot of my trades. I've found that there is no point in trading the open or the first 20 minutes. I think this is a reflection of the old cliché that amateurs open the market and professionals close it, and at that time I was trying to trade the open like a professional. Still, I always seemed to be on the wrong side of the market. I even tried to do a mental switch, so that if I thought I should buy, I would sell, but that didn't work either. In the end, it came down to a matter of discipline. Now, I won't open my first trade until 9:50 or even 10:00.

You seem to do a thorough analysis of your trades regularly, is that correct?

Yes. I put my trades on a spreadsheet to see how many I've completed that lasted a minute, how many trades from three to five minutes, how many between this hour and that, how many trades I took in this sector or another, which ones are profitable ones and which ones aren't, and I study the time of day when these trades took place. I look at the data every day, but I only crunch the numbers once a week. One of the advantages of my platform is that I can take the data off on a disk and put it on a spreadsheet. I adjust my trading to these analytical results.

Where are you trading now?

Momentum Securities.

What size position are you trading?

The maximum size position I will put on now is about 2,000 shares.

Do you scale into or out of trades?

I do both. I'll usually scale into a large size position by buying 200 share lots initially to test the waters, or so I don't spook the market. I then build on the position with a reverse pyramid.

Could you give me an example of how you would do a reverse pyramid?

Let's say I see a stock come down over the last day and test the $70 support level on high volume. Maybe it's bounced off that level by a fraction and then come back to test that level again on a double bottom. I'll put an order on the bid for 70 and a teenie ($1/16$ of a point). If it trades down to that level or the even figure, then I have my initial position with a teenie or $1/8$ mental stop loss below 70. If the stock starts moving in my direction, and everything looks good on Level II, then I'll buy another 200 shares when the stock trades up to maybe $3/16$ bid, offered at a quarter. I'll probably buy on the offer, since, if it is running, I won't be able to get it on the bid anyway. Hypothetically, the stock may run up to $1/2$ point, and I'll look for a retracement, since most stocks won't run $1/2$ point without some pullback. If I see the momentum slowing, I'll lie in wait by putting in a bid for 400 shares at $3/8$. I'm now long 800 shares. Maybe the stock runs up a bit more. There's a lot of support on the bid, possibly being led by Goldman Sachs who is on a buy program from the 70 support level. I'll buy another 200 shares on the offer at $5/8$ or $3/4$ level and maybe another 400 shares on the bid, if there is some retracement in here.

How do you get out of this position?

Let's say I had determined that 71 is the resistance level. I intend to be totally out of my position just below that level at $15/16$. I don't want to get into competition with all the sellers at the figure. So I'll start scaling out of my position on the offer at $7/8$ and $15/16$, but if it looks like the price is reversing at that point, I'll sell to the bidders. I've made about a half-point on average on these 1,400 shares, in this hypothetical example, for a profit of $700. That's a good trade.

How long would a trade like this last for you?

It could be as short as five minutes or several days. This would be a swing trade.

How would you define the difference between scalping, momentum, and swing trading?

Scalping is buying on the bid and immediately selling on the offer to capture the spread. Momentum trading is based on your reading of Level II and Time and Sales. Momentum trades could last as long as 20 minutes, which would be a long momentum trade, but that will culminate at the end of the day. Momentum trading is being able to read public emotion and has everything to do with market psychology and seeing it at work. A swing trade is based on charts and technical analysis supported by interpretation of Level II. Trading catagories are not based on the time it takes to do the trade, but the reasons you are basing the trade on.

What is the distribution of your trades by type of trade?

This has changed since I first started to trade with direct access. When I first started trading, I was doing one or two hundred tickets a day mostly based on scalping and momentum. Now, I may have two to three short-term swing trades on. Sometimes they last several days but mostly I trade them intraday. Based on momentum during the day, I may also make another five or ten trades.

How many positions would you have on at the same time?

In a perfect world, I would have four positions. Three swings and one momentum. I don't have more than one momentum trade on at a time.

How much technical analysis do you use?

Quite a bit. In the evenings after the close, I'll study charts and look for consolidations with breakdowns or breakouts. I'll set up some parameters for three or four swing trades that I may do the next day or over a couple of days. The next morning I'll open these trades, and while I watch them develop, I'll take some momentum trades with other stocks.

What do you mean by consolidation?

I believe that the 90-day high and low are very key levels to look at, so I typically look at daily charts for the last three months. I look for stocks in a narrow, congested trading range for an extended period. The more narrow the range and the longer it's traded in that range, the more I'm interested. If a stock trades between 50 and 51 for three months, for example, I'm very interested. Between 50 and 55, I'm still interested. But between 50 and 70, I'm probably not interested.

I search for stocks that may breakout or breakdown from these ranges. I'm looking for a confirmation of at least a quarter point on significant volume, sometimes on the second day. If the stock normally trades 60,000 shares per minute by 10 A.M., and the next day it trades 120,000 shares per minute by that time, I don't have to wait for the end of the day to say there is very high volume there.

What I'm looking for is a stock that breaks out of this consolidation range, but I won't buy or sell it until it retests the bottom or top of this range, and then starts to resume its breakout pattern. For example, I'll look to buy when it breaks out above its initial breakout high by a quarter point or more.

Other things have to be in place before I pull the trigger on a trade. I don't walk in blindly to any trade and just say that I'm a buyer. Maybe 80 percent of the time these breakouts are false, so you also have to know how to protect yourself if they don't work.

Are there other technical patterns you look at?

This isn't the only pattern I trade. Sometimes I make great trades just trading the range, itself. Cisco has a typical range of four points a day. If it goes down two points, I may buy on any kind of support.

What books have you found that are useful in learning about technical analysis?

There are a bunch of them. One of the best ones I've found is by Martin Pring. John Murphy's books are very good also. Steve Nison's *Japanese Candlesticks* I've found quite useful. Although I don't use them in trading yet, I'm finding that Fibonacci numbers are fascinating in measuring retracements.

How much do you use candlesticks?

Candlesticks are all I have on a graph. I believe in the law of averages, and where the majority of trades are executed. The real support level in a stock is probably somewhere in a narrow range, not a specific number. If I am trying to determine a support level, then I am looking at where the majority of trades take place. If this support level is violated by a candlestick wick or even a small part of the real body, I'm going to ignore that. I look to the corners of the real body in drawing trend lines, ignoring the wicks.

How do you find the stocks you want to swing trade?

There's a wealth of information on the Internet. One of my favorites is BigCharts, which is free and has a lot of good charts on a page called Big Reports.

How do you handle losses?

I use strictly mental stops. I never risk more on a trade than I intend to make, and usually I look for at least a four or five-to-one, profit-to-loss ratio. If I'm looking to make only a quarter point on a trade, my mental stop will be a sixteenth, and certainly no more than an eighth. If I have a larger profit on a trade, I will use a trailing stop. If the momentum stalls above the point where I scaled into my last trade, I will use the price of my last trade to get out, or no more than an eighth point below that level. I will get out by selling everything to the bid. If the move starts to weaken, I may take off 25 percent or 50 percent of the position just to see what happened next. Putting out a position on the offer on weakness is foolish, unless you can use a hidden order, because you are just going to scare the market and add to resistance. I love to SOES or preference on SelectNet in these situations. One of my disciplines is to always get something on a trade that is showing some profit.

Do you use any money management techniques in trading?

I do, which may be against what some other people recommend. I have daily maximum loss and profit limits. I will not risk more than 1 or 1½ percent of my trading capital during the trading day, and I will stop trading if I reach a profit target of 2 percent of my capital. If I am trading $50,000 and I hit a $500 loser on the first trade, then I'm done for the day. For that same size capital, if I'm up $1,000 for the day, and I'm not trading smoothly, then I also stop for the day. I have no problem taking home $2,000 a day. I've found that if you start looking for the next dollar, you will lose the next dollar. You start overtrading. Most people are human, with very few robots among us who are perfectly emotionless. If you have a $10,000 winning day, you will want to see it grow to $20,000. But there is nothing more disappointing than going home after that point with only a $1,000, because you squandered $9,000 doing something crazy.

I will check myself if I'm up 2 percent for the day. Am I really trading good today, is the market really in my favor, do I really have some good trades on, do I feel healthy, good, and friendly, am I really focused? If the answer is "yes," then I'll trade beyond that. But if there's anything that is a weakness, if I'm not really focused, if I'm really thinking about the next trade rather than the one I'm in, then I'm done whether it's the first or last trade of the day. I like coming home a winner. It makes me feel confident. If I have confidence, I tend to make quicker decisions, and quicker decisions tend to lead to greater profits. I have no problem taking larger risks for larger rewards, but I like to build myself up for doing that.

Also, if I've had a lot of winning trades where I am really up for the month, then I'll quit for a week or so. I'll do some analysis and watch the rhythm of the market. I know what will happen to me if I continue to trade at that point because it's happened to me before, and that is, I'll believe I can walk on water. And when that happens I'll become less focused and not as sharp. I assume that there are people in the market actively hunting me. I'm not paranoid, because I know that the head trader at Goldman Sachs doesn't know who I am from an ant on the ground. But when I'm in the market, I want all my hairs up— even though I'm bald—trying to feel whether there is any animosity heading my way.

You've mentioned that you don't like to trade the open for 20 minutes. Are other times of day important to your trading?

When I've crunched the numbers, I realized it's best to avoid trading during the doldrums, from 12:00 to about 2:00 or 2:20. At that time I'm usually out of the market. I do have to force myself to get up from my terminal, because if I sit there I'll try to squeeze an eighth out of another trade. I'm not here to make commissions for a broker, but to make money for Mike. I'll just get up and leave during this time.

Lately, perhaps because of age or health, I may not even come back to trade the close anymore. There are very few days that are so exciting that I'll come back in the afternoon to get in on the kill. I don't trade in extended hours. Life is tough enough.

Do you prefer to trade alone or on a floor with other traders?

I prefer to trade with others. Some people find that trading remotely from home allows them to become very focused and concentrated, but I need to go to a place of business. I get lazy if I don't. I have the best computers and terminals at home, because I can afford the best, but when I roll out of bed in the morning, am I going to be bright-eyed and ready to fight the good fight? I get up every morning at 7:30 New York time. CNBC goes on and by 8:00 A.M. Bloomberg TV is also on. I'll get on the Internet looking for news plays, upgrades and downgrades, and momentum plays. I've already had my charts put aside. I drive to a place where I will then trade. This is one of the very large disciplines in my life.

What does your screen look like?

I have a 21-inch screen with a 19-inch auxiliary screen for a Real Tick III charting package. On the main screen, I have CyberTrader 1.7 as my execution system. I used to have three Level II montages up at a time, but now I only use one after CyberTrader introduced something called Dynamic Ticker. This is a graphical display of market maker and ECN movement on Level II and the speed of the prints. It generates a green bar for upward buying pressure and a red bar for selling pressure, so I use that as a good market alert. It's nothing I trade off of, but it's a great watchdog instead of trying to read prints as they go by. Let's say I have my swing trade on, but I'm looking for some other trades. I'll put Biogen and Amgen, Microsoft and Oracle, and T-Labs and Ericsson on the Dynamic Ticker. I've got three different industries up. If two of those stocks starts to go solid red or green, I'm interested in seeing whether the entire sector is moving, and maybe I can get a good buy or short sale as other stocks in that sector play follow the leader.

I also have a minimum of three charts up. I have an S&P futures one-minute, two-day candlestick, and the same for the stock I am watching, both charts stacked in a column. I have a five-minute, three-day on the stock, and a fifteen-minute, ten-day chart. I'll be running 10, 20, and 50 simple moving averages on the ten-day chart. I use these as moving support and resistance lines. These keep me alert as to when I may want to pay a little bit more attention to Level II. That's all I'll need for a momentum play.

Not one of these things is the trigger to a trade. I'm the trigger.

What kinds of things are you looking for on a Level II screen?

I won't trade Priceline.com because I don't know who the market makers are. But if you ask me about Cisco, then I can tell you that the biggest trader is Goldman Sachs. A year ago Merrill Lynch was the second biggest trader, but this year he's been replaced by Smith Barney. Merrill is now number three. So the first thing I want to know is who is the player in the stock. Just because Goldman is the overall biggest trader, doesn't mean that he's the biggest today. But if Cisco opens at $62 and I see Goldman Sachs on the bid, and five minutes later he's on the bid at 62½, and five minutes later he's bidding 63, then what is Goldman doing? Obviously, he's a buyer. Where is he on the asked? Is he anywhere near the inside asked or is he hanging back above the market? This is more confirmation.

Who does Goldman trade for? Obviously, he trades for institutions and funds at least half the time, and for his own account during the other half. Either way, if he is on a buy program, it's going to be a large buy program. Merrill Lynch represents retail orders, who often reflect poor judgment in the market and are often getting into a move late. If I see Merrill buying, I'm probably a seller at that point. It implies that the stock's either going to drop, or I've already had the position. Knight is hard to read. They're an order aggregator, and although they are often a large player, they may not be pushing a stock in a particular direction. You do have to be aware of where they are though.

Generally, you are looking for the gatekeeper, the ax, the hammer, or whatever term you wish to call them. These are the people who give support or resistance to a stock's momentum. They define the true spread as opposed to the mathematical spread.

What is the difference in these spreads?

The mathematical spread is the difference between the best bid and the best asked. The true spread is a moving number, but is generally the same for a stock throughout the day, although there are always exceptions. If Goldman is a buyer at 70, you may find that Merrill is a seller at 70⅜. The true spread here is ⅜ and the stock will oscillate back and forth between these levels, and as the stock moves during the day, that true spread will be maintained.

Do you see deception going on in the market?

I'm also looking for what I call "scare crows" or "stalking horses," where a market maker will use an ECN to hide large share size trades. He may even display large share size to drive the market up to a selling price or scare it down to a buying level. You see it every day, in all stocks. INCA may show 800 or 1,000 shares on the offer most of the day, and then suddenly pop 88,000 shares onto the offer. This is a blatant sore thumb that would drive the market down. Who would be waiting below that on the bid but a Goldman Sachs?—although I don't mean to pick on Goldman in these examples since all market makers do this.

Large institutional brokers have also taken a large ownership stake in ARCA, the ECN. If these brokers are going to have a hidden agenda implementing a buy or sell program, then ARCA might be a likely candidate other than Island.

You said you use Level II analysis in conjunction with your technical analysis?

If I am playing momentum, I am not using technical analysis, but I am always using Level II in my technical trades.

Do you find yourself getting burnout as a trader?

I'm 51 years old and feel sometimes like I'm going on 101. I love trading. I enjoyed it a lot more when I was younger and energetic. Last year I had a heart attack, so I try to curtail some of my stress, not that I think my trading was related to my attack. But that's why I only trade about five or six months out of the year now.

I pay myself a livable wage, which covers my living expenses, and any money I make over that I take out and place in core investment holdings, including long-term stock positions and real estate.

If you hold a stock long-term, do you have a psychological problem trading it short-term?

It's not difficult psychologically, but it's hard to resist using all the leverage I may have. Trading and investing are two different disciplines. I have two separate accounts. If I kept them in the same account, I know I would fiddle with the long-term position.

Why don't you trade larger sizes than you do, if you can afford it?

I've watched other traders swing 10,000 share blocks in a trade. I don't like that risk and I don't feel as comfortable. I like the way I scale in and out. I make very good money right now and don't need the extra horsepower. A 10,000 share size in large capitalization stocks such as Cisco, Dell, or Microsoft, which can trade 40 million shares a day, is one thing. But in the universe of other stocks, a block that size will scare the market. I'm not going to be the blatant one on the board.

How many of your trades are short sales?

Over the past two or three years as the market has been going up, I've been about 60 percent long. Recently, about 70 percent of my trades are short sales.

How many losing months have you had during the previous two years?

I haven't calculated that, but probably not many. I've had some bad runs, in which I'm on the losing side of trades for two weeks. I stop trading when that happens. If I have four or five days when I've not made money, then I'm doing something wrong. It's time to stop and step back. I examine the analysis of my trades or look at me.

How long would you stop trading in that situation?

I'll just walk away for a day, do a little self-licking. Then I sit down and look at the trades and figure out why I was wrong. I'll go back to trading within a day or so.

When I'm in the market, I try to pay strict attention to it. I watch my money like a hawk. I've worked hard enough for it. If I can't pay strict attention to the market, then I don't trade. That's why I haven't been trading as much this year, since I've been working with Online Trading Academy.

How did you get involved with Online Trading Academy (OTA)?

They asked me to be a guest speaker to a very large class they had last year. I really enjoyed it, as I've always enjoyed teaching in one capacity or another throughout my entire life. I find a tremendous personal satisfaction in getting the lights to go on in someone. They liked my style and asked me to teach other classes here or there. I don't mind this, but I don't want to be a full-time instructor for a living.

Does taking a trading course make a difference in how well someone will do?

Absolutely. There is no doubt that someone who goes through a formal education, and has some trader savvy beaten into them, will do better. OTA goes overboard in making sure people understand the risks involved, the discipline, the capital preservation, the philosophy and psychology of the market, besides the pretty colors of Level II. They also teach what can happen and how fast it can happen, things like that. I'm part of that, and I'm very proud of it.

Do you follow the statistical results of people after they leave the OTA program?

As best we can. OTA is not a broker itself, so students go to a variety of brokers after leaving us. Of those who come to the office where I trade at Irvine, California, maybe 50 or 60 percent are still trading six months later. That's very good. The failure rate is many times due to poor capitalization, and some people who just don't "get it." There's always some wild person who believes it's just time to go long Rambus—as it drops thirty points—and they keep doubling their position.

OTA tells its students they are part of the trading community. If they have problems, they can come back with their trading sheets and we'll analyze them. We'll talk to them, and they're always welcome to take a class again. New traders seem to get caught up in the world of trading, as opposed to the business of trading. We're always trying to reeducate ex-students. It's free, but they don't always come.

How much capital would you say someone needs to start trading?

You can't do it with $5,000. Other than that, it depends on their talent, their savvy, their ability to grasp concepts, but I would say absolute minimum would be $15,000 to $20,000; $100,000 is way too much. If a new trader starts with $10,000 and loses $5,000, and someone else started with $25,000 and loses $5,000, which one is going to suffer the most psychological damage? The trader with too little capital becomes scared, and scared money never wins.

How much do you think people should expect to lose when they are starting?

From what I see, maybe between $5,000 and $12,000 over the course of four to five months. At about that time the lights may go on and they stop hemorrhaging money. This is with training. Without training, it may take them a year or year and a half, and I don't know how much money in losses.

The first thing an untrained person will do is read every guru book, without realizing that trading is personal, and there is no style of trading for everyone. There is scalping, momentum, and swing trading, but people need to use a blend of those, and that blend is going to be very personal.

What kinds of personal or psychological characteristics do people need to be successful?

Self-confidence is most important. Other characteristics include being decisive, being reasonably bold without being foolhardy, becoming as emotionless as possible, realizing losses are just part of business, and that they are not a reflection of you. Instead, they may point out some poor analysis and bad breaks. You need to be impervious to the market, and you can't let outside influences disturb you. If someone else on your floor is yelling that they just got into Mr. Softee, that does not mean you should take your eyes off Cisco. Discipline is probably the key thing that everyone has to have. It's the tie that binds all of the other personality traits together.

How do you teach discipline?

You can't teach discipline, but you can teach the rules of discipline. Start slowly and with small share sizes, manage risk, don't take losers home overnight, don't try to trade gaps that are for experienced traders. Hearing and doing are two different things. I am not allowed to put your feet in scalding water when you break discipline, so I cannot teach discipline. But absolutely—the skills of trading can be taught. You just can't make someone follow them.

Why have you become successful, when others have not?

Because I've been careful and thoughtful. I also believed I could do it. I had self-confidence. As an instructor, I set achievable goals to encourage new traders to modify their personalities.

Nobody is perfect. Everybody has flaws. A strength they can augment, and a weakness they can shore up. By giving them small identifiable goals, they can progress and learn self-confidence that allows them to take larger steps.

What kind of goals?

A beginning trader should trade for one month with a trade size of one hundred shares. His or her only goal should be to be green for the month disregarding commissions. This can be broken down further by setting a goal of only four trades a day during the first week, two in the morning and two in the afternoon. Stop there whether you win or lose and analyze those trades. In the next week, you can increase the number of trades. This process can be stretched out over ninety days. You can also write a business plan with other identifiable goals. By meeting these goals and going on to the next step, a new trader can instill self-confidence.

What is the most common mistake people make when they start to trade?

The single biggest mistake is the inability to recognize the power of the market. They see stocks on the news that have gone up twenty-five points and it never occurs to them that if a stock goes up that much, it can go down that much. They are too naïve when they go into the market. The second biggest mistake is they have exaggerated expectations. They believe they are going to make several hundred thousand this year, and next year they can make a million. They don't understand the incredible amount of work and understanding that they must put in before they will be success-ful. I'm talking about reasonably rational human beings. Crazy or greedy people will simply destroy themselves.

Where do you want to be in 10 years?

In Hawaii, semiretired. I will never stop playing the market. Be-cause of a broken back and broken ticker, what am I going to do? If I don't stay active, at 51 I'll get "youngzheimer's" disease. You have to use it or lose it. I can never see myself sitting in a hammock reading Danielle Steele. Yet, I doubt in ten years I'll be sitting at a direct access platform. Maybe I'll just go back to Merrill Lynch.

Is there anything you would like to say that I haven't asked you about?

Philosophically, a lot of people have problems with trading because they do not understand its civilizing force and its social value. A lot of people think of day traders as bandits who give nothing back to society. They don't appreciate that another word for trader is simply merchant, and what traders provide is liquidity to markets. It bothers me, and I feel semi-self-conscious that I am not perceived by my society as a high-ranking, honored citizen in a good profession. I have turned my boyhood curiosity into a nice investment, and then a career of trading. Yet the wins have to be weighed against the losses. I do have scar tissue. It's incredible to me that the reputable financial industry hides behind terms like "market maker" or "broker," as if there is a difference between a stage actor and movie actor. There is no difference. My dollar is as good as the traders for Merrill Lynch or anybody else's. And I work just as hard for my rewards. I don't need to apologize. I would like to see more respect from society for this profession as a whole.

chapter 4

Mayer Offman

Mayer Offman is Head Trader at Generic Trading and a principal of Carlin Equities, Inc. A most remarkable man and trader, Mayer has developed a distinctive style of trading a multimillion dollar account very successfully and consistently.

He is 49 years old and was born in the Bronx to parents who were holocaust survivors. His father was a tool-and-dye maker and his mother a housewife, both wanted him to have opportunities that they were never able to have. Mayer always attended yeshivas, where long hours of study is divided between Judaic and secular studies. He did well in math, always finding it easy to do math problems in his head, and in high school took advanced math courses. His other favorite subject was the Talmud, which involves logical reasoning and debate about the way to lead a Jewish life. Mayer has always liked challenging games and intellectual or sports competitions, and candidly states he liked to win. He went to Yeshiva University in upper Manhattan, first majoring in math and then in economics and finance.

Following graduation, he went to New York University at night and finished his MBA course work and continued studying at Yeshiva University during the day where he received his rabbinical degree. Completing his advanced degrees, Mayer was torn between working in business or the social and religious world of the rabbinate. Although he initially applied for a job as a rabbi, he changed his mind and decided to try business first, feeling he could always come back to the rabbinate if business didn't work out. Repeating Jackie Mason's joke that every Jewish mother wants her child to become a doctor, or if he's a little retarded, a lawyer, and if he's very retarded, an accountant; Mayer laughed and said he became an accountant at Ernst and Young.

When did you first become interested in stocks?

I had no interest in the stock market until I was in college. My grandfather took an active interest in stocks when he retired. He and I started to talk about stocks at the end of my college studies. I started to trade a little while I was at Ernst and Young. I would run out in the middle of the day to my broker and sit in the boardroom. I wasn't trading much but mostly did a lot of watching. I had a few positions, mostly in options, because I couldn't afford stocks.

Were you a trader or investor then?

I was always a trader. I wanted to become rich fast and didn't have time for investing. I wanted to be a millionaire the next day or I'd rather be broke.

What happened next?

I left Ernst and Young to go to a small accounting firm. The work there could be done in about five hours, so I would get in early at 7:30 and finish my work by noon. Then I would go over to visit a friend at R.F. Lafferty, where I had moved my account, and trade stocks in the afternoon. This was when I started actively trading. This was about 1980 or 1981. Actively trading in those days meant three trades a day!

How did you do as a trader?

I traded stock options. I doubled my money and lost my money. I doubled my money and lost my money. I had only about $10,000, so I said whatever it is, it is. I was learning though.

Did anyone help you at that time?

At first, I was trying to figure out where a stock would go if this would happen, or if there was a takeover, or if they got good earnings. I heard the rumors on television, takeover this, takeover that, this one's going to discover that. I was playing these stocks and waiting a thousand years for something to happen. Of course, as an options trader, I was buying the most out of the money options and losing money when nothing happened.

But then, interestingly enough, I was sitting next to a postal worker who had just retired. I learned a lot from him. The most important thing he taught me was let the stock tell you where the action is. If you're a trader, you have to see where the action is. Don't look for some esoteric stock that you think is going to invent a new Coca-Cola or treatment for cancer. Watch the market and stay where the action and volume are. He told me to forget about options. Slowly but surely over the years I've absorbed what he said.

What happened next?

I quit my small accounting firm. I knew I didn't want to do accounting anymore, because they want to work you 15 hours a day and I didn't find the work challenging or exciting. My objective was that I was going to do something I like in life, whether it's poor, rich, or in between. I knew if I did something I liked in life, I would eventually succeed.

I really wanted to trade my own account. But no one would hire me as a trader; they wanted to hire me as a broker. I wasn't interested in selling but this was my avenue for slowly getting into the trader position. So I decided to become a broker at a mid-sized firm that is now out of business. I didn't have any serious money then, but there were five or ten friends who were young and knew me from school, and I became their broker. I never did a cold call in my life but built my clients by getting references.

Even with $10,000, I was always a very aggressive trader. But big brokerage firms don't like you to be aggressive because even if you are making money, it sounds like churning. In my twenty years in the financial world, I've never had a complaint ever in any aspect of my financial life. I'm very careful.

So after about a year I left my first firm to go to a much smaller firm, where people did their own thing and there was more emphasis on trading. I took a partner who got me clients and from then on, I was trading my own account along with my clients. I did very well there and became the biggest broker in the firm. When that firm closed, I was hired by another firm, Edward Viner, to become the head options trader.

What did it mean to be the head options trader?

They gave me a $50,000 account to trade and said trade options for us. This was in July of 1982 and August of 1982 was the beginning of the bull market. I brought this account up to $600,000, twelve times my money in about six months!

Edward Viner was a conservative firm run by older people who had been in the market 50 years and had never seen a crazy options trader like me. I was very aggressive and didn't leave any money to spare. If I had $600,000, I was trading $600,000 with options. Viner never had an options business, so when I went up twelve times my money, they loved me. But when I lost back some of this, they got nervous, even though the account was still up at about $400,000.

What kind of options strategies were you using?

I was long calls. I never shorted puts or used floor strategies.

How did you choose the stocks you traded?

As the retired postal worker had advised me to do, I went where the action was, looking for events or catalysts that would move a stock, news, rumors, takeovers, earnings surprises, things like that. Really fundamental analysis. I traded stocks like Clorox, Merrill Lynch. Tech stocks weren't hot at that time and I traded almost all NYSE stocks.

I started to use some form of relative strength. If I thought a stock or a group of stocks was acting well relative to the market, that would interest me. If the market was going down, and I noticed that one stock held up, I would look at it. I might buy it, and if it was a stock in a group, I might buy the rest of the group next. Anything that wasn't acting in the norm of what everything else was doing was unusual, I had my eye on it.

I never looked at a chart and used almost no technical analysis. Technical analysis really just tells you what fundamental analysis knows. If someone didn't know the fundamentals, there would be no technical analysis.

I wasn't that disciplined back then.

What do you mean?

I was going for scores. If an option went from one to two or three, a person normally might be satisfied with that. I believed that when I went into a position, I would make three, four, five, ten times my money. I had many scores like this, but my discipline really hurt me from getting into the big time. If an option I bought went from three to eight and then to six, I should have sold it at six. I should have been out, because I was wrong after that point. But sometimes I would just wait and hope that the next day some other event would occur. I was pretty certain of my abilities, so I didn't want to say "uncle" too much. Sometimes it wouldn't sell off more the next day and sometimes it would. I saw my accounts get to a million dollars several times, but then decline again. I was very streaky. I only got the necessary discipline in 1986 and didn't start to always consistently make money until after that time.

What accounts for your change after that point?

I grew up in a family that always provided for me but I never had a lot of money. I could live on $50 a month if I had to. I was a survivor. I always said to myself before that time that I'll be rich or I'll live on my $50 a month. I was planning to get married, and I moved out of my parents' house at the time. So I said to myself let me try a method of making money every month consistently and building my savings up. I have to make a living or I wasn't going to be in the business much longer because I was taking some pretty big swings. I knew I had the talent and the skills, and I could make money on 80 percent of my trades. I just started to become very consistent.

How did you do in the crash of 1987?

My clients and I didn't get hurt at all, except for one person. This good result was partly because of me and partly the result of the crash occurring the week before a Jewish holiday when I didn't have any positions! I was bearish by then anyway and was buying puts. I was still trading mostly options, but I would let the market determine whether I was buying puts or calls.

What happened next?

I traded at different firms over the next few years, but in 1991 a friend happened to tell me about a Long Island firm that allowed you to put $25,000 in an account, and they would let you trade $500,000 or something like that. I told him to leave me alone with that kind of scam. But one day I did visit this firm, and found that they would give you a lot of leverage. I said, that's what I need. I had a few hundred thousand dollars, which wasn't major money, but I didn't want to risk it either. I figured the most I would lose in this situation was $25,000. So I interviewed at the firm and told them I knew what I was doing, and they let me open the account. This was at Schonfeld Securities.

They had about 40 traders. I probably did about half their revenues and was making at least three or five times what anyone else was.

Why do you think you made more than anyone else?

I had stopped trading options. Options were out. I didn't have to deal with premiums or market makers anymore. I started to develop a long-short portfolio strategy. I would go long and short at the same time equally.

This is a hedge fund strategy that is sometimes called "matched pairs." Could you tell me more about how you did this?

I would go long strong stocks and at the same time short weak stocks, even if they weren't in the same industry. I was just trying to take the market risk out. I had been developing this strategy for some time.

The executions were really great and much better than I had ever seen in my life. I never had access to a machine where I could execute my own orders. Before that I would have had to call a clerk with my order. This execution platform wasn't SOES, but maybe Dot or Super-Dot or its equivalent, I don't remember

because it was the firm's own software. This was the b
of when traders could have access to electronic ways o
execution. My ability is to be very quick thinking and I can inter-
pret news faster than almost anybody. So if a news story came
out on a stock, I could quickly determine which other stocks
would be correlated or react to that event. The ability to get
super fast execution was critical to me.

Let me give you a simple example. If I know that oil prices
are suddenly going up sharply, I would short the airlines immediately. I could never do that before. I could also diversify significantly with leverage going both ways with a much larger amount
of money, although I still would have to close out most of the
positions by the end of the day. I could trade my theories in full
force, which I believed worked. I could never do this before,
along with instant execution.

The momentum system most people use now, I believe I developed while I was at Schonfeld.

Tell me what momentum means to you?

I had always been a relative strength trader. When a stock
stands out among a group of stocks, or maybe the whole market
is down or even, and this stock is up two dollars, in my mind,
that becomes a momentum stock. Or maybe a stock gaps in the
morning more than it ordinarily would, opening 3 percent up. If
the volume keeps active or builds up, and the stock keeps staying up, then I would go after that stock and consider it showing
a trend. Once I decided that this is a trend that I will play for a
couple of days with higher than average volume, if the stock
closes near the high, I will go long or if it closes near the low, I
will short it.

I believed the stock was acting this way for a reason and
whatever that reason was, I was able to get into the stock generally before anyone else because I had instant execution and the
available news services at my disposal. I had been watching it all
day. If a stock closed strong, that would make some news publication, where the public would read about it the next day. Analysts who might have been working on another stock during the

day, would work on this stock overnight. People who use relative strength or other theories would also notice this stock.

Generally there would be some follow-through the next day, so I would have a very easy trade if I was able to get into that stock the previous afternoon. Until 11:00 or 11:30 the next morning I would have many chances to get out of that stock. Either it would gap open the next day because everybody's reading about it and thinking the same thing I was, or even if it didn't have a proper follow-through, during the morning the people who missed buying it the day before would get into it. I'm talking about the long side, I would do the same thing on the short side.

That's what I mean by momentum, the stock has its own ability to lift itself because there are people who have such interest in it. About 80 percent of the time, if a stock was very strong the previous afternoon, especially the first day it was strong, the next morning I would make some money.

Once I got a stock in a trend, I could play that for the next three days. I believed these short-term patterns lasted over three days. They might last eight days, or they might last one day, but generally over three days.

How were you picking these stocks?

I was a tape reader in those days and had been one since 1980. These days you don't have to be a tape reader anymore. At that time most of us watched the tape to look for stocks that traded more volume than most or that appeared more often than most on the tape. If you saw a stock with three, four, or five thousand share blocks trading, and other stocks were only trading a couple of hundred shares, then that would be one indication. If it was moving up on this volume, no matter what the general market was doing, that was another indication. I didn't watch every tick because that would distract me too much, but as long as it was moving the right direction with the right volume, I would be interested.

I would also read the news from 7:30 to 9:30 and pick any stock that I thought had a significant news story, and I would watch that stock for half an hour to see if other people confirmed what I was thinking about that stock. Let's say I thought there was some good news for a stock. It doesn't make any difference what I think, because other people have to be thinking what I was thinking. So I would buy a little at 9:30, and if I saw more and more volume, and maybe I saw it profiled on television, then I would just buy more and more as the stock held up, hoping that more and more people would see that, and since I was in a little bit earlier, maybe I could sell out at a higher price.

My whole key was trying to get there before anybody else did. Because I was in front of a machine with the most up-to-date news, the most up-to-date execution, and the most up-to-date method of analysis of stocks, which I had been doing for 15 years, I was able to have that edge. I would trade stocks that were acting remarkable well, even if I knew nothing about why they were acting so well. There are reasons people are buying these stocks, whether there is insider trading or not, because people still talk to each other, and the stock was telling me there is something there. If I was wrong, at least there is enough volume and liquidity that I could get out without too great a loss.

I always stay with the trend. If the stock is up, I never sell it short. If a stock is down, I don't go long it.

Where would you look to get out of these trades?

My biggest indicator in getting out was if the stock stopped acting well relative to the market. It the market kept going up and this stock didn't that was my first indicator that the trend had stopped and I would have to watch that stock. I would give myself pretty wide losses because I was not a scalper. So if a stock gapped open a dollar in the morning, I would probably wait until it broke even before I would get out of it. As long as it held up, I wouldn't sell it even for a day or two as long as it kept up with the market. Once that trend of acting better than the market, once the volume decreased, then I would start looking to sell it by giving it just a little room to move down before I would sell. Also, at the end of the day if I'm losing on a stock, I'll be out of it.

Did you scale into these positions?

As long as it maintained its trend, I would buy it on every dip. I always add to winning positions but never to losing positions. I never take my whole position in one shot, I want to see it confirm what I am thinking, and then I will add more and more.

Could you give me an example of a recent stock trade that illustrates these principles that you still use?

When Linux started to become important and Red Hat and Virginia Linux come out in IPOs, there was another company called Applix that was also one of the first companies involved with Linux. Now, Red Hat had a valuation of $15 billion with maybe $10 million in revenues. Applix had revenues of maybe $7 or $8 million, but it only had a valuation of $150 million. I bought a 100,000 share position at 8 or 9 and some other traders here also bought it. We held if for a few weeks and then the volume started to pick up from 200,000 to 1 million shares one day, and then to 5 million the next day. We started to buy more at 10 and added more all the way up to 15. I had maybe about 250,000 shares when the stock opened the next day at 23. They had a Linux division that nobody knew about.

   Those are the kinds of situations I look for. I know how news can affect a stock, and I am waiting for volume to pick up to reflect what the stock should be really worth. But if nobody knows about it, it's not going to help me so I'm not involved. If you're an investor, you can hold and hope you're right, but if you're a trader, you have to be where the action is.

How many trades a day were you making when you were still at Schonfeld?

I was making about a hundred trades a day.

What size positions were you trading?

I was doing between 1,000 and 5,000 share sizes. I would start with a 1,000 and start building up if I thought it was working my way. Schonfeld limited me to that size at the time.

How many different stocks would you be holding at the same time?

I could be in 40 or 50 stocks at one time. Of course, these were long and short positions at the same time

Could you tell me how you developed this kind of long-short position strategy?

What I saw in the crash of 1987 affected me the rest of my life. I saw too many people put out of business in one day and I said that's not going to happen to me. I imagined if my whole long position went to zero, where would I be? That's how extreme I got. I realized if I hedged myself, I would take a lot of market risk out, and then I would never go broke in my life. I wanted to stay in business and if it cost me a few percentage points, I didn't care.

I was at Schonfeld for two months and was doing great, and then some crisis happened and in one day I lost $38,000. Since I had only $25,000 in my account I got called into the office and was asked to put up more money. So I said to myself that's it. I think I can tell which stocks are strong and which stocks are weak, and I'm going to go home hedged every night. Even though this thing happens only once every eight or nine years, I don't preach this to others or young people, but I preach it to myself. My goal is never to be out of this business. From then on I never went home without being short something, even if I was long 70 percent and short 30 percent.

I've left Schonfeld since then but the remarkable thing about my record in the last four years at Generic Trading has been that I've been net short 80 percent of the time going home in a bull market. I have been up 2,300 percent during these past four years. I don't try to pick tops and I haven't been short the Internets until they broke down. I only take home short what's weak.

How long did you stay with Schonfeld and how did you got involved with Generic Trading and Carlin Equities?

I worked for Schonfeld almost two years. At the time I was looking for someone to take some of my money and use it to trade floor strategies with options. Someone introduced me to Ron

Shear, who had been a member of the American Stock Exchange for 15 years as the XMI specialist, and knew some good people who could do this.

At that time, I was known as one of the best traders in the industry. Ron had a small group of traders who were interested in getting into this side of the business so I also brought in some traders and we became partners.

Today we have over a thousand traders with 40 offices. I'm in charge of trading and Ron heads the administration.

What kind of stocks did you short these past four years?

Tobacco stocks have been a disaster. Some of the chemicals and food stocks have been disasters. If you weren't in high-tech, Internet, or bio-tech, you wouldn't have gotten killed shorting in general. I would go long a basket of Internet stocks, and go short a basket of tobacco stocks, food stocks, or drug stocks some nights. Cyclical stocks which haven't been super strong, paper stocks. You don't take all your market risk out, but you do take some out. And then within these groups, you might take seven Internet stocks and short two of the weakest ones, and the volatility of the Internet stocks was so great that you would still make money on the total position. If the market were up, you might lose a half point on the Deeres or Caterpillars, and on the weaker Internet stocks you might have lost a dollar, but you made four or five dollars on the hot stocks you were long. So overall I might make fifteen points for the day. I publish a list of my recommendations for the day at 11:30 for my traders, with both short and long ideas. I never go one way. Most young traders don't use this strategy, but maybe as they get older they'll use it more. This year I'm up 140 percent on my portfolio where the S&P is barely up or maybe even down a little, so the strategy works.

Do you keep an equally balanced long-short position in money?

I am very evenly balanced by money, with maybe only a 5 percent variation. If at the end of the day, I don't think I'm short enough, I'll just go after the weakest stocks and short them.

Do you ever use the stock index tradable products, such as the QQQ for the NASDAQ or the "Spiders" for the Standard and Poor's index, to hedge your position?

I don't use the Qs or Spiders because I didn't have a good experience using them. They were supposed to be very liquid, but when you try to execute them, the bids and offers aren't there. I realized I could do the same thing with a balanced portfolio. In fact, I could make money on both sides of my portfolio. In an average week, I may make money on both sides on two or three days, on the other days I may lose some or breakeven, but I don't lose enough to lose on the week. There are many weeks where I make a lot of money. Good traders have times where they make a lot of money but don't lose a lot the bad times.

Until the Qs, I used options to protect my portfolio, but it cost me too much money. The premiums were just too crazy. Incidentally, now I'm only a seller of options although I don't do it a lot. The last week before expiration every month, I will sell calls on broken down stocks, or sometimes puts on strong stocks. Mostly calls though. Even if I only get a quarter for them, I can do 10 of them. They can only hurt me so much in the last week. I also do it on very thick stocks, a Cisco or an Oracle. I do this just for fun, although I've been very successful at it.

How often are you changing the components of your portfolio that you are carrying overnight?

Generally, I'll have some stocks for two or three days, but I'm changing them every day. For example, drugs were strong a couple of weeks ago but as the market continued to rally, drugs were weak, so I shorted drugs and bought the technology stocks that were strong. The leadership is always changing. As I've said, these moves tend to last three days, although there are some that last as long as 10 days. I will take smaller and smaller size positions as I see these groups change leadership. There's a lot of rotation these days. I probably have between 35 and 50 stocks on each side of the portfolio.

Ten or 15 percent of my portfolio is composed of position that I want to hold longer than three days, maybe a few weeks.

For example, when the genomics start their powerful trend, I don't want to get in and out of them in three days. I might hold them for two months.

How many trades are you making these days?

Between three and five hundred trades a day.

That's amazing.

You have to understand that I'll rarely buy 40,000 shares on one trade. I'm buying 5,000, 5,000, 10,000, and so on. When I'm winning, I'm just getting bigger and bigger. I now do NASDAQ stocks, but I'm still one of the biggest listed stock traders.

How do you execute a 5,000-share block in a listed stock? Do you do limit or market orders?

Eighty-five percent of the time I use market orders. I know the specialist is going to take me. I know what the deal is. If I don't want to play, I don't have to play. But most of the time, I have to play because I don't have a lot of time to be too cute. I'm not going for eighths and quarters, I'm going for dollars. When you're going for dollars they can cheat you but you still can make money.

I'm no scalper. I won't take any big size position on any $200 or $300 stock that has dollarwide bid-offer spreads. No matter what I think about it. It's distracting. I go for smaller stocks where I can make five points on 25,000 shares, rather than twenty points on 3,000 shares on a stock that's going crazy. Even today, the execution in these kind of crazy stocks is horrible. They can knock it down a point and a half on a hundred shares. There are times I put a market order on these stocks and I get filled four points lower.

These stocks are too distracting. I'm a very good thinker, and a very good trend follower, and a very good poker player, but I'm not the best executer in the world. I don't want to get upset and everybody screams when they get a dollar and a half lower. I try to keep emotionally balanced during the day because when I'm upset I know I'm going to get hurt in another trade. My idea is to be completely focused and not let anything distract me.

What does your screen look like?

I have five or six screens. I have a Bloomberg machine. I have a screen that has five different news services: Dow Jones, Reuters, Professional Investor Report, Federal Filings, and First Call. I have two machines just monitoring stocks, one that monitors only groups and one that monitors my special situations that are stocks that are active or that I want to get involved in that day. There may be 45 stocks on each screen.

An example of a recent special stock is ONYX, which just passed Phase II trials for head and neck cancer. I put that right on the machine. If I see a million shares traded and the stock is bid up three points on the opening, then that stock enters my screen immediately. There is special news and the stock is reacting to it.

I also have the heavy weights on the screen, like Microsoft and IBM, so I can watch the market a little. I have the S&P and bond futures. I don't watch them meticulously, but I'll eye them every half hour. I have a chart up once a month if I haven't seen the stock before. But I know where the stock has been without a chart.

I have an Instinet machine and a Redi-Classic execution screen.

Do you use Instinet much?

I do a lot of before and after market hours trading because I think there are a lot of inefficiencies at that time compared to the openings. I've seen that if there's a large move in the after-hours trading, up or down, then the move will even be more extreme in the gap on the opening. For example, last week LSI came out with bad earnings news after the market closed. Actually they weren't that bad but the market interpreted them as bad. The stock closed at 49, but reopened after hours and traded on Instinet at 40 for two hours. It's down nine points already, so who's going to short it? I did short it after hours, although only for a couple of

nd shares because I also thought a nine point drop after
━━━━━ .vas pretty big! Yet, it opened at 31 the next day.

Whatever moves on Instinet after hours will be more extreme in that direction, up or down, the next day. I think this
mostly works with NYSE stocks, though. After market hours, you
are trading mostly against other traders. There are a lot of inefficiencies and I've had very good success trading them.

Did you cover your short on the open the next morning?

I didn't think twice. Nine points is enough. But I'll watch a stock
like this the next day. If it rallies, the odds are that I'll short that
stock again. Any stock that opens super weak in this environment right now, the odds are that it is going lower at some point
in the day almost always. The institutions and momentum players will want to be out of that stock. Traders don't want to be in
these bottom stocks. They'll try and they lose. It's a very bad
strategy, and they want to go after the next hot stock. LSI is still
trading at 31 three weeks later. Trading LSI when it's down there
is not the most efficient use of your time.

When I trade after hours I'm just trying to take advantage of
the Instinet. I want to get out of the stock on the open the next
morning, and now look at the stock as a new situation or trade. I
am looking for the inefficiencies after hours. There is not a lot of
size being done then. Most of your successful traders are leaving
early, although they may come in early. If you're a guy who has
nothing else to do with your life, you'll hang around to trade. I
have to be here anyway to watch the firm.

I'm opposed to 24 hours a day trading which I think will be a
total disaster.

The extreme thing is the best thing for a trader. A news item
that comes out before or after trading is a good way to take advantage of the market.

How do you train people or do you get involved with that?

I've tried to impart my philosophy to our traders, although the
majority of my day is still spent trading. I don't train beginners.
When people reach a certain level, they either come into my

trading room and spend a couple of days with me or anybody can ask me anything they want during a 15-minute conference call I give every day where I give my ideas about the market. I might lecture two or three times a year. We don't have a formal training program. We look more for experienced traders who want to come to us because they know they are dealing with a boss who has the mindset of a trader.

If my best people are having a down streak, I won't go after them. I'll walk over to them and ask them what they are thinking, does this make sense, or I can tell them how I went broke. I can tell them that anything I've lived through, they can live through. We've developed a lot of respect in the industry for this.

I don't have a lot of patience for beginners. I can help a trader go to the next level, who basically knows trading. They may need a little bit of sharpening on how to define a trend, how to read news, how to hedge, how to keep discipline, when to go away, when to trade small, when to trade big, and so forth. I have about 25 people in my trading room who will come in for a while and see what they can pick up. I don't force my style on anyone. If you flip pancakes to determine stock selection and I see on your profit and loss something that says "P," then I won't bother you. But if you flip pancakes and I see "L" all the time, then you might be wrong.

I think other methods work. Some traders are antitrend traders, or try to buy stocks that are washed out. I just think these are harder methods than mine. When you follow the trend, the game becomes a lot easier. And when you know not to trade, it becomes a lot easier. Because there are times when there is no trend. I say to people then, wait and don't hurt yourself.

Do you ever get out of the market completely?

I don't, but I will get much smaller. In April I may have had $60 million in positions, and now (the summer of 2000) I may have only $20 million. Stocks are like commodities, when you make it you will make a lot. Other times just don't hurt yourself or make what it gives you. Right now we have the kind of market where you just have to try to make something, the trend is just not there.

Do you take vacations much?

No. I'll take days or weekends off, or I'll visit our offices in California. I should take off more, but I don't. I do recommend it.

Do you ever get emotionally run down from trading?

From the people! But not from trading. I have losing streaks like everybody else. If you're good, as long as you don't hurt yourself, you'll come back. I'm very close to my traders, so when they go through down streaks, I suffer with them. You need balance in your life. When I conduct an interview for trader candidates I always ask about their outside life. It's not that I'm trying to be nosey, it's just that I know when I have chaos in my outside life, my trading is going to be affected. This is a business, not a game, that can make your life wonderful or destroy you.

Because I do live according to a religious lifestyle based on Torah, which is very structured and very family oriented, I think it's helped me and rarely lets me lose my balance. I have good control of my emotions. I get tired because I don't get enough sleep, but not because I'm emotionally run down.

You said that self-confidence has been important to your success. How critical a factor is that for the success of the traders you see here?

Confidence is a very high percentage of the game for winning. When I played baseball and caught six balls in a row and then dropped one, I lost my confidence. The same thing with trading. Sometimes you do get paralyzed, you're losing and everything you do is wrong. You have to totally stop. Then take very small size positions until you can make money on four out of five trades, and then get a little bigger until you are profitable on four out of five trades, and let the market tell you how to build yourself back up. When you do make it back, it will happen so fast you'll wonder why this ever happened to you.

You have to respect the market. No one is bigger than the market. You better be humble, because the market will humble you if you don't have humility right now. It happens to everyone.

How do you select the people to trade at Generic Trading?

I don't want anyone coming in who's on his last dime who has 18 kids to support. He needs a salaried job. Most of my traders are single or are married but have some money, they've been brokers or traders before, so at least I know I'm starting with someone who's balanced in trading. When their life is in chaos, they're not going to hear anything I have to say.

I look for people who can make decisions quickly. I talk rapidly, and I like people who can react to that. People who are disciplined and aren't afraid, who have gambled a little bit in their life before, not that they have gone to Gambler's Anonymous. People who know odds and are competitive. People in the military or have school honors. Or just your average kid who survived the streets under the hardest circumstances. I'm very impressed with those kids. They must have had some discipline somewhere in their lives. This is a business, not a casino, and if you don't treat trading like that, the market will take you out.

Are you hiring people to trade the firm's capital?

They bring in their own money, but we give them leverage. If they have their own money and don't want leverage, they go to Carlin Equities and can do whatever they want. Those people I don't interview. Most people in my room have been with me at least four years. We have five or six rotating seats where people leave or people just come in to visit.

Do you think trading can be taught?

I think for everyone who has the right mental, physical, and emotional framework, it's fairly easy to be taught to make some money. The amount you make will be up to you. The most important qualities are discipline and humility. You have to have enough money to do it also.

Why do those people who leave fail?

Bad luck. I try to keep them if I think it is bad luck. Some traders are comfortable with their method and they don't want to learn another, even though they are losing with their method. They blame it on the market, not themselves. Or they listen to the news or any analyst who comes on television and instead of interpreting what it means to their trading, they just say this guy says this, so it has to be so. The television is a paradise for fools. Sometimes, they do not have the discipline or aren't flexible, and we were wrong about them. It's like every other field, not everyone makes it.

How much money does someone need?

You can't do it with $10,000. You probably need about $50,000 to $100,000. With small amounts of money, you cannot do the strategies I do and be diversified. If you lose too much, your head goes into a spin. Once you're worried about your last bit of money, you can't make it. You have to start very slowly, so you get all the mistakes out very cheaply. Paper trading, unfortunately, doesn't work well.

Why is that?

People fool themselves. They think they are going to take a loss at that point, but they are never going to get out at that point in a real trade. Even if they have in mind they are going to get out at that point in a real trade, their execution is going to give them a fill a dollar lower. Or the fear isn't there. There's no money on the line. No matter how much you think it is, the fear it isn't there. All the necessary ingredients for a real decision aren't there: there is no fear, no greed, no reason to be disciplined. I've had guys make money paper trading for 20 days, and lose real money for 15 straight days after that. Every intern with no experience who comes in here, ends up a billionaire on paper and that just shows me it is not realistic.

Do you find it distracting to be in a room of traders when you have this much at risk?

Yes. Most traders only have five or six positions on, so they want the noise, they want the television on, and they don't care.

I have 40 stocks on each side and I have things to do with them if they change, so I want it as quiet as can be. Personally, I'd rather be in a room by myself. But because I own a firm, I'm always with 20 traders. They do make one concession to me and that is between 9:30 and 11:00, and between 2:45 and 4:00, they have to be quiet. The rest of the day they can chatter all they want.

You have an assistant. What does he do?

My assistant started out entering all my Instinet trades, reading Bloomberg, and doing some research for me. For example, a news item will hit a stock, and I will want to know what it's market capitalization is and all other stocks in that industry. If there's a $50 billion contract announced, I want to know whether the company is worth $20 billion or $1 billion. I want to know the average daily volume on a stock, so I can know if the volume is building up during the day. We look at the stocks that are up or down for the day. He still does that stuff for me, but I've started to let him trade, and right now he's become a successful trader. He's a smart kid and has all the qualities of a good trader. He wanted just to sit next to me to learn, and he did.

Do you follow any money management techniques?

If you average about 15 trades a day, for example, and you lose on six or seven in a row, you should stop or cut back your size. If you are trading 2,000 share size positions, you should only do 500 share sizes, or if you do 15 trades a day, you should only do three trades a day, until you build up your confidence. It might not even be you, it might be the market. Certain kinds of markets, no one makes money in.

I also think it is sometimes easier to make money in the morning. Trends are much purer in the morning whether up or down. In the afternoon, maybe for three of four months out of the year, the market tends to be all over the place, and maybe for seven or eight months out of the year, they do have trends in the afternoon that are good. So if you have made some money in the morning and then lose a third of that back, you should stop trading for the afternoon.

Are these rules you follow yourself?

I do and I don't. The rule that I have is that I am disciplined. If I start losing money, I am slowing up and lowering my size, that rule I do have for myself. Whether I would stop trading, well, I have a long track record of success. But if I lost a lot of money I would stop.

How many months over the past two years have you lost money?

Over the past 24 months, I've made money in 21 or 22 months.

What is the biggest extended loss you've had over that period?

I've probably lost 12 percent over an extended period. That happened only once. I made 140 percent on my money the first three months of this year, but I did lose some of that back around March or April when the market sold off. Even though I was long and short an equal amount of money, I lost some money because the longs went down so fast. I made it back quickly though.

Because you have a long and short position on, this statistic may not mean as much to your trading, but how many of your trades would you estimate are profitable?

If I do anything in size, which means over 10,000 shares, it is very high, between 80 and 90 percent. Anything less than that size, maybe 60 or 70 percent. When I have a size position, I have to have everything going for me. Then I'm putting on bigger and bigger size, I see everything working, I have confidence, and I'm on a hot streak.

Are there any secrets of trading that you don't want to divulge?

What I'm saying now is fair and it's not fair. It's fair because this is how I trade, but it's not fair because everyone is his or her own individual. You can give all the rules in the world that work, but there's 50 percent of success that is who you are, how you anticipate things, how you look at things, and that can't be put in a book.

If you could give me one example of an industry rotation that exemplifies how you trade, what would it be?

My biggest winners this year were the bio-tech group. I've been watching them for a while, I thought they were very cheap compared to those Internet stocks that were each being valued at $20 billion. When I saw the first movement out of Celera, which was the leading genomic stock at the time, indicating that this would be a group that would be hot, I started buying. I saw that no matter what happened to the market, these stocks were maintaining their price levels and not going down and when the market rallied they would go up double what everything else did. I made a list of all bio-tech and genomic stocks available, and any time they dipped, I would buy 20 or 30 of them. I kept them as my intermediate term stocks that were in major up trends.

Could you give me an example of a single good trade that you made recently?

I like to make money in stocks that do good things. I follow the drugs for cancer industry very closely, because I know the potential for something like that is going to be tremendous. Most cancer studies these days are in pre-Phase I trials, that means they're curing mice and gorillas left and right. Then you have Phase I, Phase II, and then Phase III trials, after which you apply to the FDA for approval. Every cancer drug I've seen till now has never made Phase I. I found this stock that had significant results in Phase II for head and neck cancer. This is trials on real humans, for a long period of time, and had remissions in tumors about 70 percent of the cases. That stock was ONYX.

NASDAQ isn't strong now, but if it were, in an ordinary time I would have 100,000 or 200,000 shares of this stock. A year ago, any story that hit the tape on a genomic stock, would have lifted it 15 points. It doesn't work any more, so you have to be a little bit limited in the size you take. I bought about 45,000 shares between 12 and 13½, when the news was running on the tape all day, and the next day I sold it between 17 and 19 when it made the front page of the newspapers the next day. This happened a couple of weeks ago.

How do you get out of 45,000 shares on a trade?

The stock traded about eight million shares that day. I never get out all at once, so I was getting out all day. I want to be happy, so if I get out of some and it goes lower, I'm happy or if it goes higher, I still have some, so I'm still happy. If I have to and I know I'm dead wrong, I'll just hit it and take it a dollar down. I'll have no choice. But in this case, it was up on the opening and just kept getting stronger the whole morning. It closed at 20.

Why didn't you just hold it longer?

You have to know the environment you're in. We're in a trading environment where the follow-through is very weak. I would have held some longer if we were back in February or March, where I had an environment where stocks could keep going for two or three days. A few months ago, I bought GERN for 9 and sold it for 35. I bought an Internet stock for 8 that went to 52 the next morning in the wild days of NASDAQ. I sold it for 27, because I'm not *that* crazy, but 18 points an hour is not bad either. You can't do that now.

Today, you have an environment, where a stock can be up five dollars today and down five tomorrow. I've had very few new stories in stocks that have made any sort of major upside move in the past month or two. NASDAQ has gone down three or four hundred points and there's a lot of bearishness. It's not a momentum market and your momentum traders are losing money. The momentum traders don't want to take home any positions overnight anymore. They've been getting hurt. I tell my traders in conference calls not to hold positions overnight, and that's not my normal philosophy. You're getting unexpected bad news on tech stocks every other day. As in every world you're in, you have to know the environment, and that's the environment we're in right now. You can't fight it.

Do you see more false breakouts today compared to the past?

I see a lot of false breakouts intraday. There are so many people sitting and waiting for them, traders are being set up. Someone breaks it, and then sells into it, and everybody else is holding it.

Electronic trading lures people into believing they can get out with an eighth loss but with so many traders on one side it multiplies and accelerates the downward move if there is a reversal. If the breakout doesn't work after five minutes, you have five hundred people each pressing their sell button. Bing. The specialist sees all this coming in and he doesn't want to lose any money so he'll bring the stock in a dollar. I think this is a very bad method of trading on a short-term basis. Over the intermediate term, you have time, once these short-term traders get out, to catch the resumption of the move.

Some of these short-term traders are so fast on electronic systems it is to their detriment. Here's a funny situation that happened. There was a stock that was the eBay of Europe trading at $20. Some irresponsible analyst comes on television and says this stock is going to a thousand dollars. Not $100, but $1,000! So one of my traders puts a short out at $200 offered. Filled! Some kid with an itchy finger took the $200 offer, because if it's going to $1,000 then it must be a bargain. He wasn't thinking. We covered the short at $70 and the stock recently is trading about $10.

Where do you want to be in your life in 10 years?

As I get older, I want to continue trading because this is my love and I know I can make money. I might start a hedge fund or something like that. But I would also like to use my position in life as an established and secure person to work in other fields. The reason I went for two degrees is because there is a financial side to me and a humanistic personal side to me. I enjoy both, and having gotten success will help me in both areas.

I already do work for a lot of charitable organizations. I probably spend five times what I spend on myself, on charity. I am a rabbi, and in the Judaic lifestyle of Torah, you are an individual that is part of a community and the whole world. Your duty is to make everybody part of that community as well off as they can be. You have to have compassion, kindness, and mercy toward everybody.

I do tell my traders not to worry about everybody else, but take care of yourself first. You can't help others if you are not okay. But if you are at the best level you can be, and you are at the top of your form, then you help other people who need it most. I believe God has been good to me and given me the opportunity to be in a field that I love and where I belong. I've been rather successful at it, and perhaps I'll be able to use what I've made to help others.

Is there anything else you would like to say?

Everything you do in life should not be solely for your ego. I hope some good comes from my interview and helps other people do better in trading or life. If I can do that, I'm happy we did this interview.

chapter 5

Michael Reise

Michael Reise trades mostly listed stocks where he has developed the art of "tape reading" into a unique style, although is he a versatile trader in all respects.

He is 27 years old and was born in Brooklyn, where his family owns a nursing home supply and institutional design company. He attended orthodox Jewish schools while growing up and has long pursued an avocation of writing music and has published a couple of popular religious songs. Michael went to Touro College in Brooklyn and began studying political science intending to pursue a career as a criminal defense lawyer. However, after two semesters, he realized he had another six years of school to earn his law degree and began to doubt whether a law degree from Touro would land him the job that he wanted. He left college after one year to take a job in his family's business and then decided that he wanted to be self-employed.

How did you first become interested in stocks?

I had a great uncle who was an insider in a publicly traded company. So my family always followed this stock. From a young age, I began asking people about stocks, reading about them and started to watch the day-to-day movements in the prices of stocks. At 15 years old, I had a system for trading stocks and I used my father's broker to make some trades. I remember one stock, North American Biological, which was trading around $3 when I bought it, and then went to $7 after some deal was announced with Red Cross. My broker was very excited and wanted to know how I found that stock. I was just watching the price action, that's all. I just looked at the Sunday financial pages, and if a stock was under $5 and was a NASDAQ stock, showed three weeks of small gains, maybe only an eighth or quarter each week, and had increasing volume, then I would buy the stock. I continued to trade off and on in high school. I bought LA Gear at $20 and saw it go to $100. Then I went to summer camp for two months, and when I came back, the stock had come all the way back to where I bought it. I finally sold it, but it taught me at a very young age that stocks can go down as quick as they can go up. Before that I really thought that stocks only could go up. LA Gear is now probably a penny stock. I've always made money in the market even from a young age. Not always tons of money, but I made my 25 percent per year before I became a really active trader.

Did you continue to trade during college?

I didn't really start trading actively until I left college in 1993. I became interested in options, so I started to trade some interesting option strategies at Waterhouse Securities. I did alright with these strategies, but I was working in my family's business and not trading full time. In 1995, I decided to try trading full time, so I got my Series 7 license and opened an account with a broker-dealer in Brooklyn.

How did it go?

At the time, the firm I was with had no direct access execution system or Level II, at least in Brooklyn, and not much analytical software either. To do a trade, I had to write out my order on a paper ticket, and then run over to an order room and hand it to a clerk who would then transmit my order.

One of my very first trades at the firm was to go short Adobe Systems. It went from $52 to $57, a five-point move, which in those days was a lot. I decided to short a thousand shares so I wrote out my ticket, took it over to the clerk and went short at 57½. By the time I had returned to my desk from turning in my ticket, Adobe was trading 59! So I was down $1,500 in about a minute. I ran back to the order desk with a ticket to buy it back at 59½, which was the last price I had seen on my screen. When I got there, Adobe was already trading $60, so I told the clerk to just buy it back for me, but he told me I had to change my ticket first. So I rewrote the ticket with $60, but by then Adobe was trading 60½. He asked me to change my ticket again, which I did, but when I gave it to him Adobe was up again. He asked me to change my ticket again. Finally, I just screamed at him just to buy me a thousand shares of Adobe, which he did. This trade cost me over $3,000. So by my second day of trading I was already down about $3,500. I realized I could lose a lot of money very quickly and after that I was much more conservative.

There was no training then, so I was learning on my own. I didn't have a system. Over the next four weeks, I broke even on my trades, which in retrospect considering that I had no formal training and really didn't know what I was doing, was not bad. But I was under pressure to make a living since I was married, had my first child to support, had a mortgage to pay, and my wife was not working. So there was too much pressure and after six weeks I stopped trading full time.

You weren't trading SOES at this time?

No. The clerk had the only Level II machine in the office in Brooklyn. I think the Manhattan office was more sophisticated but nobody pointed me in that direction. In any case, I had a Series 7 license so I wouldn't have been able to trade through SOES. I believe I might have been able to make money at that time if I had a Level II machine, since I was breaking even just writing out physical tickets and handing them to a clerk. When I later learned about Level II and how much money could have been made at that time, I was a bit angry that nobody told me about it.

What did you do then?

I went back to work in my family's business, but I started to trade through Waterhouse Securities again. I did have a handheld Quotrek device that would give me the current market prices.

as no online trading, so all my orders were placed by
e through a touchtone system. In those days, that was
considered state of the art. This shows how much things have
changed in just the last four or five years.

What kind of strategies were you using then?

I used to do options straddles on earnings. This was at the beginning of the bull market and just when stocks were starting
to move big on earnings news. I was able to buy straddles for
$4 or $5 before the earnings announcements. If stocks did even
a little bit better then the analysts' earnings estimates, then
the stock would explode. The day after an earnings announce-
ment, the stock could be up or down $10. One time I bought the
straddle on Oxford Health for $4 before an earnings announce-
ment. The next day the stock moved $15 so I made $10,000 over
night. For some reason big moves like this were becoming more
frequent but this phenomena was not priced into the options
price at the time. Today, you couldn't do this, because the
prices of options reflect the impending price effect of earnings
announcements.

I was also trading stocks, but I really had no strategy for
this kind of trading looking back on it. I knew something about
the market and investing, but I didn't know how to turn that into
a game plan for trading. I was like most new traders who come
into the business today I suppose. If a stock was down $5, I would
try to bottom pick it, and if it went up a dollar or so I would try
to flip it out for a profit, and if it went up even more than that I
might try to short it. I wasn't looking at any charts. It was all
kind of primitive.

You were involved in starting Lieber & Weissman Securities. How did that happen?

In 1996, I told my broker at Waterhouse that I was interested in
starting a NASD broker dealer and he told me about Gene
Weissman. Gene was a market maker in options on the American Stock Exchange. To Gene's credit, he told me that starting a

retail broker dealer was not the way to go. He suggested we open up a trading firm where people became members in order to trade and each member would contribute capital in order to trade the firm's capital. I had never heard of this business model but we decided to do it.

We needed $1 million in capital to start, which we were able to raise through private investors and I relied on much of Gene's expertise. This all took about a year, and I was still working at my day job. We rented an office, set up a trading room, and opened our doors for business around May or June of 1997. We started as members of the American Stock Exchange. We really started on a shoestring. We had four desks and computers in a big empty room.

How did you find your first traders?

Gene knew a few people who were upstairs traders and they came in. I think we gave one guy some money to trade, just so our trading room didn't look so empty. We did some advertising in the classified section of the *New York Times,* but people didn't really know much about the industry at the time. It was slow at first but we really grew the business by word of mouth.

What kind of software execution did you have at the time?

We were probably the first firm in the country to put NASDAQ and NYSE execution on the same system. Firms like ours were called "Dot shops" because most of our competitors had electronic Super-Dot machines, which could route orders directly to the floor of the NYSE. Since we were professional traders, we did not have access to SOES, and did not have a Level II execution platform; firms either did SOES on NASDAQ stocks or Super-Dot for listed stocks. After doing a lot of research, we did discover that one execution system was offering electronic executions on both NASDAQ and NYSE, which was also the first Windows-based system, so that's what we started using, and I believe, we became the first trading firm in 1997 to offer electronic direct access on both listed and unlisted stocks. Within about six months, however, all of the other firms were also offering this service as other software became available. Now we mostly use REDI-Plus offered through Spear, Leeds, & Kellog.

How was your own trading going during this time?

I didn't have a lot of money to trade since I was putting most of my money into setting up LWS. I was able to spend some time studying the markets when I wasn't working on building the business. I had never seen a Level II screen before, and for the first time I had access to real-time charts and things like time and sales. At the beginning of 1998, I started to trade again on a small scale and for about four months I just dabbled. I didn't make a lot, but I didn't lose a lot either. Since I started trading in a Dot shop, I tended to trade listed stocks, whereas most of our new traders tended to trade NASDAQ with Level II. I found trading Level II a bit confusing because so much was happening on the screen with bids and offers constantly changing and trade prices flying around all over the place. The NYSE listed market was simpler to follow. On NASDAQ you would see many small trades taking place and then a 25,000-share block trade, sometimes above or below where the bid and offer was. I found I was just able to read the print on the NYSE stocks better.

What do you mean by "read the print"?

I saw the actual trading action a lot more clearly. I saw a single bid and a single offer and I could see if the trades were occurring on the bid, on the offer or in between. If a bid size was much larger that the offer size, for example, a $7/8$ bid for 50,000 shares and 2,000 shares offered at the figure, then why would a trade take place between the bid and offer at $15/16$? You would think that the trade should have gone off at the offer. It was this kind of information that I started to pick up on.

What would the situation that you just described tell you?

I would have to wonder whether this stock was as strong as it first appeared. You would likely determine that the trade at $15/16$ was probably a buy. I mean, why sell if you see such huge quantity bid for? But that buyer got a better price than the offer. Why? Maybe there is more size offered at the figure than 2,000 shares, and the market is not showing it. Perhaps someone had a reason to short ahead of the offer, or maybe what was showing on the screen did not reflect what was really going on. More times than not, what you are seeing on your screen is the exact opposite of what's really going on, because it is set up to facilitate something that the specialist or some other large trader is trying to achieve. If he's showing he's a huge buyer, maybe he's a huge seller. The specialist on the exchange is not your friend. Nobody is your friend, and nobody is going to say "I have a huge bid and no offer, and I'm going to let you buy stock right now"! That is not realistic.

So would you short a stock in this situation?

It's a bit more complicated than that. This scenario should raise a flag. You would have to wonder, "Does this make any sense? Maybe something else is going on." If something subsequently proved the concept true a little bit more, then you might go with the idea. I wouldn't short a stock just based on the limited information of one trade, since there is a large size quantity showing on the bid and you don't really want to stand in the way of that. But if a few more trades occurred between the bid and offer, and then a few trades of 20,000 shares each took place at the offer and the offer size did not decrease, but stayed at just 2,000 shares, then I might determine that somebody really does have a lot of stock to offer, and I might feel more comfortable doing a short trade.

Do you consider yourself a "tape reader"?

Yes and no. For me, tape reading is the art of trying to read price movement and activity based on trades that are occurring and trying to determine a scenario that's playing out based on that. I have subsequently learned to better understand the NASDAQ system, but there is no way to "read the tape" on a NASDAQ stock the way you can read the tape on a listed stock. On NASDAQ I try to see the different activity of the different market makers to determine what they're up to and what's going to happen to the stock. That's not real "tape reading."

Tell me more about other things you see that help you read listed stocks?

The NASDAQ and NYSE markets have different mechanisms about how the trades take place. The listed stocks trade through a specialist system, with one guy essentially making a bid/offer market. He sees the order flow that you don't see, and he certainly knows many, although not all, the limit orders placed for a stock above and below the market, which is kept on the specialists' book, which you cannot see. Floor traders or brokers on the floor of the NYSE will stand around the specialist's booth, so they also can get a better sense of the real market than you can. So there is a different game plan in trading listed stocks than NASDAQ, where there is a much more open market structure with 20 market makers competing against each other and you can see more what they are doing. The specialist, I believe has greater power to move a market, which can also be something of an indicator.

What do you mean?

You have to see how a listed stock is going up or down in price in conjunction with volume. A listed stock that is going up with very large bid sizes and has trades really going off for 20,000 shares at a $\frac{1}{4}$ and then 40,000 shares at $\frac{1}{2}$, and it is still moving up is a strong stock. However, if you see 3,000 take place at $\frac{3}{8}$, and another 3,000 at $\frac{5}{8}$, and this stock moves up two more dollars on 30,000 shares volume, when you know that on a good day this stock can trade two million shares between those prices, then that is weak price movement and is probably being moved by the specialist for his own reason. Perhaps he's taking advantage of a light book so he can fill a market order at higher prices or wants to see a higher print trade for some other reason or perhaps a limit order that he wants touched so he can execute it. The price was moving up in this situation even though there really weren't more buyers than sellers. Nevertheless, you can use that information to your advantage, because you have been presented with an opportunity of knowing that that price movement is not real or strong.

In that situation, would you short?

I would be a definite short seller if I saw that happening.

How much of tape reading is just reading the specialist?

All specialists seem to have a way they trade a stock and this can be learned if you follow a stock. Every specialist has a distinct pattern no matter how hard he tries to conceal it.

They're human beings. The specialist in one popular trading stock usually makes it look absolutely horrible at the exact bottom of a stock. He flaunts it. He shows a 50,000-share offer and a bid for only 500 shares. But he also does a lot of very quick games that make it difficult to trade. So if you do buy the stock at this point, just for kicks he'll sell the 500 shares to make it look like it really is going to sell off, trying to shake all the longs out, before he quickly reverses and brings the stock up very quickly. He's entirely unpredictable, although that in itself is predictable.

I would be surprised if all specialists don't go to specialist school, since they all seem to do many of the same tricks. I don't blame them for this, but I do think they take great liberties in moving stocks more in price than is often justified by the volume since they probably are trying to make their own position better as well. If a seller comes in to sell a market order and there are no limit order bids, a specialist seems perfectly happy to buy the stock two dollars lower. Of course, they will say that they are taking all kinds of risk, and so forth, but some of these moves do seem extreme on the size volume that is traded.

And of course, they face no competition from any other market makers who might be able to improve on their price.

Exactly.

Do you have fixed stop losses?

No. I believe you should get out of a position when the reason you got in, is no longer valid.

In the hypothetical situation above, if you had gone short, where would you take a loss?

Let's look at the reason I got into the trade. I shorted the stock because it was going up on low volume. So if the stock continued to go up, but suddenly there was heavy volume, then that would be one indication I was wrong. Or I may use a round number as a level at which I believe the specialist cannot keep moving the stock up on light volume. For example, if the stock had been moving up on light volume from $88 towards $90, I might try to short at 89⅞ with the expectation that the specialist or whoever is moving the stock up could not continue to move the stock up past $90, where he is likely to encounter some real sellers for size. If the stock continued to move up to $90 and then past it, I would be wrong in my scenario at least short term and I would look to cover. I might still be right in my analysis of this stock, but it could go to 95 based on panic buying by short covering or whatever and I wouldn't want to risk losing that much.

Can you give me some examples of any actual trades illustrating these principles?

A recent example is Micron Technology, the price of which over the last five or six years has ranged from 15 to 95 dollars and is heavily dependent on the commodity price of microchips. Recently, over several days the price ran up 20 points from $60 to $80. Soon thereafter it jumped another 15 points to $95 in one day on news that microchip prices were heading up. This stock was now trading at over 100 times earnings. So I'm looking at this stock that has moved up $35 recently including $15 in one day, so I'm thinking that this move is short-term overextended. Now in principle there should be a lot of stock for sale and it was heavily owned by institutions. Yet the specialist was moving the stock up on very low volume, and in whole dollar increments, that is, $91, $92, and $93. He probably added $2 billion in market capitalization on a couple of hundred thousand shares traded. When the stock broke $96, it was trading at its all-time market high. I expected that at this price, there would be some institutions that would become sellers, so I thought a good short would be between $96 and

$100, which is a good round number. I started shorting above $96 and intended to build my position up to $100. But if it broke $100, then I would determine that I was wrong.

So what happened?

It went up to almost $100 like it was water, 96, 97, 98, 99. I had accumulated a short position of 2,000 shares and was probably down about $6,000 at that point. I did not leg into this trade properly though. Normally I would short the smaller amounts first and then build up to the larger amounts. If you have a 2,000 share target, you should begin by selling 200 shares, then 400, then 600, and finally 800. Anyway, the highest price of Micron that day was $99^{15}/_{16}$. It sold off a little, and then went up to $^{15}/_{16}$ several more times and then it sold off at the end of the day to $98. I didn't make money that day since it was still about a dollar above my breakeven price. But I held it overnight, figuring with the action it had at the close and that this was a very overextended move, the specialist would probably open it down the next morning.

Do you usually leg into positions this way?

No. In fact, most of the time I don't leg into positions, but I do it sometimes if there is a reason. When NASDAQ was first approaching the 5000-point level, I began shorting the index (QQQ) from above 4800, figuring that it would sell off from that level at least temporarily, which it did. But I didn't know exactly where people would be selling, thinking the same thing I was, and I didn't want the NASDAQ to sell off from the 4900 level and for me not to make any money. So I don't always leg in, but when I do I like to use an increasing progression.

Did Micron sell off the next morning?

Boy, was I wrong! A large brokerage firm came out with an upgrade before the open the next morning. I believe there was a big seller out there and this was part of the plan to create a large buying interest to unload stock. Anyway, the first trade that morning was at $105. After this trade, the specialist made his market $105 bid at $110 offer. This is the specialist at his best, making an orderly narrow market. Well, my pain was unbearable at that point, since I was now down close to $20,000.

Why didn't you start covering at least some of your short position?

I was really lost at that point since the trade had gone totally against me. Fortunately, this kind of trade is very rare for me, but I could not see covering at $110 either. One thing I've learned over the years is not to panic in these kinds of situations and to keep your sense about you. You don't want to do something completely stupid, just because your game plan has been blown away. To me, covering at $110 would have been stupid. So, I looked at this as a new trade, and put out another thousand to short at 109½, figuring that if 110 trades, I'll get my short and this was more than likely the top. The next trade was 108¼, which told me something was about to change. It sold off very quickly back to 105, and I didn't get my short position off, but I did get a short off just above 105, before the stock dropped to about 101. Then the stock rallied back to 107, where I did finally cover all of my positions. That was the high price for the rest of the day, and the next day Micron dropped pretty quickly after the open to $95. A perfect example of being right, but too far ahead of time.

Do you have days like this often?

No. This was actually my largest losing trade and my largest losing day ever. This also happened to be my maximum draw down in my account over the last two years.

So what did you learn about this trade?

I still believe I was correct in reading this stock, but obviously my timing was off. I believe the market has changed character recently, and I've had to change the parameters I use to judge moves. Price patterns now can take one or two days to adjust, whereas in the past these patterns would have adjusted more quickly. I think that although the markets are doing record volume, the liquidity is actually less. Obviously, there are more day traders, but I think hedge funds, institutions, and mutual funds are secretly short-term trading these days as well. This means that there is, in a sense, less liquidity, as there is not as much real stock being bought or sold. I cannot believe mutual funds are long-term buyers of Yahoo at 700 times earnings.

How does this make it more difficult for you to trade?

As a tape reader, I am trying to determine where the real buyers are accumulating stock, or sellers are distributing stock. But if there are no real buyers or sellers, then the prices of stocks are being pushed around by short-term traders and speculators. The markets are becoming more influenced by sentiment. That's why there are more crazy swings in the market. Traders take the market up when they're in a good mood, and down when they're in a bad mood. They're very susceptible to good or bad news, and so forth. It used to be that if the market moved 100 points, this was considered a strong move or reversal. Now, it happens three days out of five for the week. This is an indication that the markets are having less to do with real buyers or sellers, and are being dominated by traders.

This kind of market is not good for a tape reader, although it probably is very good for a momentum-style trader. At firms such as ours, experienced traders have been doing well during this market environment. But less sophisticated traders, trading through E*Trade, Ameritrade, and firms like that, are going to suffer. I think for this reason, the fundamentals of online brokerage firms are going to be weak in the future.

You sound pessimistic about the markets?

I believe there will be a day when there is a huge crash, or it will sell off in a slow horrible death. We will have to pay for the excess in this market sooner or later. I cannot look favorably at stocks, even though they are growing at 20 percent a year, at 200 times earnings.

Do you use market orders or limit orders on listed stocks?

I never use market orders, unless maybe Alan Greenspan unexpectedly says he is raising interest rates several points. Giving a market order to a specialist is like giving him a blank check with his name on it. I will put a limit price on my order that may be above or below the current bid or offer, just so I can be reasonably sure I will get filled, but I will not use a market order. If the current bid is ¾ and I want to sell, I may put in an order to sell at ½ or better. I'm giving the specialist room to move on my order, so that if I don't get filled at ¾ and even don't get filled at ⅝, then I can reasonably expect that there is a buyer at ½. If I gave a market order, the specialists may sell all the bids down to ⅛ before he will fill me. If for some reason, he doesn't fill my order to sell at a half, and trades all the way down to ⅛, then I will leave my order because I am fairly confident that the price will trade up again, at least short term.

Some people may use stop loss limit orders, but this makes sense only if the stock is highly liquid. Otherwise, your stop is bound to be hit and the price will probably reverse at that point. For example if the market is 60¼ bid and offered at 60½ for small sizes, and you put in a 2,000 share order to sell if the price trades down to 60, as I've seen some traders do, the specialist will certainly look to see how many shares are wanted down to 60 on his book. If he sees only a couple hundred or a thousand shares are wanted to 60, he may sell the price down to 60, just so he can execute your order to sell, which he will then buy, to cover his shorts and maybe even go long, and then run the price back up now holding an inventory of a thousand shares or more composed of your stock which you sold at a loss. This is why generally stop loss orders don't make sense to me in illiquid stocks.

How do you take a profit?

There's an art to getting out of positions as well as getting into them. I don't usually sell out my whole position at one time, at least on listed stocks. What I usually do is offer out my stock in pieces above the market. As a general rule, if I have no definite expectations, I look to get out at the next highest big dollar figure to get out, such as 65 if the stock is now trading at 63. If I don't think the stock can move two dollars in a short period, I'll look to get out at the next dollar figure or half dollar, again each of these sell orders is only part of my order. You want to take money off the table, which never hurts anybody.

I should also mention that I put my orders in to sell a little bit below the whole or half dollar figures, which means that if my target is to sell at 65, I'll place my order to sell at $64^{15}\!/_{16}$, or if I'm trying to sell at a half, I try to sell at $^7\!/_{16}$. If the whole or half figure trades, you are entitled to a fill. Whereas if you had used the whole or half number, traders ahead of you might have been filled, but not you. This works to your advantage also, because when large institutions place orders to buy or sell, they will usually say buy 50,000 shares up to 65, not up to $64^{15}\!/_{16}$. It's a small price to pay for making sure your order will get filled. Often even when you place an order like this, the specialist will fill you at the dollar figure anyway, since he doesn't want to write down an order where he sold 1,000 shares at $64^{15}\!/_{16}$ and 49,000 shares at 65. In these quantities, nobody cares about giving you an extra $^1\!/_{16}$ on a relatively small size just to save themselves the trouble.

Do you ever double down on losing trades?

No. But I do trade around losing positions sometimes. I was trading LSI recently when it dropped in price to around 32. It was down significantly for the day. Anticipating a short-term bounce I bought 1,500 shares at 32 and a teenie. It had traded down to 32 on the open, bounced up, and retested 32 several times, and the next time it got to that level, I bought. Of course, I'm looking at the general market during this time also as confirmation.

Now, if the price drops below 32, I'll get out of half my position, but not all of it, because sometimes, the market will drop though round numbers and then bounce right back. So if it broke that number I'll sell 700 shares. If the stock falls quickly, I might now look for a good spot to buy back the 700 shares.

Aren't you doubling down on a losing position by doing this?

No, because my predetermined trade size is 1,500 shares, and I'm willing to sell out half this position if I can buy it back lower, especially if it sells of sharply, say to $31^1\!/_4$. I will look to buy 700 shares at that price, and then sell out that part of the position if the price goes up, say at 31⅝ or ¾, even if it doesn't reach my original entry point. I will do this immediately by putting out an offer of 200 or 300 shares at ⅝ and another sell order at ¾. If the stock really doesn't look good at 32, I may even sell 1,000 shares of my position, holding only 500. I am leaning long but trading around the stock. I don't recommend this on stocks that move 20 points in a day, but LSI was trading in a range of $32 to $35, and I did not feel I was going to get clobbered doing this.

Well, if the stock dropped to 31¼ and you bought more, where are you going to take a loss on this whole position?

That depends. If the stock sells off slowly below 32, trading 31⅞, 31¾, then I would have gotten rid of my whole position. If it goes down sharply, then more times than not I can make at least a quarter point profit on the 700 shares I buy at a ¼. If the stock continues to go lower, I will continue to do this. If at any point I feel this is not happening as I anticipated, I will get out of the stock completely. Remember, I'm still looking at how the specialist is making the market in this stock and how the prints are trading.

Anyway, I was riding LSI down to 30⅛ in this fashion. I had been up about $800 in LSI at one point, but by the time it reached 30 I was down maybe $500, and I was long again 1,500 shares. I don't think this was a bad position to be in, since the stock had dropped two points and was approaching a round number such as 30 where I thought it would hold. My average price for those 1,500 shares was now about 30⅝. This was getting near the end of the day, and I also thought the stock would bounce by the close. LSI is a real company that recently had been selling for $65 so I thought there would be some bargain hunters who would come in, and that short sellers may look to cover also. And that's what happened. The stock ran up like crazy to 33 at the close. I didn't make all this as profit since I legged out of my position on the way up, although very sparingly since I saw how strong the stock was. I had gotten out of 1,000 shares by 32, but when I saw a strong bid, I bought another 500 shares. I got out of all my position by the end of the day and did end up making a couple of thousand dollars on this stock. So by trading this way, I ended up making an additional $1,200 in LSI.

You were in this trade all day?

No. I had been watching or trading in and out of this stock all day, but I only initiated this particular trading pattern at 3:15. So I was in the whole trade maybe 45 minutes.

Do you ever buy more stock if the stock goes your way with a profit?

No, at least not usually. If I do I'm looking at it as a new trade. Generally, I'm scaling out of my position if it goes my way, although there is some discretion about how much of it I will sell off as it goes my way.

Do you use technical analysis much?

No. I don't use charts at all. You might say I keep my charts in my head since I am watching and remembering prices and levels. I do look at the general market though, and I will watch the S&P futures for indications of changes in general market direction.

Is there any significance to large block trades?

There is no significance in itself to a large block trade. It could be a negotiated cross-trade, although this is somewhat unusual on the NYSE. If it's in the context of something, then it may mean something. If the market was ½ bid with a small size offer at ¾ and then a large block traded at ½ or ⅝, it might mean that there was a large seller standing on the sidelines hiding. And when people came in to buy stock because it looked strong, he stepped in to sell. This might even be more significant if the stock had been moving up in price just prior to this point. This would make me think that there's a lot of stock to sell and they are using the rise in prices to get rid of stock. Of course, if this trade went off and the price continued to trade up, I might not think anything of it, but if another trade for size occurred below the offer, then I might think there is something going on. If I were long, I might think of getting rid of it at that point.

Or if a stock has sold off to 30 as in my LSI trade earlier, and large blocks started to print at 30, well it is understandable that there may be large buyers at 30 as well as sellers. The only thing that would concern me in that context is if continued large size traded at 30 and then the offer came down to 30 for size. At that point, I would get scared if I were long. On the other hand, if large sizes had traded at 30 and then size traded at 30⅛, that would be a good indication that a buyer has been found, and the stock is getting ready to rally. Large blocks are important only in context of what is happening.

Do you hold positions overnight?

Occasionally. I think of my risk/reward ratio. How much can the stock open against me as opposed to how much I may make if the stock opened my way. The odds would have to be in my favor. Of course, in any trade you make, you want a good risk/reward ratio of at least 1:1. If I am willing to lose a half dollar on the trade, then I should expect to make at least a half a dollar.

How many months over the last two years have you lost money?

For the previous two years, I didn't have a losing month, and maybe I've lost money in only five or six weeks during the year. This year for business reasons, I haven't been trading as much. I haven't had a losing month this year either, but I notice I'm having more breakeven months than I've ever had before this year. I changed the execution system that I had been using on NASDAQ and this I think has been part of the reason since I was trading more NASDAQ stocks than I have in the past. Also, as I've mentioned before, I think the markets are changing their liquidity patterns and I've had to learn to adjust to new parameters, but when I trade listed stocks I have remained profitable overall.

Can trading skills be taught?

Yes and no. The skills themselves can be taught, but there is an element of personality that a person has to have also. A person has to have a sharp mind and be able to analyze and make quick decisions. There is a lot of information coming at you, and if you are the kind of person who has trouble deciding which toll lane to get into, you are not going to be a good trader. Of course, you can't be stubborn and you have to have good discipline.

How do you get discipline?

I think you have to have some already, although some of it you can teach yourself. I wasn't as disciplined when I started to trade as I am today. I believe that traders should have three things absolutely clear in their heads before they do any trade. One, why are you making this trade? Two, where are you going to get out on the profit side? And three, where are you getting out on the loss side? I know the exact answer to all of these questions before I go into any trade. If you keep this in mind it is easier to be disciplined. Unfortunately, I see many traders who don't have the answer to all or even any of these questions before they do a trade.

Is gut feeling important in trading?

Yes, but I don't mean it in the sense that if my eyes were closed I could have some kind of "feel" for what the market is doing. My gut feeling is probably a part of my mind, which is analyzing every trade and interpreting what is happening on the screen, even if it is not always conscious or I am realizing it.

What kinds of misconceptions about the market get people into trouble?

That market prices are real in any fundamental sense. I think that if people see Intel trading at $100 then they think it's really worth $100. Because of this they don't understand the risks of trading. Perhaps they are unwilling to control their losses, because they think Intel is really worth $100 so when it begins to sell off they think it must come back. But the prices are just what people are willing to pay at that point in time. They don't mean anything else.

Do you ever trade options?

Options can be useful in trading a position, but day trading options is a stupid thing to do.

How many of your trades are short sales?

Maybe 20 to 30 percent or less overall.

Do you enjoy trading?

When I'm making money. I do enjoy it, but it can be also very stressful, especially if you're banging your head against the wall breaking even for several months.

Do you take vacations?

Not many. I'm always thinking that the one week that I'm gone will be the best trading week of the year and I will miss it. Last year I probably made half the money I made for the year in November and December. I've had days when I will make $10,000 or $15,000 and in a slow market it may take me several weeks to make that much. So because I never know when I'll be making my money, I'm reluctant to leave.

How then do you handle getting run down or being stressed?

I'll take days off from trading if I'm having a rough time, but I'll be in the office and keeping track of the markets.

What do you want to be 10 years from now?

I don't know specifically what I want to be doing, but I probably don't want to be trading. I don't believe anyone can trade for 10 years without their brain turning into fried bananas. I don't believe the brain was made to make that many quick decisions and go through that many ups and downs for that long of a period. After three years, I'm feeling a bit burnt out already. I go to sleep at night thinking about numbers, everything is a number to me, everything I talk about has some connection to the market. If I go into a store I ask what's the bid on this thing. Still, I probably would want to stay involved in the financial industry in 10 years, perhaps swing trading more.

chapter 6

Brad Luce

Brad Luce is notable for being consistently successful in trading a distinctive risk arbitrage style which he calls "scalping with a crutch."

He is 35 years old and was born in San Diego. His father was an officer in the Marine Corps. After leaving the Marine Corps, his father became a lawyer for Standard Oil and other firms. His mother has worked as a teacher and social worker. His family moved to several different states as his father changed job locations, including Kansas, North Carolina, Maryland, South Carolina, and Connecticut. When he was living in Maryland, Brad was selected by Johns Hopkins University to participate in a "study of precocious youth." This was the first time Brad had ever heard that term. He completed algebra 1 and 2 in the seventh grade as part of the program. He skipped eighth grade and was a member of the National Honor Society in high school. He attended Georgia Institute of Technology and graduated with a degree in industrial engineering. While at Georgia Tech, he worked for IBM in a coop program for eight semesters, and took a job with IBM when he graduated in 1988. This first job was as an IBM sales representative to the Department of Defense in Washington, DC. Within months of starting this job, Brad won an IBM award for $34,000 for developing a process that cut the time for doing an existing procedure from several days to less than 30 minutes.

When did you first become involved with stocks?

After I won my $34,000 award from IBM in 1989, I went to a financial planning firm which recommended a diversified portfolio of mutual funds. I invested in an international fund, large capitalization fund, and a growth fund. These funds didn't seem to be going anywhere although the money they were making seemed fine. But around 1994 or 1995, I thought I could do better on my own. So I started looking at technology companies that were involved in my business. I had some business contacts with people at Oracle and I thought they had a really good relational database product. I wanted to buy their stock, but determined that I didn't have enough money to buy as much stock as I wanted. So I looked into options because of the leveraging capability and bought Oracle calls. I also bought Sybase calls, another technology company. Using no real technical analysis, I was just buying companies that I thought had good products because I worked in the technology business. I started to read a lot about options and options strategies, and started to do more complicated strategies using spreads and covered calls.

What did you read?

I read a number of books including your book *Options Market Making.*

Well, I hope you won't hold that against me. How did it go with these strategies?

I had a fair amount of success and I really thought I knew what I was doing. But I think it is real easy for people to confuse skill with luck. In hindsight, a lot of what happened to me in my early trading was luck. I thought I was good at it, but when I started to lose money in the 1997, early 1998 period, I realized I had been very fortunate and a lot of things just went right for me when I started options trading.

What did you do next?

At the end of 1996, I wanted to do some other things at IBM, but management wanted me to stay in my existing job. So I left IBM to pursue full-time trading although I did take a two-month job with another technology firm after I left IBM. I would call my options orders in to a regular broker. I had a DTN data feed for live stock and option prices, and I wrote my own software for some analysis as well as using some commercially available software that helped me in valuing options, calculating the potential profitability of spreads, and identifying unusual activity in options. I put a lot of time into this and it wasn't just a willy-nilly effort. But I just couldn't consistently make money. Consistency was the biggest thing for me. My strategies would work sometimes, and then sometimes didn't work. They weren't consistent.

Did you do any technical analysis?

I did some technical analysis with stochastics and moving averages. I looked at a lot of charts, but I didn't have any tool that I used consistently, whereas later I developed more advanced methods that could give me probability outcomes. It wasn't as refined at that point.

How did you become more involved with trading stocks rather than options?

I read about day trading in a magazine, and when I considered the business a little bit, I thought it would be great to be on the other side of the table collecting the commission. So I met with a group who was involved in the business and we talked about expanding their operation by going to Atlanta. But I never got a really good feeling about the business model from them, and so I decided that I was going to do this on my own. I decided the best way to do this was to learn how to day trade and understand the business from the customer side. I thought if I could do this, I'll understand the business better before I become an owner. So I contacted Block Trading in Atlanta and ended up moving to Atlanta and going through their training program for new traders.

What was their training program like?

It was a two-week program. They explained how to use the software, what market makers were doing, and what ECNs were. The course was taught by a fellow who was a former market maker and I thought he did a really good job. The problem that I saw with this program was that they didn't really teach you a trading method. Not even one trading method by saying you can be a scalper and this is what scalpers do, and this is what their risk/reward profile is, or you can be a swing trader or whatever. There was none of that. They did give us some rules like, don't lose too much money in one trade, and don't trade stocks that are really high priced or are very thin and very volatile.

But if I were teaching this program, I would try to find some proven methods that work and show those to the potential traders. There was also two weeks of trading in "demo" mode, which is a simulation program that allows you to place orders and get filled without risking any money. After finishing this course, I made my first trade on April 1, 1998.

Sounds like a fun day to start. How did it go?

I traded at Block Trading making 10 to 15 trades a day on a size of 300 shares. But I was consistently losing money, and at the end of those two months I found myself down about $15,000. Was I learning and getting better? I didn't really see that. I knew that I should try to figure out a better method than scalping. So I stopped trading.

What did you notice about the other traders who started trading about the same time you did?

What happened was that people would say their method is scalping and they would make a little and lose a little, and then make some and lose some. Then on one trade they would get into a position that would go against them dramatically for one, two, or three thousand dollars. What they would do at that point was to say, "Well, that's my long-term holding." And the next thing you know, they would be down $20,000 or $30,000 and then they were done. A person would make a thousand trades over several months and one or two trades would knock him out of the business. They would change their strategy during the trade and didn't want to admit they were wrong.

I was fortunate because when I first started I wouldn't take any positions home and I'd get out of all my losers.

How did your trading go after that point?

I had stopped trading but continued to work on trying to figure out a trading method or algorithm. About this time, there was a man often in the office late determining whether he wanted to buy this branch office as a business. He saw me working at night and we talked about what I was doing. I use the word method rather than system because the word "system" means to me something more defined than the things I was working on, which are more techniques. Anyway, I presented my algorithm to this man, who gave me some money to try it out. Incidentally, this man did become the owner of the firm, which he renamed Capital Gains.

You don't have to divulge any proprietary details about your program, but I'm curious about what factors you took into account.

I had a program that scanned the market for stocks that had an average daily true range greater than a certain amount, and also met certain minimum volume levels. This would give me several hundred stocks and then I would run an algorithm that would determine whether the stock was a buy, sell, or neutral. The algorithm was based on where the stock closed within its previous day's range, what sort of volume it had relative to previous volume, and I put some mathematical equations around all that and came up with a factor or multiplier. All this was automated and the program would spit out a sheet of stocks based on the buy, sell, or neutral classifications.

But we would not trade on these classifications alone. The data file, containing the list of stocks, would then be put through an intraday signal generator. For this generator, I used moving averages and regression lines, and only when we would get an intraday signal that confirmed the initial classification would we trade the stock. For example, if Cisco was classified as a buy on the daily algorithm, only when the intraday signal was triggered would we buy Cisco. When I back tested this model, I found a success percentage of between 67 and 72 percent.

Our money management strategy was good for handling our losers but I think we capped our winners a little bit because we scaled out in the direction of the trade. For example, if Cisco had a four-point average range and we received a buy signal, we would buy 500 shares and sell 100 shares each point up letting only the last hundred shares run in our favor.

How did the trading program work out?

We were successful. We made a little bit of money, generally between one and three thousand dollars a day. We had a team of four traders and were able to trade about a hundred stocks a day. It was very consistent and we probably lost money on only two out of the 20 or 25 days we traded this method. We were on our way to something good, although I didn't want to be fooled into just being lucky.

You only traded this method for 20 days?

Well, after 20 days, another customer in the office lost $70,000 trading one day. Since he only had $30,000 in his account, the firm lost $40,000 since it was obliged immediately to make good on the remaining amount of that customer's loss. When that happened, the man who had been backing my trading stopped everything. Even though everything I was doing was unrelated to that loss, he now owned that firm and realized he was on the hook for traders in his office if they lost more than they have. So he shut our trading program down. I was very discouraged. At some point in the future I would be interested in trying this program again.

But your stock trading took a different direction. How did that happen?

At the time we were trading this program, I heard about another fellow who was trading Intel and Intel warrants in an arbitrage. Intel and Intel warrants should have been trading on a one-to-one price relationship, based on the price of Intel and the terms of the warrants, but he noticed that Intel would sometimes move more than this spread. I don't remember what the exact relationship was, because the terms of the warrant had other conditions if Intel's price fell below a certain level. But that level was far away at the time. When Intel moved ahead of the warrants, this gentleman would short Intel and buy the warrants, and when that relationship came back to parity, he would unwind the trade. It didn't happen all the time, but it would happen a few times a day and he would make a point or half point. I thought this was really a good strategy, and I thought I could make some money if I could find stocks that moved in a relationship of this sort.

So you traded Intel and Intel warrants?

No. I think by the time I learned about this, Intel warrants were no longer being traded. But a couple of us in the office started looking at mergers as an alternative. I thought that this was the same thing except for the fact that the deal may not go through, or a white knight may come in and bid higher for the acquiree, or that the terms of the deal get changed. But I still thought that there was enough potential to give this kind of trading a crack.

How did you do this?

I figured out the ratios of the two stocks and the ranges of the discount of the acquiree to the acquirer. For example, WorldCom was buying MCI. I don't remember the exact terms, but for illustration let's say it was a deal for one share of WorldCom for each share of MCI. WorldCom was trading about 50 and MCI was trading about 35 before the deal was announced. After the deal is announced, WorldCom comes down to 48 because often the acquirer's stock declines a little, and MCI goes up to 43. So the spread is five points. MCI is trading at a $5 discount to the merger price at that point. The discount is a reflection of the uncertainty of the deal going through, and there are multiple factors that affect that uncertainty level.

But as time goes on, that $5 discount changes because the stocks continue to trade without enough arbitrageurs making sure the stocks trade in an exact relationship. A big mutual fund, for example, may want to buy WorldCom, and it goes up in price, without another big mutual fund buying shares of MCI to make it go up as fast. There are many reasons why that discount changes.

How do you trade this spread?

What I do with the software I've developed, is to track those changes in the discount. In my mind I have a good idea of what I consider the right discount level, which in this example, would be $5. The discount may get as narrow as two points, for example, if WorldCom remained at 48 but MCI traded up to 46, or the discount may get wider.

When the discount is wide, I short the acquirer and go long the acquiree. And I wait for that discount to narrow or decrease. And then I take the position off.

How did it go when you started trading this arbitrage spread?

When I first started trading spreads I was making about $1,000 a day. Again, I wasn't going to be fooled into confusing luck with skill. I wanted to make sure I could do this and I understood it. I did a lot of things early on that I've refined. I don't play big size as much as I used to do. As far as my profitability, I was making between $1,000 and $10,000 a day, and every now and then there would be a fluke where I would make a ton of money like $30,000 in a single day.

I imagine you watch your news sources pretty carefully trading arbitrage?

That is correct. We have a Bloomberg machine in the office. There are several other people in the office trading arbitrage, some of whom I've taught. We get on the Internet at night looking for news about deals, and we share information. When new deals come out we research the deals. We call the company to find out things like shareholder voting dates, and things like that. The younger guys who are new to arbitrage are real excited about finding these deals, so it is a very powerful group.

When you talk about trading arbitrage, I am reminded of the 1980s when the big risk arbitrage traders were much in the news. Is what you are doing what they did then?

I still feel like I'm an outsider to what the big arbitrageurs do. They don't trade like I do. I assume they put on large positions and use options to hedge them. I would like to get to where I am trading like I am now but have options to guard against a deal blowing up. I wish I could talk to these guys and understand what they do. I am pretty confident that they put on such big positions that the time value of money is critical to them and I imagine they use sophisticated models.

In an arbitrage spread, even though you are long and short an equal value of money, do you still have to put up full margin for each leg of the position?

I do, and that's another big disadvantage that I have compared to other professionals who may have more lenient leverage or margin requirements.

Since you've been trading arbitrage, in how many months would you say you've lost money?

One month.

How do you control your potential losses in this kind of spread trade?

Before the deal was announced, the discount between these two stocks might have been $15, for example. I take the preannounced deal discount and I say that's as wide as it can sensibly go. When I used to trade large size on a trade, I could not let it go out to that level, so if the discount dropped a lot, I would say this is getting way out of the range and it was a subjective determination to close down the trade. But now as I've progressed, I'm trading smaller sizes so I can let it run out to that predeal discount. If it breaks through that level, then I know there's something seriously wrong and I'm out of the trade. Also, any time I hear bad news about a deal I normally get out of it.

Did you ever experience any large losses using this strategy?

I put on a spread between JDSU and ETEK, in which I was long about 10,000 shares of JDSU and short about 22,000 shares of ETEK. In March of this year, this spread moved against me 20 points, and each point spread against me represented $10,000. What happened was that there was a rumor that the deal wasn't going to go through and ETEK just tanked. I was out of the office at the time, but even if I had heard the rumor and made the decision to get out of the trade, I don't know that I could have because there was nobody to sell to on ETEK. It was almost like they halted the stock; it was going down so fast. I ended up taking a $200,000 loss.

That must have been painful.

It was painful. $200,000 was a lot of money. I didn't trade any more that day, but the next day I made $12,000. When the weekend came, I reflected a little bit. I kind of felt sorry for myself for another three days and then said, you're a good trader, let's keep going. And that's what I did. I have made very consistent profits, except for that particular trade.

I think it's very important for a trader not to look at the dollar amount of a loss, but the time involved to make that money. You can't think that you just lost the price of a house! We were making $5,000 to $10,000 a day trading and had a terrific January and February. I said, okay. Let's look at it this way, I just lost between 20 and 40 days of trading. And that makes you think that isn't that bad. So you get back on the horse.

You said that you had refined how you trade these spreads. How did that occur?

It kind of jumped out and hit me in the face early on. For example, I would have one side of my spread on and I would be showing a profit. And then I wondered why was I so anxious to put on the other side? The spread's still fine, but I have $500 in profit already on my short, so why am I so excited to buy the other side? Why not just take the profit? I did not have a mentor or an expert to answer these questions for me. It seemed to make sense to take the profit on the first leg of the spread and then try to look for another opportunity.

So I wouldn't put on a lot of these spreads because I was scalping. Seventy to 80 percent of my trading would be on only one side of the deal. There are a few people in my office that put the spread on every time because they're nervous about their trading. They'll get over that, but putting on both sides of the spread is a good way for a new trader to gain confidence.

Were you able to read a Level II screen sufficiently to determine the short-term direction of the one leg of the spread that you traded?

Oh yes. I had enough skill on Level II after the first two months when I lost the $15,000 that I knew what I was doing in putting the spread on. There are multiple things that are happening though. First of all, the market makers are getting better, so the Level II is getting tougher. But I think my skill on Level II is also always improving. Now I'm not as concerned about my executions because I'm at a level where my chances are pretty good inside that box.

How many of these arbitrage spreads are you trading or trading around at any one time?

Three to twelve.

How many new mergers happen in a week or month?

You can go a long time without a good merger being announced. A lot of mergers announced are not stock mergers, for example, but a cash deal. I don't trade these. But what normally happens is that every few months there is a really good one that lasts three to six months. So it's not really the quantity of new ones that is important, it is the volatility of the spread and the volume in the stocks that are important.

How many would be going on at one time then?

In my software there are about 30 mergers that I'm looking at. I'm actively trading only five or six of those. The others I am looking at, but they're not volatile and aren't moving. The discount may only be a dollar, for example, and the only place it's going is zero and it trades very tightly around this figure. The other reason I may not trade a merger is because the acquirer does three million shares volume a day, but the acquiree only trades sixty thousand shares a day. If the volume is this low, the market makers keep the bid-offer spread so wide you can't trade it.

How many trades are you making in a day?

This summer I'm trading between 35,000 and 60,000 shares a day. My average trade is between 500 and 1,000 shares. I know it's less than a thousand because on a lot of these positions I'll scale into them. For example, the current spread I am trading is JDSU and SDLI. This spread is 380 shares of JDSU to every 100 shares of SDLI. SDLI is a stock that can move two points just by two traders dropping their bids. I trade it a hundred shares at a time, and then I put on 380 shares of JDSU. And then I'll go back and do another hundred shares of SDLI, and then 380 more shares of JDSU. I scale into the position because I don't want to do 300 shares of SDLI since I might not be able to. I also scale out of the position in the same way.

Do you do any other kind of arbitrage?

I've started to wonder what I would do if there were no good deals to trade so I investigated trading stocks that are a component of an index. For example, HHH is an Internet holding stock traded on the American Stock Exchange, and Yahoo is a major component of HHH. I've done some back testing with some factors to determine the range of where the HHHs trade relative to Yahoo's price. I have done some trades where I will short the HHHs and buy Yahoo. That's worked okay but I'm not comfortable enough because all these holder products have only been around for the last year and I don't have enough data to feel comfortable trading them. Another reason I'm not trading them is that while the liquidity is okay, the HHHs are a specialist driven product and he keeps the bid/offer spread a half point wide all the time. So you have a lot to overcome in execution costs to trade them.

I did trade an arbitrage with the QQQs which are much more liquid that the HHHs. This product is heavily weighted with Microsoft, Cisco, Intel, and I actually built a little model tracking the spread of this basket of stocks with the Qs. There are a lot of ECNs, mostly Island, trading the Qs so you do not have a big bid-offer spread. We actually traded this basket against the Qs, and found a consistent tradable spread range. The problem is that it's a slow mover, so you can tie up capital for multiple days.

There are tons of things out there. If you had more capital and the ability to sit on the spread for a while, you could make a decent return.

How many trades do you do that are outright speculative, compared to how many trades involve an arbitrage spread?

This summer, maybe 5 percent are speculative, whereas last winter and spring, when the market was really moving I and two partners were trading a lot of directional trades. There were a lot of small stocks that had not done anything for years, but because the high flyers had already run, they were starting to get some money. We were picking off these small stocks like the bio-techs for something like $6 to $8 with 5,000 shares that were running two or three points. So back then, it was fifty-fifty between arbitrage and speculative trades.

Is technical analysis part of how you trade?

If you call technical analysis looking at a chart, that's what I'm doing. Let's say I am looking to short the acquirer's stock in a deal. If I see on its chart that the stock's going to break through a support level, and the S&P and NASDAQ futures are going down, and if it looks like the market is going down, I will short that stock. If there's no reason for me to put the other leg of the spread on, and the acquirer's stock keeps going down, I stay short that stock.

Do you use trend lines or things like that?

I've found that when I draw trend lines I draw them to suit the situation that I want to happen, so I'm not objective. I think a lot of people are like that. I don't draw trend lines because I know that I'm not good at it. If anything, I draw support and resistance levels because they're just horizontal straight lines. There's some subjectivity in that, but not nearly as much in drawing a trend line.

Do you use moving averages?

Yes. Moving averages I do use. I also use Bollinger Bands a lot. I've studied a lot of his work. I put them on stock charts but not futures charts. They help me. It tells me that if a stock has run a long way and the band is wide, then it might be time to get out of a position. Or the stock made a high outside the band and then came back inside the band and made lower highs, so maybe that's a good stock to short. Maybe it's done running.

Are you using Bollinger Bands to countertrend trade?

I think some people do use them that way, but you need to be careful about doing that. What a lot of people do, I think, is to say that because a stock price might be outside the two standard deviation band, an extreme area, they are going to short the stock. The problem with that is, the stock can stay outside that band for a long time. You can really get your head handed to you, and you really don't have a good stop loss level. This is because you haven't allowed the stock to pull back inside the band level. If you waited for this pull back, then your stop is that previous high. If you short when the stock goes outside the band you're messing with fire. I just use those bands to get a feel for where the stock's going. I don't have any method that says every time this happens with a stock relative to the Bollinger band, I short it.

My partner and I are looking at some position trades for the next three to five days. We are trying to find a divergence between money flows and the stock price trend. For example, if the money flow is positive and the stock price is moving sideways or going down, there may be some reason to believe that the stock will soon go up.

Do you have any special money management techniques that you use?

I keep $100,000 in my account. When my account gets up to $150,000, I take $50,000 out. If you do this, you don't change your trading style just because you have more money. This keeps me from putting on too big of a position because I don't have enough money in the account to do it. I think this has worked out well. Even with this size account I find I still have $5,000 or $10,000 days. Although this summer, if I have a $5,000 day, I take my wife out to dinner, because the summer has been slow.

How often do you take your positions home overnight?

I take one or two positions home just about every night. If I'm in a position that I don't feel is that great or I'm down or up a little bit, and it is getting toward the end of the day, I'll try to take it off. If I could go home flat every night, I probably would. But I always seem to have two or three stragglers which I have to take home.

Do you pay attention to the time of day while trading?

Most definitely. Volume is important and you can't get good fills when there is a lull in the market mid-day. It's much better to trade when there's high volume and there's fear and greed working and you can take advantage of that. When nothing's happening, there's nothing to take advantage of. I'll watch the market mid-day because maybe a spread is getting to a point where nobody is paying any attention and I'll trade it. But I definitely trade less mid-day.

Do you pyramid your good trades?

I should. I don't do it enough in my directional trades.

What software have you used trading?

I've used CyberTrader, Mtrade, and Gr8Trade. I haven't had a lot of difficulty learning the mechanics of execution, but in general, I think, a lot of people have trouble with that.

Have the systems been satisfactory?

Yes, for the most part. However, I think day trading firms allocate a very small portion of the money they make to the information systems department. I know that the Wall Street firms have the most state-of-the-art computer equipment, the brightest computer minds of any business, and they allocate a large portion of their funds to make sure that their systems are the best.

But day trading firms have no real time operating system, for example. We're using Windows which is about the furthest thing from real time you can get. It's just amazing to me that more money is not allocated by these firms to that side of the business.

You are now trading with Protrader.com. How did that happen?

The man who financially backed my initial trading algorithm bought the Block Trading office where I started to trade and named the new firm Capital Gains. At one point, Capital Gains developed computer problems, and I transferred my trading to Momentum Securities. I traded there until July 1999, when the tragic shootings occurred in that Atlanta office. During that time I just started trading with Cornerstone Securities, which is now called Protrader.com. Actually, this is the same office location where I first started to trade in April 1998!

You were in the office in Atlanta where the tragic shootings occurred?

The murders by Mark Barton occurred on Thursday, July 29, in the Atlanta office where I traded. This office was a small single room with one entrance. There were only about 10 traders and four people who worked there. You were friends with everybody because it's a close-knit group.

Every now and then we would get a new trader who would come into the office. Mark Barton was new to the group. He came in and traded for a couple of weeks and nobody really knew anything about him. He was very quiet. We never said anything to him and then he left. The rumor was that he lost some money. I guess he got more money because he came back and traded the Monday and Tuesday of that week. He had a bad position and was losing money. Tuesday and Wednesday I was out of the office and then Wednesday night I went on vacation.

On Thursday, July 29, Barton came in and shot everybody. There were four people killed in that office who were good friends of mine. One of the guys who was killed was a guy I had taught to trade risk arbitrage, and he had become successful. I was really upset about it and sad for them and their families. We were a close-knit group. I realized I could also have been there.

Everybody there was mourning this tragedy and then all of sudden out of nowhere comes this media storm about how day trading is bad, and how day trading made this guy kill these people. I felt that the media was blaming my livelihood as a cause of somebody harming other humans. I feel very strongly that this is ridiculous. When the postal workers go in and shoot up the post office, people don't say that mail is the cause. Day trading has never made me think about killing anyone.

What do you think motivated the media? Is this just part of the sensationalism of the media today?

Every time the media comes to our office to interview people they always want to know the amounts of money you are making. I will not talk about this. We've all heard about how people are making tons of money day trading and losing tons of money day trading, for some reason, that is of interest to the public. Hell yes, they sensationalized it.

Do you think the public has a misconception about the industry?

Oh, yes. I'm a pretty competent person I think, but I am almost embarrassed when I am introduced to people I don't know, at church say, and they ask me what I do for a living. I don't want to say day trading because then I have to have a 15-minute conversation and explain to them actually what I do, and they don't want to hear it. The minute you say "day trader" they have this preconceived notion. It's kind of like people who just hate lawyers. But being a lawyer is at least prestigious. It's very frustrating. My business card just says "proprietary trading."

What do you think we can learn about this tragic experience?

I would like to see several things happen. It is my understanding that Barton lied to Momentum Securities because he had lost a fair amount of money over at another firm and never told them that. Now, I am a firm believer in protecting the professional environment where other traders exist to make a living. If you day trade from home on the Internet and lose money, that's your business. You don't have any affect on other people when you are at home day trading by yourself.

I see guys who come in here and have absolutely no chance in hell of making it. And what I think day trading firms should do is give them some sort of test on their competency. I'm not saying they should pass a test to determine whether or not they can lose their money because people start businesses every day and there is no competency test that determines that they know how to run a business. And this is a business. But I do think that they should pass a competency test on using the software, understanding the market, and when they pass those tests if they want to lose their money, that's fine. But if they cannot pass those tests, they should not be allowed to trade in that office but go home and do it on the Internet. It's my office and I have to work there.

Many people in the industry oppose restrictions and regulations of day trading by regulators. Are you asking for that?

No, I'm not saying that. I think the trading firms ought to do it. Regulation as far as I'm concerned just hampers all businesses. But self-regulation can make businesses better.

Is there a reason why you prefer to trade in an office with other people rather than with your group off somewhere else?

I'm really considering it. I am working with someone checking out the feasibility of moving off site to another office where we have to approve the person who comes into that office. That person would have to meet certain requirements and skill levels. If they can do this, we'll give them an environment where they can be successful and make a living.

Can trading skills be taught?

Definitely. But they are not being taught. I think the trading firms are so scared that if they tell someone to look at a method or pattern, and then if that person loses money, he is going to come back to sue them.

You've said you've done a little training. What's been your experience with that?

Protrader.com saw me as a new trader who became consistently profitable relatively quickly. They asked me if I would mind putting together a little class to talk about how you trade risk arbitrage. My trading is risk arbitrage, but it's really what I call "scalping with a crutch." The crutch is when you put the spread on. But if you can scalp the initial leg of the spread and put money in the bank, then do it. If the scalping does not work exactly as you planned, then you put the spread on and wait for it to go your way as the spread narrows or widens to your profit target.

Anyway, I've done three or four seminars. You would not believe it, but people try it and give up. The people who stick with it are set financially and should always make money unless they make trading illegal. The biggest thing I noticed about those who became successful was that they had perseverance. If you give most of the people a trading method, they'll try it for a while. And then a bad thing happens, and they give up on it. And they go to the next style, and then the next, until they run out of money. I can sit there with my record right in front of them and tell them exactly what I am doing, and they just don't believe it or have the patience to do it. It's absolutely amazing to me.

There are two people in my office who persevered and now they are making a decent amount of money consistently every day. Probably one out of eight people I have talked to about it, pick it up and becomes successful.

I hear that again and again.

They have an advantage over normal day traders because I am giving them a proven method. Most day traders fail because they have absolutely no method.

What in your opinion distinguishes successful traders from those who are not?

Successful trainees don't give up because of one bad experience. They're persistent and keep focusing on what they're trying to accomplish. I think decent keyboard ability and computer skills are very helpful. There are some people who just aren't that fast on the keys, and if their trading method doesn't require them to be fast then that's fine. But most of the trading methods I've seen require some sort of keyboard agility.

Do you think good trading is an innate skill?

I think you can be a good trader without innate skill, but I think to be a great trader you need a little bit of innate skill. Great traders can have a "gut" feel for a chart and have their emotions under control, and I don't know if you can teach those things. But I think I can teach someone to be successful even if they don't have that edge.

Do you feel you control your emotions well?

I control them well most of the time. I think I handle loses real, real well. But I think when I have a winning trade I have more excitement than I should. But when you're in a trading office and the other guy is losing money, and you shout "Woo Woo!" that doesn't make him feel too good.

One of the things I had to work on is that I really like to be right. You go through your entire life being schooled to be correct. In trading you have to throw that out the window quick. That's one of the things I had trouble with. I overcame it by just starting to expect that I would be wrong. Then when I was right, that was a pleasant surprise versus something that was expected.

What kind of misconceptions about the market get people into trouble?

The general public thinks that stocks always go up. Maybe they will. I don't know. But I think about fundamentals. Why is this Internet company that is never going to make any money have a market capitalization of $4 billion? I don't understand that.

What makes you different?

I think I'm confident, disciplined, and have math and computers skills that helped. And I'm dedicated to this. Some guys think they can just come in at 10:30 and just pick up the trend in the market and you can't do that.

What time do you get in the office in the morning?

I wake up and check the Internet for news and then am in the office by 8:30. I live three and a half miles from the office so it's real nice that I don't have a lot of travel time.

How often do you take a vacation?

I never go on vacation because if the market's really moving with high volume, then a week's vacation can cost me $25,000. I try to take weekend trips to a house we have near the ocean, maybe leaving on a Friday afternoon and returning Monday morning. I have been able to trade from there on my laptop.

Do you enjoy trading?

Oh, I love it. I love the independence and doing something that I really enjoy. I like the fact that I am gaining expertise in this business. And I really love teaching people. When you can teach young people to make money, that makes me feel terrific.

And then the money's good. One of the things my wife and I have been discussing is once we get to where we basically have what we need, what are we going to do? I think we would like to take the money and do something for other people. Or if she needs capital to start a business, we'll do that.

Where do you see yourself 10 years from now?

I think I'll still be trading, and I'll keep working on trading ideas that I haven't had time to work on. It's eating at me that I don't have time and eventually I'll make time. Maybe I'll have a team of guys working on these ideas I have, and maybe they can build on those ideas. I'm the first guy to say that's way better than what I was thinking of, let's work on that. I definitely see myself still in this business.

chapter 7

Matthew Andresen

Matthew Andresen is the 30-year-old president of the Island ECN. He has been described by CS First Boston analyst James Marks as displaying "the vision, expertise, and technological capabilities that make Island the thought and innovation leader in alternative markets." Certainly Island, which every trader is familiar with, will need this leadership as it confronts the challenges and complexities of the changing marketplace on NASDAQ and listed stocks.

Who started Island and why?

Island was one of those companies fortunate enough to be a solution to a pervasive problem. And the problem was the way NASDAQ existed prior to 1997, which was as a dealer monopoly. The only people that could see the orders that came from retail investors were the market makers or dealers. So it was very difficult to be a retail trader. It was like being in a poker game and having everyone else hold their cards in normal ways while you're holding them the wrong way. Clearly, you couldn't be a very good poker player in that kind of game. This situation made it a very uphill battle for traders. So what a guy named Josh Levine thought was: Why don't I build a system where the orders of retail investors could interact with each other, in addition to being sent out to the NASDAQ marketplace. And the system he constructed he called Island. And when the U.S. Securities Exchange Commission recognized the advantages of this kind of system that was put into place to help retail investors, they enacted the Order Handling Rules in January 20, 1997 which, in our minds, at least to this point, is the single biggest shift in how U.S. equity markets operate in the last 200 years.

Recent statistics show that Island has gained about a 12 percent of market share of trades on NASDAQ, more than any other ECN, and is the second dollar volume ECN. How did Island gain such a market share in such a short time?

I think any network's job, and Island is really a network of over 350 broker-dealers, is to match buyers and sellers as quickly, as efficiently, and as cheaply as possible. We've competed successfully on speed. Within milliseconds, Island can match trades. We've competed on reliability. We've gone three and a half years without a single capacity related degradation of service. And of course, price. Island is the cheapest ECN. We charge only seventy-five one thousandths (75/1,000) of a penny per share per trade. But with all that said, I think that what the most important metric is for trying to quantify the value of a system like Island or Instinet or eBay or the New York Stock Exchange, is the liquidity on that system. Because you might be fast, you might be reliable, and you might be cheap, but if you're giving someone a cheap, fast, and reliable way to get nowhere, you don't have a very good business. And the liquidity is what really matters. If you have sellers, do you have buyers? When you have buyers, do you have sellers? And it's that liquidity of the sum total of buyers and sellers that really creates an efficiency for a marketplace. And I think that's what has fed the success of Island. It's why Island's 1999 trading volume was over 26.5 billion shares, with a total dollar volume of 1.56 trillion.

Many traders have execution systems that allow them to place their orders by routing them to the Island book. Can a broker use Island as

their primary execution system rather than having to do that kind of routing?

There are 6,500 brokerage firms out there and they're all going to do different things and all have different business models. Some trade proprietarily, that is for their own companies account, and it will be up to the traders themselves to figure out where and how they want their orders to be routed and displayed. We've found, and I think this is the underpinning of our success at Island, that when a brokerage firm gives control of where orders are routed, shown, or displayed to the customers, those customers have in overwhelming numbers selected Island. A lot of customers don't think about their order's routing. They're looking at charts or they're looking at fundamentals, and when they're ready to buy or sell, they'll just try to execute. They're not thinking the way institutions are. Institutions have known for many years that the most important thing isn't the commission, it's the execution quality of the trade. And if over time you can be right for an extra sixteenth, or an extra eighth, or an extra quarter point every single time, that may very well be the difference between success or failure. So we think that when put in the cold light of competition, people select Island. And they select Island for those metrics we discussed earlier: speed, price, reliability, and liquidity. I think once someone's given those clear choices, it is an easy decision.

Doug Atken, CEO of Instinet, has been quoted as saying that "Those of you who are ECNs, you better make your money in the next few years because it's a dead business model." What do you think of this?

The first time I heard that was from Doug at the Baruch Conference, almost exactly two years ago. I am still waiting. I know Doug very well and have a lot of respect for him, but what I think he meant was that ECNs in their then current form would not exist in two years. I think there is some truth to the spirit behind that comment. An ECN is, in its regulatory definition, a sort of historical accident. It's a broker dealer. Island is actually registered as a brokerage firm, yet we match trades for other brokerage firms and have no customers in the traditional sense. This doesn't make a lot of sense to me or probably anybody else. That's why Island filed last year to be the nation's first for-profit stock exchange. I think what Doug is saying, clearly from his purchase of a big chunk of Archipelago, one of our much smaller competitors, is that the for-profit stock exchange model is the wave of the future. The hybrid broker dealer ECN will have to change into either a for-profit exchange model or the strict broker dealer model. I disagree with the statement in so far as it suggests that the direct electronic matching of orders is not the wave of the future. I think it is.

You said that Island has applied to become a stock exchange. What does that mean and how is it going to affect the marketplace?

It's funny you phrased the question that way, because "what does it mean?" is a question that is evolving very quickly. This is very important to us, because filing to become an exchange is the only method laid out to Island by the SEC to be able to compete with the New York Stock Exchange for listed stocks. To compete on NASDAQ, you have to be a broker dealer. Okay, we're a broker dealer. To compete for NYSE listed stocks, you must be a stock exchange, just like Cincinnati, or the American, or NASDAQ, or Boston, or New York. We're not that type of entity right now, so we filed to be that kind of entity. But what that means, I think, will change considerably over the next year. We don't want to just buy a regional exchange. A lot of people have suggested that we just buy a regional stock exchange. They're known to be out there on the block. Then suddenly we would be an exchange. The problem is that being an exchange at the moment is a mixed blessing. It's mixed because the current rules and technology governing the communications between the exchanges is incredibly archaic and obsolete. Even SEC Chairman Levitt has used those words. By going through the effort of being an exchange, not only will we be successful and become an exchange, but we will bring these issues to the attention of the SEC and the public, who will take a real interest in making sure that the exchanges themselves communicate in a modern way.

If you become an exchange, would a trader still be able to route their orders through Island on NASDAQ?

Absolutely. Our model has always been: Show the orders that we have to as many people as possible and allow as many people as possible to come in and interact with those orders. That's our philosophy. So anything we can do to further advertise the intentions of our customers, which we believe insures best execution, anything we can do to insure that more potential buyers and sellers can access our network, is in our interest and the interest of our customers. What we don't want to do is to be forced to route orders on to inefficient markets. People come to Island because it's fast, cheap, reliable, and liquid. They don't come to us to have their orders shunted off this beautiful system on to an inefficient system like that governing NYSE listed stocks. So we are always going to allow ourselves to be accessed by as many people as possible.

If you became an exchange, would that mean you could show listed stocks?

We're actually able to trade listed stocks now on Island. This gets a little bit convoluted, but welcome to the world of market structure. It seems so simple, just buyers and sellers meeting. Unfortunately in real terms, it's quite complicated. We're allowed to trade NYSE listed stocks now. In fact, if I punch up our book for IBM, you will see a nice deep book of buyers and sellers. The problem is the prices on our "Book Viewer" and Island itself aren't shared with people on the American Stock Exchange, the New York Stock Exchange, the Boston Stock Exchange, the Pacific Coast Exchange, and so on. That's because we're not allowed to have our prices incorporated into what's call the Consolidated Quotation System, or CQS. It's strange that regulators allow us to trade listed stocks, but insist on us doing so in a fragmented way. We think that's kind of silly. I think the regulators agree with us, and that's why they have allowed us to file to be a stock exchange. And why they've dedicated a significant amount of time lately toward policy initiatives to strengthen competition in the equities markets.

Archipelago has also applied to become an exchange, and perhaps other ECNs will also. How is this going to affect Island's being an exchange?

I always believe that we have been a huge beneficiary of competition. We've been in an incredibly competitive environment here on NASDAQ, not only because there are so many cut-throat competitors here, including us, but also NASDAQ itself has created quite an unlevel playing field for us. Yet we still manage to do very well. The extra challenges and competition will insure that we will be as sharp as possible. It's interesting that Archipelago has largely abandoned their exchange filing in favor of doing a deal with the Pacific Coast Stock Exchange. So they are actually going the route of doing a deal with the regional exchange. Island is not interested in such a deal.

NASDAQ has recently asked to become its own exchange with a central order book, with the name, I believe, of "SuperMontage." What is this and how will it affect Island or trading?

I don't know if you are a big basketball fan. Obviously I am, as you can see from the Duke poster over my shoulder. My favorite time of year is March Madness, where you get 64 teams in the NCAA field. What makes it great is the feeling that anything can happen at any time because it's so relentlessly competitive and fair. Well, imagine if the NCAA themselves, based in Overland Park, Kansas, decide not only to run this tournament, host it, regulate and referee it, but also field their own team, the NCAA team. Imagine them in the tournament. You'd probably get some eye rolling, the NCAA team, good luck getting some good calls here. That's basically what's happening. The NCAA, in this case it's NASDAQ, might look at Duke having all this relentless success and say, why is Duke getting all the press attention in the NCAA tournament since it's the NCAA that puts it on?

Well, NASDAQ is not a central meeting place, it's just a group of different market places, like Island, Instinet, Goldman Sachs, and so on. These different places have all competed very well and have had a lot of success, which has fed NASDAQ's success since they are just an approximation of these markets. What NASDAQ now wants to do is field their own ECN in the marketplace and not only be the regulator but also a competitor. Certainly I find that disturbing from a competitive sense. No one should be in a position of trying to compete with their regulator.

So if NASDAQ went ahead with being an exchange, would that mean that Island would be off creating its own market with its own liquidity?

I think we already are our own market with our own liquidity. The question is whether NASDAQ can duplicate that. They don't have any of their own liquidity and they don't have their own market. They are just a connectivity system for other people's market. So the question is, can they compete on speed, reliability, cost, and liquidity. We have a big head start in all four of those and we welcome the competition.

What regulatory action from the SEC is now being considered that will change the marketplace on NASDAQ? Could you tell me a little bit about that? I know you have been in Washington, DC, recently.

You had impeccable timing asking that question, because there was a little noticed concept release coming out of the SEC about 10 days ago. I believe that in time this concept release will go down as one of the seminal moments in market regulation. This is a concept release so it is not a rule yet, but something the SEC is putting out to see what the public thinks. The SEC gives us the chance to rethink some issues in today's NYSE listed markets. Specifically, no market, no matter how quick, fast, efficient, and fair, can ever go at a faster pace than any other market. We all have to agree to be as slow as the slowest market. The rule that enables this to happen is called the "trade-through rule." It basically says that, no matter how efficient, for example, Island may be, if there's a better price advertised somewhere else, you as a trader will have to route your order to that other market.

Have you ever shopped at a Seven-Eleven? Is anything at Seven-Eleven the cheapest? Absolutely not. Seven-Eleven is the home of the four-ounce carton of orange juice for three bucks. Yet people go to Seven-Eleven all the time. Why? It's convenient, open later, reliable, and has high quality products. Well, imagine if you went to Seven-Eleven at two in the morning and you were really hungry and you absolutely had to have a Moon Pie. So you go to Seven-Eleven and you say you would like this Moon Pie for $2, and I'll be happy to pay for it right now, and they say, I know you think you want that Moon Pie, but you don't. You want to go to Sam's Club 40 miles over that way. They've got Moon Pies for $1.98. But by the time you get to Sam's Club, the Moon Pies are gone, or they're not open, or the price has changed, or any number of bad things. You get my idea. That's what the trade through rule does for markets. It denies the customer his right to choose his market.

If you don't make things competitive by price, though, don't you make it more advantageous for large institutions that have large order flows simply to route their orders to themselves?

This is why this concept release is so important. Right now, remember, Island is trading NYSE listed stocks without its prices being shown on listed stock exchanges. So what this rule says is, take Island's orders, immediately show them on the consolidated quotes for New York stocks, and let everyone know where the best price is. We want to be in that mix. But, let's do this without forcing traders to route their orders off their system. In return, the broker-dealer sending the order would need to disclose that you are "trading through" another market price. That is, if we're trading at 60, and you at the Boston Stock Exchange are at 60$\frac{1}{16}$, and I get an incoming order from a trader, I can go ahead and fill him at 60 and not route him off to Boston. You know how long it takes to route an order through the intermarket trading system? Two minutes. You know how far the PalmPilot IPO moved in the first two minutes? Twenty-six points.

I drove in this morning from New Jersey, were I live, to the Holland Tunnel. You know how I came through the Holland Tunnel? With EZ-Pass, the electronic ticket sensor. I use EZ-Pass despite the fact that it is no cheaper than the full service lane. It's four bucks in either lane. In fact, it's actually more expensive because you have to prepay EZ-Pass thereby giving the EZ-Pass folks an interest free loan on your money. Yet I use EZ-Pass. Why? Because it saves me 30 minutes. I know I can get through the lane and I know I won't get stuck. You make decisions all the time based on criteria other than price. Have you ever been a victim of the "bait and switch"? They'll say we've got water for a dollar and you go there and they say no, it's two dollars. And you say, but you advertised a dollar. The price changed. Well that happens in markets all the time.

The only thing that concerns me about what you're saying is that I've talked to people who traded before the Order Handling Rules were passed and they say they would put orders on NASDAQ, for say, $7/8$ offered, I think they did use Island at the time, and they would see trade prints go off at even, simply because the market makers preferred to trade their spread rather than the cheaper price.

That's still the case today. There is no trade through rule on NASDAQ, which is why NASDAQ has such incredibly small spreads, why they have such incredibly strong competition, and why it's such a vibrant marketplace.

The trade through rule meaning?

You can trade through another price. Remember Wall Street is not about losing money. This is the place in the world where you find some of the most sophisticated financial people in the world and these people want to fight for every last dollar. Let me tell you something. People don't trade through because they want to lose money, they trade through because the price that you are seeing at seven eighths, isn't really there. If it takes you two minutes to get to a price, it isn't really there. If you go to that other marketplace and they have 90 seconds to review your order, like NASDAQ market makers do, to decide whether they want to trade with you, is the price really there? If you go there, and you sometimes don't get a fill, it's not really there. Immediacy, accountability, and speed are what counts.

How do you feel about "payment for order flow"?

I think Island is the antidote to those kinds of systems. I think putting a human being with a profit incentive in between you and an execution will over time adversely affect you. But I certainly don't think that any regulation is necessary. It's a business model. And people over time, and I believe Island's growth is a validation of this, will eventually choose what is right for themselves. And it is my job to get out there and convince them of that.

You don't think that payment for order flow will hurt Island because of loss of liquidity?

Payment for order flow has been around for a long time—long before Island was around, and we've been able to be successful despite that. Brokers realize that the three dollars they might make off selling the order, might in the end upset their customers about not being treated properly.

Is the merger of all ECNs into their own exchange a possibility?

A guy named Bill Burnham, who is one of the smartest guys I've ever met and who was the Credit Suisse analyst for a long time before becoming one of the general partners at SoftBank, has been saying for a long time that there's going to be increased mergers or consolidation. I've heard that about online brokers. I've heard that about ECNs. And I haven't seen any evidence of that whatsoever, even in what is getting to be a somewhat mature industry. I believe the reason why is that when we think about mergers we think of economies of scale. With ECNs you talk about the need for more liquidity. But why would you expect to see mergers in an industry of 12 participants where two of them—Island and Instinet—have 85 percent market share?

Let's say NASDAQ goes ahead and gets approval for their own ECN. Wouldn't it be possible that the other ECNs would form up on the other side?

But again, what is the benefit of adding someone with marginal liquidity?

Well some of these ECNs, although they are showing marginal liquidity, are actually owned by pretty heavy institutions and maybe at that point they would be interested in routing more of their orders on them—REDI for example.

I think REDI has been doing a very good job, but I think if you look at Archipelago or Strike, there is not much volume or liquidity. Strike is the best example, which has had 37 brokerage firms and major luminaries on Wall Street invest in them, yet they don't amount to much volume. And I don't buy into the argument that well, if they are filing to become an exchange, they would be interested in adding liquidity if something changed. I disagree. If those investments had value in terms of liquidity, they would be adding liquidity today. They're not.

Is Island looking to expand to the European stock markets or other world exchanges?

Certainly we're always open to considering all the alternatives to take the Island model and bring it to a wider audience. I've always felt though, that a mistake a lot of businesses make is to stretch themselves thin and bite off more than they can chew. Island has always been careful to focus with razor precision on our core business. And that I think has been one of the secrets to our success. We currently have 93 employees. And we spend a significant amount of time pursuing the public policy goal of trying to get representation on the consolidated quote for NYSE listed stocks. Andrew Goldman and I have spent at least a month of total time in Washington, DC, in the last year if you add it all up, to try to get that access to listed stocks. And this is a market that is three doors up the street from us. And it's taken me a year, and I'm not there yet. So when I think about trying to go to say, France, and commit significant resources to engage in a regulatory process, I am not convinced. And the barriers are not technological, but regulatory. I used to live in France and I remember being unable to get a dishwashing job because I didn't have an EU passport. So I am keenly aware of the regulatory barriers that are going to confront us over there. All to get to a market, which compared to the NYSE, is very small. That said, we are always open to licensing our technology and expertise, or doing a joint venture where someone else can do the groundwork.

What other products or features does Island intend to introduce in the future?

I think that we've proven ourselves to be the thought innovation leader in this industry. We were the first ones to put our limit-order book out over the Internet two years ahead of anybody else and are still the only one who do it with any degree of reliability. We were the first ones to file to be a for-profit stock exchange. We were the first ones to go after hours for retail brokerages. We were the first U.S. equities market, not just ECN, to go to decimals. We did that on July 3, 2000, and we're already seeing 11 percent of our orders being submitted in decimals. We think that's a testimony to both our vision for what the customers are really going to want, and also reflects how inefficient the current system is. The next thing we'll do is go after NYSE listed stocks, and also go after the buy side, which we have never gone after before.

I've found that when I route my orders on Level II to Island's book I frequently get partial fills, which I find quite a nuisance. Once I'm filled, I have to do another odd lot trade only with Island to get out. Not only does it mess up my position size, it means I have to pay an extra commission on this odd lot, which is sometimes just one or five shares. It's one thing I don't like about Island.

You're not the first person to tell me that. Probably 10 percent of the people we talk to bring that up. I was a trader for a long time, and before the Order Handling Rules came out, I used to consider an odd lot anything less than a thousand shares. Now it's less than a hundred shares. I think in two years, all trading is going to be odd lot sizes.

Why is that?

I think the most compelling reason for including odd lots on the system is that people want Island's liquidity. If you're trading

Qualcom and can get 30 percent of your order done every time on Island immediately and anonymously, then that's a huge benefit. Obviously, that's why a trader uses Island a lot of times. But that ten thousand share bid on Island in Dell that you're hitting when you are trying to get filled is not a single ten thousand share order. That large bid is actually a five share order, a seventeen share order, and hundreds of much smaller orders that may annoy people. But they love all those smaller orders when they are put together in one huge pool. So I do not want to turn away 50 percent of my orders because people may get filled on an odd lot. If you have 1,500 shares to trade, would you not be willing to trade 1,497 shares? In the end I think the logical and rational trader will eventually realize that the value of Island is that you get to interact with an enormous pool of retail liquidity, and that's what its advantage is. And to say that I want the retail liquidity without the retail liquidity, is, in the end, a spurious argument.

You were a stock trader for a time. Could you say just a little bit about this and what your background was?

I moved to New York in 1993 after graduating from Duke. I worked at Lehman Brothers for 2 years on their commodities derivatives desk. I think Lehman actually exited the business about 6 months after I left, although I'm pretty sure that was only a coincidence. It was a frustrating experience for me, since Lehman did not see fit to give me much advancement. They worked me very hard, I fetched a lot of coffee but I was not given a lot of responsibility. So I went out on my own and became a day trader. I was a day trader for 3 years.

Where was that?

I traded at a couple of different places, but mainly Datek.

How did your trading go?

I did okay. I was profitable. But of course, that was in the days when you would say "Don't buy that stock, it's already up a point"! Of course now, 70 point moves seem to happen almost every day. It was a much different game back then. Commissions were much higher then.

And how did you make the transition from trading to where you are now?

Island's founder Josh Levine hired me. I was lucky enough to catch his eye and have a couple of conversations about market structure. I was fortunate enough to be in a situation where Island was a company that no one had ever heard of, in an industry that no one had ever heard of, and I might have been someone no one had ever heard of, but that was a perfect fit at the time. I became Island's fifth employee, I think, all working in one cramped office. Now we are over 93 employees on three floors, so it is a much different company now. But I was lucky to get in at the right time. I was lucky that Josh saw something in me which I hope I have in some way backed up.

Many traders like Level II because it gives them a lot of transparency about what is happening and how the different market makers are acting. Do you think that if NASDAQ becomes an ECN or its own exchange, and all orders are placed on one book, that this visibility of participants on Level II will disappear?

Anything is possible. Certainly Level II will appear different. One thing to remember is that liquidity in the real sense, as you well know as a trader, exists for the most part on ECNs. When market makers play, they are in the background, and if they want to trade, they zing in and zing out.

I think that many traders would disagree with some of those last statements.

Let me give you a statistic. We've been told that in the top 10 stocks on NASDAQ ECNS are the best price up to 90 percent of the time. And as long as ECNs exist and continue to grow, there'll always be an opportunity for private people to encapsulate market data in ways that traders want to see it. That can be called Level II or an improved private version of Level II which is much faster. Look, a lot of market makers don't use Level II. They use

Level II but it's Level II data for the market maker quotes which they then combine with direct feeds from the ECNs' books and then combine these into one super book. They do that now and they make a lot of money, I think, because of that. When that kind of service is given to retail investors, which I think it will be once NASDAQ changes their display, then there will be a huge benefit for the individual investor.

chapter 8

Joseph Conti

Joseph Conti was one of the earliest electronic SOES traders when he began trading with Harvey Houtkin's All-Tech Investment Group in 1991 and has been successfully trading ever since. He is 39 years old and grew up in Rockland County outside of New York City, where his family was in the restaurant business. He went to Rockland Community College for two years before transferring to Kenisaw College in Georgia where he majored in science intending to follow his brothers by becoming a chiropractor. But Joe decided this was not what he really wanted to do in life, so he left college in 1982. A six-month stint as a runner on COMEX in 1984, the gold and silver futures exchange in New York, left Joe feeling that he was not temperamentally suited to commodity trading. For the next seven years, he worked as a bartender and restaurant manager, opening up his own night club in 1988. When this closed in 1991, Joe reconsidered what he wanted to do for a living.

How did you get involved in the stock market?

I was always interested in the stock market because I was interested in who the richest people were and how they got that way. My general impression was they got that way either through the oil business, real estate, or the stock market. I tried to find which one I liked best and spend time around it. And that was the stock market. So I knew a friend who worked in an office building where she thought people were trading stocks in an office next to hers and she thought they might need an assistant. So I went for an interview at All-Tech Investment Group.

I'm not sure the interview went that well but I was persistent and got the job. This was as an assistant to Harvey Houtkin. I did whatever he needed—you need coffee I'll get you coffee, write down what I just bought or sold, whatever. He was a trader at the time. He taught me a lot of things about trading and strategies that I use in my trading to this day. After working for Harvey for about six weeks, I said I needed to move on. I said I want to do what you're doing. He asked me if I thought I was ready. I said I was, and so in 1991 I became a customer of All-Tech. That was the beginning of my trading career and I never looked back.

How did it go for the first few months?

As dangerous as it sounds, I started making money from day one. Now, having been exposed to the market as long as I have, I know for new traders that can be the worst thing in the world. But for me, luckily, it was not. The first day I made 180 trades, and in those days commissions were a lot higher than they are today—about $50. That was the first day. I probably made money on about 85 percent of my trades back then, and probably 48 weeks out of the year, because the follow-through of moves was much stronger back then. I never went below the $24,000 I started with.

How could you make money trading that often with such a high commission charge?

Back then markets were not as saturated with participants as they are now. It was not as difficult as now to trade. When I would buy a stock back then the move would not be as limited as it is now. The move would be more real or true. Back then you could buy a thousand shares and watch it go a half or whole point and sell it within 30 or 60 seconds. Today, moves tend not to go that far at all and it's much rarer that a stock will make a move that far in as little time. Back then moves consistently moved that far. Today, you might only make a quarter, an eighth, or a sixteenth point, when back then I would more routinely make a half or whole point.

Why is it different now?

I think because a lot more people are trading actively now. Back then I might have been just the fifth person day trading as we know it today. Harvey Houtkin was the first, and maybe he had four other people trading with him at the time.

You were using SOES back then?

Right. There were no ECNs back then. Instinet was the only one of what we would call an ECN today.

Could you tell me more about how markets were different then than now?

Back then with only so few traders, market makers would not hesitate to continue to move their market. It wasn't a big deal for them to buy or sell a thousand shares to so few independent traders who "SOESed" them, and they would allow the move to be true. There was no one in their way for them to sell their hundred thousand shares of stock a point higher. A thousand shares from me was not going to affect them. Now, with so many more traders, market makers I believe are trying to trade against day traders. I think they try to determine from the volume and lot size that these are day trader trades. From this information, they know how to get these traders out, and then take the market up. Or to get them in and then take the market down. I believe market makers know how to manipulate day traders. I have no love lost for market makers. Yet I make my living trading with them, so there's no animosity there either. I know what their mentality is, and am basically trying to beat them by being one step ahead of them. I'm trying to think ahead of the market maker when he tries to make his move. This is how I try to pick my entry points and trade against market makers. I believe that market makers do try to trade against day traders.

Did you actually trade a thousand shares in size from the start?

If the SOES rules allowed me to trade a thousand shares, I traded a thousand shares.

other five or six traders back then that you know, also con-sistently profitable?

To my recollection, absolutely. All of them. I don't remember anybody I knew back then who was losing money. It was a less competitive business back then. Some may have lost, but I don't remember any at all.

How did you decide back then when a move was about to occur?

What I looked at back then was what I look at now. That hasn't changed. I'll look at momentum by which I mean the movement of the bids and offers in a stock and the thickness or thinness of bids and offers. I start with momentum because I need movement to make money. There is a lot more to momentum, of course, based on what you do with it. I shouldn't say that you always need movement to make money. If the spread of the stock between bid and offer is $1 wide, maybe you don't need movement, but I don't trade stocks with those kinds of spreads.

Nothing has changed since I first started trading. What a Level II screen looks like now it looked like then. When stocks begin to go up now, it looks exactly like it looked like back then. But now what market makers do is that they make moves look like they are about to follow through, but they will put the brakes on the move and reverse it, which rarely happened back then. You can call these head fakes or jiggles. Sometimes it's window dressing, where they want to make something look like it's not. They are more likely to do window dressing near the end of the day.

I should add that I also look at time and sales. This is not rocket science. Time and sales tells me that if it's trading the offer, it's bullish and if it's trading the bid, it's bearish. So if I see stock consistently trading at the offer, my initial thought process is bullish. I am not saying I'll buy the stock, but I have to have a reason to start looking at things. If it's also set up properly on the bid, I may buy the stock.

Can you give me an example?

If a stock is trading at $20 and there are five market makers bidding at 20 and three market makers offering at 20¼, and then there are 15 market makers bidding at 20 and only one offering at 20¼, and if time and sales indicate that a lot of buying is occurring at 20¼, that is an indication that there might be a potential profit in this move. This is because market makers are being forced to buy out those other market makers on the offer because they have orders to buy. This kind of momentum or movement is what I'm first trying to identify.

What is a jiggle?

If I buy a stock at 50 and the market makers determine that there are a lot of day traders who also bought at 50, they will press the stock down to 49⅞ and drop their bids, forcing a lot of the traders out of the stock even though it was a good buy. At that point, the market makers will bring the stock back up to 50½ or 51. That's a jiggle.

Would you get back into a stock in this situation?

Possibly. If I thought I was caught in a jiggle and had a reason to believe that, I immediately bid back the stock at 49⅞ to see if I could buy some on the bid.

Weren't the bid and offer spreads wider when you started trading in 1991?

Yes. This shows another difference between now and then. I remember that Oxford Health used to trade in a two-point spread between bid and offer. Yet I would have no hesitation paying the offer on that spread and still be able to make two dollars on the trade. That's because there was follow through on moves back then. I believe market makers kept those spreads wide because that was their margin of profit over and above the thousands they would make additionally in commissions. Customers, of course, were paying for this extra profit to market makers and didn't realize that they had the ability to pay in between that bid-offer spread.

I believe that Harvey Houtkin is largely responsible for these spreads being tightened. I've been around him for many years and saw him fight this battle to reduce the wide spreads often maintained by collusion among market makers. Customers did not realize that you could try to buy or sell stock in between those wide spreads and no market maker would tell you otherwise. But Harvey did. He told me and a lot of other people. You must remember that NASDAQ was governed by the National Association of Securities Dealers, a self-governing body. Until somebody from outside decided to fight for the customer, nothing was done and rules were not enforced. I think Harvey Houtkin deserves a lot of credit for fighting this battle for everybody.

How long did the good times last?

For me the good times are still here. But I noticed that the markets started to change their character in terms of strong trend follow through and consistency about 1995. It is my personal theory, but I think there were more independent traders trading entering the markets and market makers didn't like this. They began to act differently as a response and try to shake traders out before moves occurred.

Did your profitability suffer when this happened about 1995?

Yes. Before 1995, moves might have gone for a half or whole point, of which I may have made three-eighths to seven-eighths profit. Now, since moves aren't as consistent or strong, I may be limited to only a one-eighth point profit after commissions. I also became more selective in the stocks I was trading.

How did that happen?

I became more selective in having taken the first of my hard lumps early on trading. I didn't take that many of them, but the ones I took shook me up a little bit. If you were trading a thousand shares as I started to do from the beginning and that stock moves against you five or six points because I was just wrong and misread the momentum, then I found myself taking a big loss. I was able to sustain those kinds of losses because I was making a considerable amount of money back then, but it is a dose of reality when you lose $4,000 in one minute. That's a lot of money. That shook me up. I decided after that not to jump in a stock just because it was moving. Momentum does not mean execution. I had to understand why I was buying or selling a stock and movement was the beginning of that understanding but it was not the definitive factor. I was becoming more selective.

After about 1995, I became more selective by hesitating to buy a stock with a wider spread, whereas before then I would not hesitate because I could expect to make the amount of spread I was paying in the follow-through trend. I began to hesitate to buy stocks and now start looking for stocks that have smaller bid-offer spreads. If I bought a stock at $25 I wanted to be sure that at most, if I am wrong, I could sell the stock at 24¾. I didn't want to look at a bid of $24 as my only out. More often than not now, moves do not consistently follow through, and if you buy the stock at the offer and it jiggles down and you don't have enough cushion in that bid, you are going to find yourself with a loss of a half or whole point. I do not play that game. Taking small losses is the key to making money in this business. Period.

Could you tell me a little bit more about how you handle losses?

I've done hundreds of thousands of trades. And every single one of those trades has been a guess. An educated guess. And that's the only guess I'm going to make on each of those trades. If I am wrong and my entry point is wrong and my loss tolerance is met, I am out of the stock. I am the most disciplined person I know and have no hesitation whatsoever in taking a loss. None. Zero.

Market makers know that traders feel pain at losses and like to move a stock back and forth to force traders out. But since I've been doing this so long, my entry points now are very accurate. If I think a stock is going to $32, my entry points are at the point at which the market makers are ready to take the stock up, not when the stock is still being moved around. I'm on the ride with the market makers so they can't get me out because they're on the same ride with me.

Why do you think most traders have trouble taking losses?

When I watch people let a stock go against them, I've never understood it. People seem to say, I've just paid $20 or $25 to get into the trade and now I don't want to take a $\frac{1}{16}$ point loss on top of that. So they end up taking a whole point loss and still paying the commission. People who trade with commissions in their mind will not make it in this business. If you can't afford to do the trade, then you shouldn't be trading. But trade it like it should be traded, not with the thought of a commission in mind. That should be irrelevant to your trade. I don't like saying to new traders, cut your losses, since cutting your losses from a whole point to a half a point is not acceptable. I like to say, take small losses so new traders should not trade Internet stocks. They should trade stocks that are thick with bids and prepare to take a small loss if they have to.

Are you recommending that traders start out by trading a thousand shares to get the benefit of an economy of scale on a $25 commission ticket charge?

No, no. I don't recommend that. When I first started to trade and traded a thousand shares it was much less risky. The market now is much more challenging and you have to be more astute. You must be a student of the market and you don't want to start doing that with thousand share trades. I would recommend they start with two hundred shares. I think All-Tech has an introductory rate for new traders so they pay a lower ticket commission charge on small size trades.

Do you have a fixed stop loss point?

Because my entry points are pretty exact, my stop loss point wouldn't be more than an eighth point. That's the discipline. There's no reason to take a loss larger than that.

Doesn't your aversion to losses larger than an eighth point mean that you don't trade many stocks over $100?

Yes, I would say I don't. For me, if I can make an eighth point profit on two thousand shares of a stock trading at $12, why do I need to trade a stock over $100 to make a quarter point?

How do you identify when the market makers are ready to move a stock?

It's not something that you can just say that if a market maker does this it is going to happen. You've got to have a feel for a stock, a feel for market makers and what they've tried to do throughout the day. Without watching that all day long, it's tough to say this is just what's going to happen. If Merrill Lynch goes to the bid and then the offer and then the bid again and then the offer, that's not going to tell you anything. But if Merrill is the only market maker on the bid when there is trading at the bid and they're buying everything, then you may assume that Merrill is a real buyer since he's the only one holding the stock up as it's coming down. So after you see that you may want to follow Merrill Lynch a little bit since they seem to have a position and reason to buy the stock. Now I don't know if they're covering a short or initiating a new long position. I have to determine that. And I do that by instinct.

What is instinct?

Instinct is a guess. That's what gets me involved in my first trade. An educated guess.

Can instinct be taught?

I absolutely think it can be taught. I look at market makers as people who are not trying to do me a favor here. So I am going to look at them as people who are not trying to help me, and if you decide to buy my stock at my offer, you have not done me a favor. So if I sell stock to them and they take it, or if I buy stock from them and they sell it to me, it helps me make a decision and determination of what they are intending to do.

If I sold a stock at 30 and I bought it at 29½, was I wrong to sell the stock? Never. I am never wrong to take a profit. Even if the stock then goes up to 35. If you are looking to buy the low and sell the high of the day, you will bust out of this business faster than anyone you've ever seen. The objective is not to buy the low and sell the high. I may have done that once in hundreds of thousands of trades.

Do you scale in or out of trades?

I scale in and out. I don't believe in cost averaging on the downside, that is buying a stock at 30, watching it go to 29½ and buying some more, and then some more again if it goes to 29. That's guessing once, twice, three times. I don't guess more than once and that's the initial trade. After that it's whatever the stock does. If it's down, I'm out, and if up then I make a profit.

I do scale in on the upside. If I buy a stock at 30, I may want to buy more at 30¼ or 30½ or even 31, because my first guess was right. Now, that first guess is no longer a guess but has become a profitable trade. Now that I have a profit, I may be willing to make another initial guess, which is really my first guess and the second trade. I don't do this on every trade, but I will do it on some trades.

Do you scale out of the trades you take in parts? That is, on a 500 share trade, will you sell out 200 shares and then 300, or do you sell out the entire 500 shares in one trade?

It depends on how well I am trading that day. If I am consistently right and have the feel of Dell Computers today, then I may scale out. If I have a thousand shares I may sell out 500 and 500 or 300, 300, and 400. This allows me to participate in the more extended moves than if I just sold out everything for a quarter point profit. On the other hand, if I am not so right on the market that day and am just fighting for eighths and quarters, then if I bought a thousand, I'll sell a thousand. I never say, though, that I want to make a quarter on this trade. I have no fixed profit objective. I offer my stock into strength. I will never wait for the momentum to stop, then offer it, then try to hit bids that are disappearing, and then breakeven or lose money on a trade, that I could have made three-sixteenths of a point on. I'll always offer my stock into strength.

How can you be so accurate in your entry points?

Patience. In the last five years of trading, I try to do more what market makers do. For example, if a stock is 25 bid and offered at

25¼, I usually don't pay 25¼ to buy the stock. I will have the patience to bid the stock and try to buy it when the price is coming in. I'll base these buying points on several things. One is the intraday support and resistance. If I see a pattern in a stock that by 11 A.M. has not been able to go below 29½ on three attempts, I now have a reason, an educated guess, to buy some of that stock at that price or just above it.

How much do you use technical analysis?

I do use some technical analysis intraday, but I don't use charting much at all. I've never met a chart that will tell me what this stock is going to do in the next 15 seconds. I do use one-minute candlesticks in the charts I do watch, but I don't look at trendlines or things like that. You can't do the kind of volume of trading I do and look at charts that much. If I do several hundred trades, then I've tried to execute another hundred, and passed up another two hundred that I've thought about doing. I have no time to read that many charts. I have to read a market. When I make a decision to really get involved in a stock, I will look at intraday support and resistance. That's about as far as my technical analysis goes. What is going to tell me what is happening in the next 15 seconds is not a chart, but how it is set up, what it's moving like, what its momentum, time, and sales are, whether market makers are joining the bid or leaving the offer, and things like that. That tells me more likely what's going to happen in the next fifteen seconds.

Tell me what your screen actually looks like?

My screen layout is the same every day. I have three Level II windows and time and sales linked to those Level IIs. I also keep up a list of stocks with current prices. I used to keep about 250 stocks up at any one time, but now I usually watch only 50. I feel it's important to get to know a stock well, to get to know its personality, and I can't keep up with 250 stocks any longer.

How do you select those 50 stocks you keep track of?

Trial and error. What other people are trading and how they are doing with some stocks. Someone may be trading ABCD and I haven't looked at ABCD. I'll take a look and maybe it has nice volume and it's set up pretty thick on the bid. Maybe I'll trade it, but I also choose not to do 300 trades in a day. Why? Because although they're moving great and they're fast-moving stocks, but I cannot guarantee myself a small loss. And if I can't do that, then I prefer not to do the trade. It's important to feel confident that if you are wrong, you are not going to lose that much money. That's one of the important aspects of being able to read a Level II screen.

Do these 50 stocks you monitor change that much day to day?

Yes. I'll be adding and deleting stocks throughout the day or week or month. A stock may have been trading two and half million shares a day and now it only trades 25,000 shares a day, and if I haven't looked at it in several weeks because it hasn't been really moving, then I will take the stock out. It's not a good trading stock, and maybe I will replace it with something more liquid, or maybe I won't.

How do you trade news?

I also have Bloomberg and Dow Jones news on my screen, not just linked to my stocks but all news stories. I do not want to trade with the news story in a stock. News stories are definitely, in my opinion, traded ahead of by someone who already had access to that news story. News stories are sucker plays. The move has already happened by the time the news is released. The reason I believe this is if you look at a chart before the news story was released, the stock price has already moved and reacted to that news.

You may want to trade against the news story if you do anything, that is, to trade against the public who are less educated traders. When the public thinks it's right, it's wrong. Market makers are well aware of who is buying a stock after a news story is released, and now will try to sell to them and then reverse the stock's advance. In that case I may choose to sell the stock short. I may not do it immediately, but wait for that slight push up. I may do this maybe twice during the day.

Is there anything else you have on your screen?

All-Tech has something called "Analysis Client" which I keep up. It's a software system that allows the user to input parameters of a stock that you may be interested in and it will return all stocks with those features. For example, I may say I want to see all stocks between $20 and $100, that have five market makers on the bid or offer, that have no more than an eighth-point spread, and that have an average volume of 200,000 shares or more. The software will kick out all stocks that have all of those parameters combined. Another feature of this program is that it will continually list all stocks that have just made their 52-week high or low.

What are the parameters that you look for?

The kinds of parameters I would watch might be different than a new trader would watch. I would want to filter all stocks between zero and 200 dollars, that have at least two market makers, an average volume of 90,000 shares a day, no more than a half point spread between the bid and offer, and five market maker moves in 10 seconds. I open these parameters as wide as I can. I'm in the information business, so give me the information and let me make my decision.

This program just scrolls up shooting stocks out all day long. When I have a free moment during the day I'll take a look at some of these stocks, see how they're set up, I may quickly look at a chart, and if I feel confident I will not lose a lot of money, I may trade the stock.

How many monitors do you use?

I have one large 21-inch monitor.

What execution system do you use?

Attain. I also use Island sometimes. Island is good for certain things but not others. Island is good for liquidity, although I will trade with another Attain bid or offer first, before I go to Island. I actually prefer to trade with a market maker rather than an ECN. When a market maker executes me, it gives me information, that an ECN doesn't.

I should mention that every time I buy a stock, I assume I'm wrong. That allows me to expedite my getting out. I will immediately set up my execution system to sell for a small loss if necessary.

What kind of information does trading with a market maker give you?

As I said earlier, a market maker is not doing you a favor by trading with you. Trading with him, however, does give me information. If he sold me a stock on the offer at 50, then I'm not thinking bullish. Maybe I remain bullish for a "teenie" or ⅛, but I'm not thinking long-term bullish on this stock. If a market maker sells stock at a price, and then refreshes with more quantity and then sells to me, that tells me something.

Is being able to use SOES a very important tool in trading?

SOES is a good tool, but I do not think it is essential to trading. Of course, when I first started trading as a customer, almost all my trading was done through SOES. I actually prefer to use SelectNet which allows me to preference the market maker I want to trade with, but does not obligate him to trade with me as he would be required to do under SOES. That really helps me decide what's going on. If I SelectNet preference Morgan Stanley or Goldman Sachs and he chooses to accept my order to trade that tells me something. If he sells me the stock that suggests to me that I'm not as bullish as I was. Of course, he may be testing me with disinformation and I have to take that into account. I notice that some market makers do seem to honor their markets more than others, Morgan Stanley being one.

What kinds of differences do you see among different market makers?

The first thing I notice is who has the deepest pockets and who has an order here. They are not taking their own risk but have an order. I want to find out who has an order, say, of a million and a half shares to buy. Generally, those are the market makers with the biggest pockets. Morgan Stanley, Goldman Sachs, Merrill Lynch, Knight Securities, Lehman Brothers, Sherwood, and Piper

Jaffray I find are the biggest market makers, although this depends on the specific stock.

How do market makers tip their hand that they are doing something important?

They show their hand by continually buying, staying on the bid, always being the first to jump up on the bid, never wanting to be low bid. These are signs that they are going to dictate the direction of the market. Or their being the last to leave a bid if all the day traders are buying heavily. Maybe the stock will go up another eighth or a quarter, but I'll bet within a few minutes that that market maker who sold all that stock will make money on all those sales. I'll follow that and maybe put stock out for a short sale when that market maker finally leaves the offer and starts selling again at the next price level up.

How does personality or emotion affect your trading?

Trade your personality. I'll go one step further and say you better stay within a certain parameter of personality and if you don't, don't trade. If you are someone who has a problem admitting when you're wrong, if that's your personality, then don't trade. If you are going to trade with an ego, don't trade. I have no hesitation whatsoever in taking a loss. None.

Also, I take no overnight positions. The most important thing in day trading is always having a clear head for your next trade, otherwise you will not be astute. Overnights interfere with this clear head theory, so I keep most of my excess money in cash instruments, although I do carry a small portfolio. One hundred percent in cash and proud of it.

How did you gain that discipline to take small losses?

Because if I know I'm right 80 percent of the time, I have no problem taking a loss two out of ten times, knowing that I am right the other times. And knowing that I'm right that often, my goal is to keep that loss as low as I possible can. I never want to play catch up during the day making up losses. I find that emotionally shaken traders are worthless as traders. If you have just taken a thousand dollar loss and that is enough to emotionally shake you, then you are now worthless to yourself, to your bank account, and you will not make it. You cannot be afraid of the stock market. Like the ocean, you cannot fear it, but you must respect it and what it can do if you don't have discipline. I don't get shaken by the market, because I don't put myself in the position to get shaken anymore. If I don't feel confident that I can only lose a small amount of money on a trade, I just don't do the trade.

How many weeks in a year have you made money in the market over the last two years?

About 40 or 45 weeks each year. Although this is about the percentage I was making when I first started, I am not making as much as I did then. I'm working for smaller profits now. But it's all relative. You still can make a good six-figure income trading in the stock market.

Is there a size constraint in the amounts you trade? Why don't you just double the size of your trades and make twice as much money?

First of all, it's more difficult to get out of a position twice the size. It's not as easy to get out of a position of 2,000 shares instead of a 1,000. If you were wrong, you may be able to get out of the first thousand shares at a sixteenth or eighth point loss, but not for a quarter-point loss on the second thousand shares. You've more than doubled you potential loss by doubling your size.

Also, trading larger means you are not the same trader. I am personally uncomfortable trading two thousand shares. I don't need to trade two thousand shares, since I am very content with what I make every year. I don't want to be greedy. Bulls and bears make money in the market, and pigs get slaughtered. I try not to be a pig. If I can make $250 on a trade and do it a hundred times a day, what's wrong with that?

What are the mistakes beginners most frequently make that you see?

Several things. Reflexes may not be where they need to be initially. Their eye-hand coordination is not where it should be. The speed of their decision making is not where it needs to be. And they are less likely to understand how important it is to take small losses. This requires discipline and most people don't have discipline. They get discipline by having their asses kicked fast and hard. That's the best way to get discipline in my opinion. Your best trade is your first big losing trade. This is going to determine what's going to happen in your trading career. Are you going to try to beat it by doing it again and again and eventually get knocked out, or are you going to say I didn't like that feeling and I'm not doing that again? If you shape up, then you are going to be one of the ones that make it trading. Never compromise discipline.

What stocks have you been trading lately?

It varies. Right now, Dell, WorldCom, and Oracle. I will not trade the more volatile Internet stocks because I am not willing to take a big loss. I will not compromise my discipline about taking small losses. Small is a sixteenth or an eighth.

What about IPOs?

Ninety-nine percent of the time I will also not trade IPOs for the same reason. There are occasions when IPOs will be set up for a profitable trade in which market makers are thick on the bid. Also, ECNs like Island and Attain are trading so far above the current offer which gives me the confidence that if I buy it here on a lucky fill a half point below where the market is trading, I'm confident I can make money on this trade. But mostly I don't trade IPOs.

How many stocks are you trading simultaneously?

No more than three. When I first started trading I had 15 or 20 stock positions at one time, but I learned not to do that. I found I couldn't control these positions as well as I liked, so I choose not to trade that many.

What's the largest loss you had in the last year in one trade?

Three thousand dollars. I lost 3 points on a thousand shares in about 45 seconds. It was an IPO that just got out of control. My reason for getting in was justified, or it looked justified to me who has a lot of experience, but it just wasn't there.

Out of the hundred trades you may make in a day, how many would be in one stock that you are trading most frequently?

Maybe 30. Ninety percent of my trades will be in the three stocks that I'm watching most closely, which right now are Dell, Oracle, and Worldcom. Ten percent may be in other stocks that my Analysis Client may kick out to me.

What time do you get in the office?

About 8:30. I look at some pre-open trading, where the futures are, my stocks and whether they are being bid up or down and who is doing the bidding. I start to develop ideas about what I might want do. But I try not to have an opinion. Because if I have an opinion, I may be more likely to trade that opinion rather than trade what is actually going on.

Do you trade right from the open?

I don't trade right from the opening. The opening and close can be a lot of window dressing, but by 10:00 or 10:15 stocks are going in the direction they really want to go. I'll probably trade my first trade at about 9:45 and then become more active after 10:00. What I'm eliminating by waiting is a lot of head faking, and there probably is more head faking at the open than at any other time of day. I would say I make 80 percent of the amount of money I will make for the day between 10:30 and 12:00 and between 3:00 and 4:00, and that is evenly divided between those two periods. Between noon and 2 P.M., I pull back on my trading. Generally, I would say that stocks will move more truly in the morning and get to levels where they will then trade between for much of the rest of the day.

What is your percentage long trades to short trades?

Maybe 80 percent long and 20 percent short. I am more comfortable trading from the long side.

Does that mean you don't make as much money when stocks are selling off on down days?

Not at all. Because stocks always bounce. I'll bottom fish stock trying to determine support levels. If it's below any support level, then it's like trying to catch a falling knife, don't do it. In that case, I'll wait for the stock to reverse and then try to buy on the offer.

Do you trade listed stocks or mostly NASDAQ stocks?

Probably 95 percent NASDAQ. I like to see what's going on, and I can't do that with a listed stock. The only time I may trade a listed stock is if I'm next to a trader who is very hot on a listed stock and I may piggyback him. Sometimes you follow people who are hot, there's nothing wrong with that. People can piggyback me if they want. I'm here to help you and you should be here to help me.

Could you describe how the trading room works?

There are several strategies and techniques I teach to All-Tech's proprietary traders. Everybody that wants to trade in that room, must call out their executions. If I bought Dell from Merrill Lynch on SelectNet, I may call out "Merrill a seller of Dell at 50." That's good information. That's a fact. No opinion is involved in call-outs. If I am offering Dell and someone lifts me, then I'll call that out, "Dell out at 50." If I'm on the bid at 50 for 500 shares and someone sells 200 shares to me, I'll call out "Dell in at 50 partial." We don't want to hear anyone's opinion about who sold me the stock. That's an opinion, not a fact. The people I trade with use that information all the time, which is the best information. Knowing factual executions takes out 90 percent of the guessing if I choose to go long or short Dell. You must call out your executions. The group tends to trade the same stocks, and we tend to work together.

Doesn't that mean that the trading group is competing against one another?

No, although that's what people think. I would say about 30 percent of my income comes from using other traders' reports of executions, and that is about the same for everyone else in the room. For example, if you are short Dell at 49⅞ and I call out that I've just been taken out of my long on the offer at 50, you say thank you and cover for an eighth loss, whereas without knowledge of my execution, you may have lost ⅜. You just saved $250 because of me. That's trading with each other.

How many people are in the trading group?

About 25 in the room I trade in. No one has to trade the stocks everyone else is trading, they can trade whatever stock they want, but whatever trade they make they must call out to everyone. If a trader thinks their two eyes are better than 50, they are going to find trading difficult. If you can work along with people that give you factual information, not opinions, and use that knowledge and information to trade, you are eliminating 90 percent of the guess work in an intraday momentum based move in stocks.

How are people selected for the trading group?

Well, there's not that many women that get involved in this. I don't know why that is, although we would be happy to work with women. For the traders we select, we want people who I would want to date my sister or brother. If you're not that kind of person, then we don't want you in our room. We want to create a peaceful, trustworthy environment. We want people who are willing to help and be helped, because we have to spend every day here and want to enjoy it. We all need a clear head, that's the number one most important thing, after being disciplined to take a small loss, and really they go hand in hand.

How many of the 25 people you trade with make money?

Seventy percent to 80 percent, at least on a monthly basis.

Can trading be taught?

If 10 new people joined the group, probably most could be taught if they were willing to listen. But about 40 percent of them wouldn't be able to listen, and of the 60 percent who would be willing to listen, maybe 80 percent could learn to trade profitably.

Where do you see yourself 10 years from now?

Strangely enough, in 10 years I would like to see myself doing exactly what I am doing now. I love what I'm doing. Maybe in 10 years I won't love it as much, but so far that hasn't happened. Buying a bar on an island that I own would be nice, as you see on the commercials, but that's not reality. What I do now is reality. Perhaps I might like to slow down a little, but I still enjoy it. If you are going to do this, then enjoy it.

chapter 9

Anthony Mariniello

Anthony Mariniello is the unusual day trader who not only has not had a losing week in the past three years, but also makes more extensive use of fundamental analysis in the selection of his stocks than most short-term traders. He is 31 years old and was born in Livingston, NJ, where his father was a pharmaceutical salesman. He was not a great student in high school, but was able to enter Kean College to play football. After two years there, he transferred to Rutgers and studied for another three years. By his own admission, he didn't care much for school and frequently changed majors. He describes himself at the time as very anti-establishment and wasn't into conforming. He left school without graduating for personal reasons during his third year at Rutgers.

So what did you do after you left college?

I left college to come out to California to get my Series 7 license with my mother's brokerage business which needed some help at the time. I tried selling stocks. I discovered I didn't like this and wasn't really any good at it. But I did become interested in the stock market and started to learn by reading everything I could about it.

What did you read?

I read *Barron's* and *Business Week,* but my favorite book back then was Victor Sperandeo's *Trader Vic's Principles of Trading.* That book taught me the most. I still use many trading techniques from that book, although I have also developed my own style now.

Has anyone every helped you or been a mentor?

No. Aside from Sperandeo's book, I've had to learn everything on my own.

Did you start trading at this time?

Yes. A friend of mine from high school, Peter Kearns, who also was working for my mother's brokerage company at the time, and I decided to set up an account together and do some trading. Peter later went on to start Lexit Capital, a brokerage firm where I am trading today.

Anyway, we borrowed about $20,000 on our credit cards and started buying a lot of options on the first-wave technology stocks. I was listening to all these analysts talk about stocks such as PairGain, ADC TelCom, and Iomega. So we bought calls on these kinds of stocks and our account went from $20,000 to $80,000. We thought we were geniuses and even rented expensive offices for ourselves. Looking back on it, it was all really stupid. But nevertheless, we did really well for about a year. I was playing mostly from the long side. I don't remember ever buying a put. We didn't do any electronic or SOES trading, but would call all our orders in to our broker on the phone.

Sounds like a good beginning. What happened?

The first technology correction in 1994 put us out of business. Micron, PictureTel, PairGain—stocks that we were trading—all went from 60, 70, 80 dollars all the way down to single digits. I wondered, "What's just happened"? It certainly gave me a new negative experience on markets after that point. After this experience I wasn't even sure I would stay in the business, and I didn't know what I wanted to do.

So what did happen?

I happened to meet a guy at a basketball court, who was a lawyer, and he said he was working with these three guys who were starting a new brokerage company. One was a trader and two were salesmen. I showed him my track record before everything started to go bad and they invited me to join them. These guys didn't know anything about the markets, but were selling penny stocks as it turned out, at least that's my perception of it.

The firm did have a little bit of money, however, and I traded it. I did well, not great, just well over a couple of months. Meanwhile, this firm had sold a lot of stock to clients in a fingerprint technology company called Comparidor, the symbol of which was IDID. Anyway, this stock just took off going from nine cents to two dollars and at one point had the largest volume stock on NASDAQ. Their clients made several million on this stock.

So with some money I set up a hedge fund where I could go long and short depending on market conditions. This was around 1996 and I was thinking the market was due for a correction. I thought that if I was correct and the fund made a lot of money, we could sell the hedge fund. So we set up a limited partnership and got some outside investors to invest.

How did that go?

I was successful. We had raised about $100,000 and I was always very conservative. I started out just doing 200 or 300 shares trading 80 percent NASDAQ stocks, and the rest listed. Eventually, I was making about $8,000 to $10,000 a month. Although I was largely buying and holding stock I did do some options again. I made a lot of money in one month in one technology company, Bay Networks, and they thought I was a genius. It was more luck than anything though. The stock had just gotten crushed to about $30 and I bought lots of 30 strike calls. After reaching that low point, it proceeded to rally eight or nine dollars on a takeover rumor, really not that much of a move, but enough to make a lot of money.

I remember the market became more volatile around 1998 when the public started to get involved more in the stock market. I was amazed that they thought things were still cheap enough to buy as investments. Microsoft at the time had about a $200 billion capitalization with about $15 billion in revenue, and it seemed to me that could not continue higher much more. I read that at the end of speculative cycles, valuations could reach extremes, and I thought that was where we were. I just didn't know how long things could last though. I certainly didn't realize it could last another three or four years.

At first I wasn't day trading per se, but when the market got to the point of such volatility and apparent overvaluation, I didn't want to take the overnight risk any longer. So I stopped holding stocks overnight. I got into day trading by default, since I thought it was the best risk.

What kind of execution system were you using at this time?

I had a Web relay connection to my computer and I would type in my orders which would then go to my broker, who could fill me directly with them or send the order to some market makers or the exchange. I think they dealt with some market makers like Herzog, Knight, and Tri-Mark who could fill me directly, by what is called auto-execution, meaning that they became the counter party to my trade without actually sending it to the exchange. I didn't have a Level II direct access at that point but still, my orders were filled very quickly. I now trade at Lexit Capital and do most of my trades on Level II or Super-Dot.

Why were you successful during this time?

I was conservative. I honestly think that being conservative and disciplined makes money in the long run. I never get too greedy. Ever. I also think that it's been relatively easy in the past three or four years to make money. The markets just have kept going up. I used to look to buy breakouts and they would just keep going. It was easy.

What do you mean by breakouts?

You would have a stock trading in a long base, say in a trading range between $50 to $60 for six months. Fundamentals looked good. And then they would break out of this range on high volume with good news. This was textbook technical analysis and it worked. I think this kind of technical analysis has been working well up until about six-months ago.

But this doesn't work anymore?

Up until about a half year ago, maybe 70 percent of these kinds of breakouts would be profitable. Now, maybe only 10 percent have that kind of follow-through. I think technical analysis eventually will not work, because everyone is starting to use it. Everyone is using the same tools.

Now, I really like to look at a stock and how its acting before I make a trading decision. I look at market makers for a long time. You could see if a market maker is accumulating a stock over a period. I'll watch a stock for several days. Intel two weeks ago is an example. I was short and Intel was trading between 115 and 125, although it had traded as low as 107. Around that time I saw Goldman Sachs was a buyer day after day and I kept covering my shorts for small losses.

Why didn't you just buy it?

I didn't think NASDAQ would rally that much at that point. That's not listening to the market, of course, but I did think that Intel was still too overvalued at that price for me to go long it. But I was getting long other stocks that were getting beaten up that I thought had a better chance of rallying.

Are you still trading this hedge fund?

No. About one year ago I started trading for an investor, who was willing to give me half the profits I could make for him. He gives me a salary if I don't make money for him, but that hasn't happened yet. My style of trading or results did not change that much after I started trading for this private investor.

Why don't you just trade you own money?

It's psychological. If find it easier to be less emotional with someone else's money. I did some position trading for myself, for a while, but now I don't keep anything in stocks.

You said you don't like to trade in a room with other traders. Why is that?

I like to trade alone because I can deal with my emotions better. I avoid getting involved with a group mind-set. I don't mind someone trading in the next room, where I can go out and talk to them if I want. But when I'm trading, I want to be one hundred percent alone. My ego gets in the way if I have someone near me trading who may be looking over my shoulder. I think this happens with most people, but perhaps they are just less honest with themselves. When I'm around other people, I find that I want to show them that I'm right, and then I start to break my discipline.

I should say that I am a very emotional person and get very upset when I break my discipline. I do have a tendency to break my discipline when I'm up a lot of the day and just try to go all out for maximizing gain. But I never break my discipline when I'm down for the day, which fortunately is not that often.

How do you handle such strong emotions during trading?

I have a "Slam Man," which is a big dummy full of sand. I punch it. I put holes in my wall. I also try to relieve my stress by just walking out of the trading room. But I think my emotions don't interfere with my trading. In fact, they help me, because when I feel the pain, I just get out of whatever stock is not working out. People who stay in a stock too long are not listening to their emotions.

Do you ever add to your position on a trade?

If I have a profit in a stock, I may add to the position if I think it's still going up. I have sometimes added to a stock where I have a losing position, although I don't like to do it and I think it's bad discipline. But I have done it. But where I do it is in a stock that has been showing a strong up trend, and is selling off a bit, not in a stock that is in a downtrend or if the general market is selling off.

How do you determine where to take a loss?

Very quickly. As soon as I start losing I will get out. If I am up two or three thousand dollars for the day, and I have 500 shares of a stock that can move five or six points then I may stay in the stock if it moves against me for several points. On the other hand, if I'm in Intel with a thousand shares I will get out much sooner, maybe with a ¾ point loss.

There are many variables I consider so it depends how much loss I will allow myself to take in a stock. I like looking at longer term daily charts, rather than intraday charts, to find longer term support and resistance levels in the stock's trading range. I like to buy stocks at the lower end of their longer term range and sell stocks at the higher end of their range, unless it's breaking out of its range to new highs. I will buy or sell with these support and resistance levels in mind and set my allowable losses according to these range levels.

More recently, I have noticed that frequently even stocks that will not be able to break through their resistance levels permanently will go through them temporarily before they reverse. So, sometimes I will go short after a stock breaks out of its range on the upside and watch to see if it continues to go up. If it is a true breakout and does continue to go up, I will cover my short and that is the point when I can lose the most money. I will then go long on what I think is a true breakout.

How do you choose the stocks that you watch?

From different sources. I check the new yearly high and lows every day. I check the most active stock lists. I listen to CNBC for stocks that are in play for some reason. I very rarely will trade a stock the first day I start watching it, since I like to see how that stock acts for a while.

I like to categorize stocks I watch in industry sector groups. I like to watch the correlations and divergences within these groups of stocks. Once I've categorized stocks by sector, I will look to go long stocks that are acting strong, or short stocks that are acting weak based on this reference group and the market as a whole. Stocks in similar sectors usually move together but not always. When stocks start acting good in a sector even when bad news is coming out, that is often a signal of a reversal.

For example, in the semiconductor group I will be watching Intel, Applied Materials, Novellus, and so forth. When I start following a stock, I like to know what kind of business it's in and what kind of market share it has. Those are the kind of fundamentals that I'll look for on a breakout, in which case I'll buy the stock.

Semiconductors are really tough to call though. Stocks react here way before the fundamentals change. But if Applied Materials blasts off, other semiconductors may be a buy and the beginning of a trend.

Isn't it unusual for a trader to pay so much attention to the fundamentals of a stock?

Yes. But I try to look at everything because I believe that nothing is going to work all the time. Sometimes studying fundamentals works. Sometimes technical analysis works. Because I think technical analysis will increasingly not work, as I've said, because too many people are following it now, I like to break away from reliance on that method or try to find something new emerging. You must be alert to new patterns or how they are changing.

For example, last quarter Yahoo came out with earnings which were down. Then other Internet stocks started not meeting earnings expectations, so I began to short some of these stocks just before earnings were announced. If you can catch little changes in patterns, you can make some money. You make the most money in the early parts of those new patterns if you notice them.

How else do you use fundamental analysis in trading?

I like to start by looking at the macro picture and taking it down to the micro picture. How is the overall economy doing? How is this sector doing in the overall economy? How is the best stock doing in that sector? I do like the fundamentals of the company, although the fundamentals of a company right now often seem unimportant to the market. I think 10 years from now people will wake up and wonder what happened. Yet I've still made a lot of money being 100 percent wrong, so I can't complain.

I don't look at the old economy sector much any more. It's hard to look at the auto or paper sectors when there is so much volatility elsewhere in the market. I look at cyclical stocks here and wonder whether I should buy. But even though they're down about 40 percent I don't think it's over. I have tried to buy some of these stocks, but I get out right away when they keep going lower. I keep waiting for them to act good and they're not.

How many stocks are you watching at any single time?

Well, I'm changing the stocks I watch all the time, but at any one point, I'm watching about 200 stocks.

And out of those, how many will you trade in a day?

On an average day I'll trade about seven or ten. When everything is going perfectly, I have traded up to 30 stocks in one day. Some days I'll trade the same stock all day long. I won't be in it all day, but I will be in and out all day.

How many trades do you make in a day?

Most of the time maybe around 50. When I'm trying to take it easy, maybe 30, but if the market is busy, more than 100 trades.

Could you give me an example of some trades you've made recently?

Last Friday I thought the market was due for a little sell off after the Federal Reserve meeting on Thursday and the uncertainty going into the weekend and maybe people getting a little nervous. I had been watching Corning Glass and SDLI for a couple of days, which both have almost exactly the same daily chart patterns if you look closely enough. SDLI had dropped 25 points before rallying, and then the next day dropped another 25 points. Corning had been holding up but had hit resistance at 247 three times. So I shorted a couple of hundred shares at that level. I got out at the close on Friday for a seven point-profit.

What kind of profit objective do you have for your trades?

I'm usually looking for several points profit or at least a half point. But, of course, I let the market determine what I will actually do in the trade, whether it's a profit or loss.

How long are you holding your trades?

On average, maybe 10 or 15 minutes, although I can be in positions as short as two seconds or as long as several hours.

Are you in more than one trade at a time?

I tend to trade just one stock at a time. But I am looking at other stocks during this time and see how they are acting. Sometimes I will trade more than one stock, but my preference is to trade only one at a time.

How would the market get you out of a stock?

Most of the time, it's just that the stock is going against me. But I may get back in again, if I feel the market is about to move in the direction of my original trade.

How do you decide to get out when you have a profit?

It really depends on why I got into the trade in the first place. If I got in because the whole market is rallying and all the semiconductors are rallying, for example, I wait for the market to start to reverse against me, or I may just take some points in profit if I no longer know where the market is headed. In another case, a stock may be getting close to a double top and that will get me out. If I bought a stock on a strong breakout and it shows signs of strength all day, I'll often wait until the end of the day to get out. If I have several points profit on a trade, and it starts to move back to where I got in, I'll get out because I don't like letting winners turn into losers. If the stock is at a bottom and it doesn't rally, I'll just get out. I do many different things at different points, so I can't say that there's a single way I take profits.

Do you watch the S&P 500 futures as a short-term indicator?

I look at it sometimes, but I don't really use it as a tool.

Do you use charts at all?

I look at the Dow chart, the NASDAQ chart, the Transports, and the sector indices. I don't look at intraday charts that much. I find they make my brain work less.

What other indicators do you look at?

Victor Sperandeo has an indicator which he calls the "2B" signal. If a stock is near a bottom or a support level, breaks down through that level, when a lot of technical analytic traders will sell, and then reverses above the support level again. This used to work really well.

Doesn't it work well any more?

It does, but I just don't see stocks at their bottom as much. The market has been so strong recently.

What does your screen look like?

I have a Bloomberg machine which has rows and rows of stocks sorted by my sector categories. I use Real Tick III as an execution system. I have two Level II montages up, but I don't keep any charts up. I will pull up a chart on Bloomberg for reference when I need to.

How often are you short compared to how often trading from the long side?

I'm short in maybe 60 percent of my trades. I do like to trade from the short side, and if you just listened to me, you may think I short all the time. I probably would like to short more than this, except that the market has been so strong, that I have to follow what the market is doing and go long frequently. I'll short at the low and if it doesn't go lower, then I'll cover and go long.

How important to your trading is the time of day?

I do most of my trades in the morning and late afternoon. I will stop trading about 11:30 or noon for a break, although it depends on the volatility of the market. If the market is raging up, I may just trade all day. I never trade after hours, although I've tried it.

How has your style of trading changed over the last two years?

I don't think my style has changed that much but the market has changed. The market has become much more volatile, and that's been good for me, because I've been making more money. If I can control my losses to the levels I try to maintain, but the market just moves more when I am right, then I'm going to make more money.

What makes a good trader?

The ability to be wrong or allow yourself to be wrong, and the ability to change are two extremely important features of a good trader in my opinion.

Can trading be taught or is it just an innate skill?

I believe anybody can learn anything. It's just that some people learn faster than others.

Why have you become successful as a trader?

When I'm by myself, it is very easy for me to say I'm wrong. When I start to be wrong on a stock, I can admit to myself that I don't know anything. And then I just mechanically get out. I think it's very important to understand who you are as a person, and trade that personality. Some people can trade the way I do, other people may have to trade differently.

How do you trade your personality?

I think I'm a hypercompetitive human being, and that's why I like trading. I'm also an obsessive compulsive, so I have to trade. But I don't like large risks and I don't feel comfortable losing. Some people feel comfortable losing, and they may make more money than I do because they can take bigger risks.

How many weeks have you lost money in the last two years?

I haven't had a losing week since 1997. In the past three years, I may have lost money on only 30 days. The most I've ever lost on one day was about $3,000.

How much have you made on your best day?

Probably about $29,000. Honestly, I think if I was less disciplined as a trader I would have made a lot more money over the last three years. But I think being disciplined cuts down on my losses. I very rarely lose. Maybe only once or twice a month.

How many shares do you do on a trade?

Volatile stocks I'll trade two to five hundred shares. Less volatile stocks such as Intel, I'll trade up to a thousand shares. Recently, I've traded Microsoft for up to two thousand shares.

Why were you trading Microsoft recently?

It had dropped into the $60 range below all recent levels of support. Yet given all the negative news at the time, it just wasn't going down any more. So I bought a couple of thousand shares and started trading around that position.

Do you take vacations regularly?

I've never taken a break from the market and even when I've taken a vacation, I have taken along my computer and continue to trade. But for the last few weeks, for the first time, I've just gotten away from everything and am not trading right now. I guess, I'm on trader burnout right now. I've been doing this for a long time. I almost fainted in my office recently I was so upset about trading. It wasn't that I was not making money, it was just that I was not making as much as I felt I should have. Yet there's no reason for me to be that upset about anything given my track record. Everyone who knows me wonders what I've been doing to myself. I think my personality started to change also. I'm always tense. So I said to myself, I need to take a real break. And I have. But you know, I still watch the markets. I guess I'm afraid I may miss the big breakdown in the market if I'm away too long. I think we're close to that point. But who knows?

Where do you want to be in 10 years?

I don't really know. I think and grapple with the idea of money a lot, whether it's good or evil. I think money makes a productive society, but doesn't always bring out the best in human beings. I don't know what I like any more. I do play basketball three or four times a week which has been very good for me. When I get out into the Rockies, I enjoy the mountains, but only for a short time. Right now when I'm feeling so burnt out, I think I might enjoy going to a relaxing spot or having that lifestyle, but then, what am I going to do? I could probably retire right now if I cut back on my expenses. But I think I would miss the adrenaline rush of what I do now. Unfortunately, I don't think I'm growing as a person right now, so I don't know where I want to be in five or ten years.

chapter 10

M. Rogan Labier

M. Rogan Labier is the unusual trader who has also become an author, writing unique books devoted to NASDAQ execution, *Tools of the Trade* and *The Nasdaq Traders' Toolkit*. He is also unusual because he is a trader who had professional experience as a NASDAQ market maker.

He is 33 years old and was born and mostly raised in Washington, DC. His father was a psychoanalyst and his mother designed computer software. In high school he showed an aptitude for mathematics but did not do as well in most other classes. He's held full time jobs after school since he was 13. Not getting into any college he wanted to, he attended Union College in Schenectady, NY, where his father had gone. Disliking it there, he was able through persistence to gain admission to Columbia University which had rejected him as a freshman. He majored in economics, but also got involved with theatre and acted in several plays. He wanted to be one of two things, either an investment banker, which it seemed everyone at Columbia wanted to be at the time, or act. For him acting became the priority since he wasn't enamoured with college. He left Columbia after a year and a half to go to Los Angeles in 1988 where he found a job acting in an after school television special for teenagers. The show was nominated for an Emmy award and he briefly became a teen magazine idol. He stated that he thought he had it made, but it turned out to be the high point of his acting career. As a member of Screen

Actors Guild, he acted in small roles and did some film production work for the next 10 years.

When did you first become interested in stocks?

When I was at Columbia, I would watch stocks although I had no money at the time to do anything. It's always impressed me that you could make money buying and selling something where you saw value and others didn't. For a while in California, I restored classic American cars and resold them. But it wasn't until about 1992 or 1993 that I started seriously watching the stock market again.

I started by paper trading for eight or nine months and analyzing my results. After a while I opened a brokerage account, but I was scared to make my own decisions. So a highly recommended broker at the top-five firm where I had an account suggested a Mexican telecom company. I bought it, on margin, and almost the day after, the stock dropped about 50 percent. After this, I decided to learn as much as I could on my own about stocks. I figured I could do at least as well as this highly recommended broker from a top five firm! So I undertook a serious program of self-study and started to read books.

What books did you read?

Everything from Graham and Dodd to options evaluations models. One book that I really enjoyed was *Reminiscences of a Stock Operator* by Edward Lefevre. This was the ghost written autobiography of Jesse Livermore. Since then, I've found a copy of *The Livermore Key* which is a little-known book that Livermore wrote describing his system. I'm writing an introduction to this book now and it's going to be republished shortly.

What was your style of trading when you started to trade on your own?

I was position trading. I would hold stocks for weeks or months. I used a discount brokerage. I found that the fills were not great, but it took me a while to catch on to that fact. I wasn't trading a large account since it was hard for me to save much money working as an actor.

Did it go well?

No, at least at first. I was losing everything and making stupid mistakes. But I kept at it, gradually becoming more familiar with charts and patterns. The first time I had a really great trade was when I bought Starbucks, and saw the stock go from 13 to 40 dollars over a couple of months. About 1996 I opened an online account with Datek and started to trade more actively. Sometimes with success and sometimes not. I looked at a lot of chart patterns. I didn't really understand the difference between momentum trading and a value approach. I was swing trading, and overall I started to get good at it. A typical trade I might make, although it happened a little bit later, was when I saw Yahoo go up from $13 just like a rocket. It was a no brainer to buy it. It would have been great to hold it. But I didn't, since I started to get out at the end of each day. I had gotten killed once holding an overnight position when some biotechnology stock gapped down next morning.

You were trading all day at this time?

Yes. I would get up and go to my computer at the open. I would trade until the market closed at 1 P.M. California time. Then I would go for acting auditions in the afternoon. I didn't do badly. I would quintuple my account, lose it, and then do it again. My results were erratic. My problem back then was that I would do well in a stock, hold it when it dropped, and continue to hold it waiting for it to come back up. Which many did. I didn't really know what I was doing, but I did do alright. In retrospect, I'm not sure how much of my results were the really strong bull market and how much was skill.

However, I realized that the best way for me to gain knowledge about stock trading professionally, was to become one of them. So I took my trading results and started knocking on doors of market makers in Los Angeles explaining why they should hire me. Everyone either laughed at me or cursed me when I told them I was a day trader. Finally, one guy looked at my P&L and said that although he wouldn't offer me a job, but would let me hang around the office. This firm didn't make a market in any high flying Internet kind of stocks. They were a very traditional firm making markets in small value-added stocks.

How did that work out?

I did hang out in the office and the head of the firm would periodically ask me some questions to see how much I knew. I had never seen a Level II screen at that point, but he showed me the market maker workstation, which was actually a Level III screen. Level III screens contain the same information as any Level II screen except that a market maker on Level III can move their bid and offer separately or simultaneously. That's the only difference.

At the time, market makers had to show, at best, 1,000 shares on their bid or offer no matter what their real size was. That's one reason why SOES trading was so great at this time. Stocks may not have moved as much in the early 1990s but SOES traders could get executed much more easily on a thousand shares. After the summer of 1998, the rules changed and market makers were allowed to show their actual or minimum size, which was often smaller than a 1,000 shares. Now market makers will typically show only a 100 shares, even if they might have more size behind it. So, with much greater volatility, there is less liquidity from market makers, and it is more difficult to get executed for size. Today, you really have to know what you are doing.

Some early SOES traders believe that there was actually greater follow through to moves in the early 1990s than there is today.

Perhaps that's true over small price ranges for scalpers in liquid stocks, but I don't think you had as many 20 or 30 points moves in a day in stocks back then. Today, I think there's more opportunities, but also more danger.

Did you ever work for this market maker?

Eventually he hired me. I started to make markets in about a dozen, nonhigh-flying, value-added, big companies. The firm I worked for had great, top notch analysts who did great for their clients. I learned a lot there about fundamental analysis of companies. The clients for these stocks tended to be high net worth individuals and institutions. Our firm did its own research on these stocks, and I would make a market in them, that is, I would be willing always to provide a bid-and-offer quote at which I would trade these stocks. Generally, they were somewhat thinly traded and did not have a large following. These were strong regional stocks as far as the fundamentals would go, and would often trade close to their fundamental values. But they did get hit hard in the summer of 1998 when small caps sold off for a brief period.

What happened in the summer of 1998 when small caps took a hit?

Well, of course, some of our stocks went down too. It was too bad, because many goods stocks were hammered unfairly. Unfair I think, because you may have had a stock with a $9 book value now trading at $7, while the Internet startups of the world were trading at record multiples.

How did it work as a market maker?

We didn't carry a large inventory but facilitated customer order flow. Clients came to us because they liked the research and execution. Typically, I would get calls or I would call someone we didn't know, such as a pension fund, and talk to them about the stocks. If someone wanted to buy 20,000 shares, I would handle the execution. We didn't usually keep that size amount of stock in inventory, but there were other market makers in these stocks that I could look to buy from. Or a client or fund might want to buy a block of stock at a specified price and we would look to see if someone else had that amount for sale at that price. We had relationships, and we might call around. Of course, I wouldn't say to them do you have X amount of shares to sell at this price, because that would tip our hand. Sometimes we could find parties on both sides and just cross the stock. It depended on the situation what I would do. Sometimes people would just want to sell a large block right away, as quickly as possible. It wasn't normal, but sometimes that happened.

What would happen if someone wanted to sell a large block quickly?

This happened rather dramatically once, when I had an order to liquidate a 500,000 share block of shares for a fund manager. I had been selling this position off slowly for a month because I could only sell a little bit at a time, since the stock only traded about 60,000 shares a day and there were few market makers in this stock. When I was down to the last 22,000 shares or so, the fund manager called to tell me to sell the remaining block out immediately no matter what price it would sell for. So I did what I received the order to do. Prior to this point the stock had been trading around $8 a share. I just started to sell to all the market makers showing bids. The market makers panicked because they began lowering their bids as fast as possible. I sold the stock down to $4½ in about two minutes.

Incidentally, within a few minutes of this trade, I received a call from StockWatch, the market monitoring division of the Securities and Exchange Commission. They wanted to know everything about this trade and its circumstances. Fortunately, everything had been recorded on phone, so I could show them that nothing had been done that was wrong. But traders should know that StockWatch is paying attention even to little out of the way stocks and they can be aggressively complete in their surveillance.

Traders on NASDAQ could SOES you?

Of course. But it happened rarely since our stocks were not the kind that day traders usually traded. If it did happen, I often found it a nuisance, because Level III did not have a position monitor. I would have to keep track of my position size mentally in a fast-moving market in not only this stock but a dozen others. However, if someone wanted to trade 5,000 shares, we would sometimes do it even if the trade was not profitable, because we wanted people to know we were always there for size.

In this hypothetical situation, if someone bought 5,000 shares from you leaving you short, would you immediately go into the market and bid the stock?

Not necessarily. I would manage the position. Five thousand shares short would probably not be a massive risk to me.

What if someone came in for another 5,000 shares, and then another? Did this every happen to you?

Sure it happened. What I would do next would depend on the situation.

What if a news story came out suddenly and you were short?

Well, I would be taking a big risk, but that's what it means to manage a position. If I were getting short in this example, I certainly don't think I would start to bid up the stock. If I showed a higher bid, I would just be telegraphing to the world that I want to buy. How I would manage that position would depend on the situation. I would look at my risk, my inventory position, what is going on with the stock, what's happening in the general market, and what my client orders happened to be at the time. If I were desperate, maybe I would buy stock from another market maker. There's no standard response to this situation.

Did you trade the firm's account in the stocks you make markets in?

We tried not to carry heavy inventory but because we believed in the companies, we did take speculative positions in the stocks I made markets in.

Did you manually set the bid and offer on your stocks?

Yes. Goldman Sachs or Morgan Stanley might have some kind of automatic algorithm to set prices, but I set the prices manually. I monitored all my stocks on just one Level III workstation. Of course, I would have to be aware of what was happening in each of the stocks. Some market makers may be watching as many as 40 stocks at one time. If you are not paying attention to all your stocks and one starts to run up or down, you could find yourself in deep water real fast. I got caught once.

What happened?

I was told it wouldn't happen again or I wouldn't be employed there any longer. I just wasn't paying attention momentarily, and some news came out on one of my stocks and it just started to run. My offer was still available a half point below the market. And boom, I got both SOESed and preferenced. I was now short a stock that was running up. I held the short thinking the market would sell off, and it did.

Do you think market makers have any special advantage?

The advantage they have is knowing their own order flow. If you know a pension fund has an order to buy 700,000 shares over the next week, that's an advantage. But if you use that advantage, you are guilty of insider trading. It is a big misconception among many traders that market makers somehow know the order flow of other market makers. Some traders seem to believe that there is a central book that describes all the market makers orders, which market makers must know. But they only know their own order book and they cannot use this information. Market makers may not even know the total picture of their own firm's order flow. They may receive an order from one of their clients to sell 30,000 shares. Then they may be told to sell another 30,000 shares, not knowing that these pieces are part of a much larger order that has not been disclosed to them.

So the answer is no, I don't think market makers have any special advantage that they can use. They may even be at a disadvantage since their execution systems on the Level III are older software that can be very slow.

Would you use other ECNs when you were making markets?

Sure. I would use Instinet or Island when I didn't want to disclose it was me doing the order. If I wanted to look like a seller when I would really want to buy, I might do that. If you have pegged me as a massive seller for the day because you have seen me return to the offer, obviously it is in my best interest to appear like someone else with a disguise. If you are clever enough, you might watch and still be able to determine that it is me.

Do you think that because you've been a market maker, you have greater insight into how market makers trade on Level II?

Absolutely. But it's not that complicated a game. The fact is that you will never know with one hundred percent certainty just what someone is doing. You never know exactly what kind of order they're sitting on, whether the 5,000 shares they've just sold is just 5,000 shares, or is part of a million share order that will drive the stock down 10 points over the next two weeks. But individuals can learn to decipher this by observation day after day.

What would they be trying to observe?

Which market makers are constantly bidding or offering. Who's holding the offer down or the bid up. Someone who is showing small size on the bid or offer but trading much more. A market maker who may buy up to a certain price and then lowers his bid.

Can you give me an example of these points?

Let's say a market maker has a large order to buy a stock up to $46. He may bid and buy the stock up to $45\frac{15}{16}$ but no higher, since he wants to sell it to his client at $46. If the stock looks strong at that point he may lower his bid and may even lower his offer too. He would do this because he would like the stock now to come down in price so he could buy more at a price lower than 46, since that is the price at which he is going to fill his client.

Is this how large orders are usually handled?

A market maker can fill an order on either an agency or principal basis. Agency basis is where a market maker acts as a middleman only. I charge you a commission on top of the price at which I bought the shares for you. I buy a stock at 45, give it to you for 45, and then charge you a commission for that service. Principal basis is where a market maker buys stock which goes into his own account, which he then sells to his client at a price which is inclusive of a small mark-up in price over that which the market maker paid. There are NASD rules and regulations about how much a market maker can charge as a mark-up. What is so interesting about the ready availability of Level II, is that it allows large institutions and pension funds to watch whoever is handling their order and see where market makers are buying their stock. Institutions can now more readily determine the mark-up they are being charged and whether it is fair and competitive.

When you look at NASDAQ times and sales, you will typically see many trades for a couple of hundred or thousand shares being traded and then may see a very large trade of 25,000 shares trade, often just above or below the current best bid or offer. Is this block trade related to what you are describing?

People may wonder about this. The reality often is that a market maker is buying or selling a large amount of stock for a client, and when this order is completed at some average price, the print of this trade then appears on time and sales. He's actually been buying or selling this stock before the print, perhaps all day. There is a sense in which this is double printing of this trade. Let's say you are a client and ask me to buy a block of Microsoft for you. I start buying some portion of this order in the market that gets printed on times and sales, and I continue to do trades this way. When I've completed the order, I then sell the shares to you, the client, and this also gets reported as one aggregated trade on time and sales. There are rules and regulations about the timing of those prints and when they may be done relative to the price of the stock.

Why did you leave market making?

It was very restrictive in that I was no longer day trading my own account. So I quit and opened accounts at a series of firms. I started off swing trading, holding positions for minutes but sometimes hours.

What was the execution system you were using?

Several platforms, got mostly Townsends' Real Tick III.

What happened next?

I was trading remotely and I was a bit lonely. It happened at this time that the broker I was using was hiring professional staff for their office, and I offered to run their trading desk. The firm did not trade a proprietary account, but it did need to manage errors in client trades, solve software problems that traders might have, or handle orders that clients might phone in instead of executing them for some reason. This job was exciting and I built their trading desk, of which I was very proud. But I became increasingly frustrated that I could no longer trade my own account.

You wrote _The Nasdaq Traders' Toolkit,_ which is the only book available devoted to execution and execution systems. Tell me about that.

I started the book when I started to trade using ECNs on Level II, and I realized I was not getting the kinds of fills that I imagined I would. I didn't understand why at the time. So I started to call the heads of all the ECNs and sat down on their phone doorsteps, so to speak, until they could tell me exactly how their machines worked. Perhaps because this was all so new, they were all willing to tell me. From that point on, I knew how all the ECNs worked. I realized a lot of other people were going through my experience of not getting good fills with their ECNs. They did not understand how the ECNs functioned. For example, they would be using SOES in a situation where SOES could not work. So I basically wrote the book so that other traders would not sit on the phone with me all day long while I explained all this.

When did the book get published?

In October or November 1999. I had some initial conversations with standard publishers, but I went with an electronic publisher who put it out online in two weeks. The online version is called _The Tools of the Trade._ I didn't know if anyone would ever buy it, but it's become something of a bestseller. I update it all the time when new information becomes available on any changes to the execution systems. The book doesn't teach people how to trade, but it does teach them how to execute, which is one of the most ignored things in many books and courses on trading. If you don't know how to get in when you need to get in, or out when you need to get out, you're going to be in trouble. The best trading plan in the world is useless if you cannot execute it. Many traders don't understand this, but I've been gratified at the many letters from readers who have been helped. The book has led me to be invited to consult and speak at numerous events, like the Online Trading Expos, where my presentation has been voted best and most useful. So I'm happy with the response. This book is now due to be published in a hard back edition by John Wiley & Sons later this year. It's called the *The Nasdaq Traders' Toolkit.*

What is the most common mistake that you think traders make when they try to execute trades?

They don't have a full understanding of how the different routes work. They may work differently in different situations depending on who is on the bid or offer. For example, if a trader sees that NTRD, ATTN, and STRK are the only bidders in a stock for a thousand shares each, and he tries to SOES them, he will not get filled because they are ECNs and SOES will not execute against an ECN ever. The stock may crash at that point, and the trader may still be wondering why he was not filled. He will have to cancel that order and then place another one which may also be inappropriate. You have to know which specific tool works to do the specific job. It's not brain surgery, but it's not explained anywhere. And Super SOES, which is scheduled to come online the third quarter of 2000, will completely change order routing dynamics.

How would you recommend that someone execute a short trade?

It all depends on who's on the bid and offer. If an ECN were on the bid and it were an uptick, you would not use SOES. You would either use SelectNet, or route your order on that ECN if your broker gives you access to that ECN. And even if you have access to that ECN, ECNs have all kinds of configurable options that brokerages either enable or don't enable. The fact that you use Island and I use Island, does not mean that we can use it in the same way. I may have much more functionality than you do.

What do you mean by functionality?

For example, Island has hidden and subscriber orders. Subscriber orders will appear on the Island book, but will not appear on the

Level II screen montage to other traders. Hidden orders won't appear anywhere.

Why would someone want to do that?

For obvious reasons. If you wanted to buy stock on the bid and you don't think much stock is going to trade there, and you don't want to make the bid look any stronger perhaps because there is a wide bid-offer spread, you could place a hidden order. You've increased your chances of getting the stock. I don't think these hidden features are being used that widely, since most brokerages do not configure Island for these features, although a few do. You may want to ask whether your broker has these features, and if they don't you may want to go to another broker.

Do you see any changes in how Level II may work in the future?

Super SOES is scheduled to be coming out. That will eliminate SOES and SelectNet as they currently work in NASDAQ national market stocks, and create a new system called NNMS. What it will do is auto-execute against a market participant, market maker or ECN, up to his size showing. It will function similarly to SOES, but will make things a lot easier because you won't have to think about SOES or its five minute rule, tier size, or whether to use SOES or SelectNet for national market stocks. There are some other features to this new system, when it is introduced, that will make market execution must faster and more liquid. However, because of technical problems I think the system's introduction may be delayed.

What advice would you give new traders?

You must be ruthless in your discipline. This has been something I've had to work on and still need to work on. Know what discipline means. If you don't know what you are doing, not only do you need to find someone who can show you, you need to limit your risk by trading smaller. If you have a loss, don't try to trade you way out of it by trading larger size or trading more volatile stocks. I've also gotten hurt trading just taking shots, just trading because you've wanted to do something. Watching and analyzing markets, is doing something. A trader can get into a lot of trouble wanting to buy or sell all the time.

I think it is real important to have a mentor. It's a very tough game and it's probably different from anything they've ever done before. If a new trader doesn't have someone who knows what they are doing helping them, they are at a disadvantage.

What are the psychological pitfalls of trading?

I've done a lot of thinking about this, because I'm still working on this myself. Here's what a gambler does. A gambler gets into a bad position hoping that it will turn good. And if it does turn good, he takes the profit right away. What a good traders should do is the opposite of the gambler. If it goes bad, immediately get rid of it. If it goes up, then you want to keep it. Why get rid of it? When momentum stops then you want to get rid of it, but not before then. You have to aggressively fight the gambler's mentality. If you don't, it will all end in tears. That was my first lesson in trading.

Did trading ever wear you out?

Every day.

How do you handle that?

Sleep.

Do you ever take vacations?

Trading is a vacation. I enjoy trading and being with some of the best traders. It doesn't get any better . . . Well, maybe the month I spend in Bali was better.

Where do you want to be doing 10 years from now?

I don't really know. Retired on an island.

chapter 11

Matthew Walsh

Matthew Walsh began his trading career as a specialist on the floor of the Chicago Stock Exchange in 1983. In 1996, he left the stock exchange and moved to Colorado to trade his own account using remote electronic access. He is 40 years old and grew up in Chicago where his father was an oral surgeon and professor at the University of Illinois Dental School. When he was 16 his family moved to Idaho, where Matt developed a love for the West and the outdoors.

After graduating from high school and several years at community college, Matt transferred to the University of Idaho where he studied electrical engineering. Asked why he studied electronics, he said that it was as far from oral surgery as he could get and that he had friends in the field. He was good at mathematics. Trim but muscular, Matt is an avid sports practitioner. He's been skiing for 30 years, has run marathons, and is an endurance bicycler. Matt is married and has two young children. One of Matt's special causes is raising money for the Leukemia Society of America and Children's Hospital.

How did you first get involved with stocks?

I had been studying at the University of Idaho and was close to graduating but I got a little burnt out, so I decided to take a year off and moved back to Chicago where I grew up. I had a friend who was dating a girl whose dad owned a brokerage and specialist firm on the floor of the Chicago Stock Exchange. I met Jim

Niehoff and he offered me the opportunity to go to work. He warned me though that as a clerk I wouldn't make much money. I took the job as a clerk regardless and began my career on the floor on the Midwest Stock Exchange, which was later renamed the Chicago Stock Exchange. I had so much fun doing this that I just never went back to school. This was in 1983. I stayed on the exchange until 1996 when I moved to Colorado.

What did you know about stocks before you got this job?

Nothing. Before I came to Chicago, I used to make fun of a friend of mine, who worked for a major mutual fund company in Chicago, asking how he could end up wearing a suit and commuting downtown to his job. I thought you'd never catch me doing that; next thing I know, there I am doing it myself!

So what did you do on the floor?

I started as a clerk, which meant that I filled out trade blotters and answered phone calls. I did not think of being a trader myself at that time, but after six months, a trader left the firm and I was put in her position. This was a specialist firm on the exchange, so I became a co-specialist. I fell in love with this job. It was intriguing, fascinating, and a fast-moving environment. A big day then was less than ten million shares a day. Of course, by today's standards, trading volume was at a snail's pace. Technology was very rudimentary, and I'm not even sure at that time I had even heard of the NASDAQ market!

Tell me what it was like to be a specialist.

As a specialist, I provided a bid and offer at which price I would trade specific stocks with brokers. I made a market in about 20 stocks including some big name stocks, such as Hewlett-Packard, Dupont, Eastman Kodak, and National Semiconductor. As a specialist on a regional exchange, you're the shadow of the New York Stock Exchange. You make a market, but you make a market based on what the market is in New York or by the orders that come into your book. Investors care about what the best (highest) bid or best (lowest) offer is, which is called the BBO. With all regional exchanges and the NYSE taken into account, you had what is called the "composite quote." Sometimes you're the best quote and sometimes you're not. The regional exchanges provided a very good alternative route for brokerage houses to send their orders. Some of this order flow was based on the regional exchanges having the best bid or offer. But this whole business, more then than now, was built on relationships. You have a buddy over at a brokerage house that you go golfing or skiing with. Based on this relationship, he may send you some percentage of his order flow provided you are not worse than the BBO. And that's how a lot of this order flow worked out. Generally, it would come in small trades of a few hundred or thousand shares each, or part of a larger block, which I was instructed to do my best to fill. Still, the NYSE got about 90 percent of the order flow back then.

When you were put into the specialist position, did your firm give you any special instructions how to fill this role?

Not really. No formal education aside from studying for my Series 7. Most of the training was on the job. The fellow I worked for was also a specialist and I learned a lot both by watching and by listening. I really then learned by doing and making mistakes.

Did you know who the specialist was in you stocks on the NYSE and did you have a relationship with him?

In some stocks I knew who he was. But our relationship was pretty distant, except when he would yell at me if I got in his way with a better quote or something. I can't say that we went out of our way to be kind to each other.

How did the floor trading change while you were there?

When I started, the Midwest Stock Exchange was located on a small trading floor that still used gas jet tapes. It was loud and very crowded. Our technology as I mentioned before was rather rudimentary. In 1985, the exchange moved to its new and modern location with a very large floor that was deathly quiet, but it was much more electronically sophisticated. It took some getting use to.

What kind of systems did you use as a specialist?

We had the RICH trading station that had four screens reflecting the different functions of the system. We had a quote system, which was Quotron. This allowed us to obtain general market quotes and statistics of various kinds. We also had an auto-quote system where you, as a specialist, maintained your quotes. This was all done electronically. We had the MAX system which was one of the earliest electronic trading systems. This was used primarily to receive and execute retail orders automatically from brokerage houses across the country that also had a connecting MAX terminal. Finally, we had an ITS system. That allowed all regional and New York exchanges to link to each other. So that if the NYSE specialist saw that I was offering the best price he could take my offer by typing in this order. His order would then show up on the screen in front of me and would be executed quickly and efficiently.

In 1993, I went to Melvin Securities, another specialist firm. One day Congressman Edward Markey paid a visit to the floor. Everyone at Melvin was directed to wear Melvin jackets and caps for the visit. I refused. When the Congressman visited the floor, he ended up talking to me for about 10 or 15 minutes. He asked me how fair the markets were, how I felt about the NYSE specialists, were they representing orders fairly and accurately, and so forth. I told him exactly what I thought. Well, a half hour after Markey left, I got a call from the head of the firm and I expected I was going to be fired. Instead my boss said that Markey had enjoyed his visit with me and that I was a real maverick. Later, when I started my own company, I choose the name Maverick Trading.

Do you think specialists treat public orders fairly?

For the most part, I believe they do. When public orders are not represented fairly, it's not always the specialist's fault. The big brokers and specialists often work closely together. They have to work together. If the broker has a large order and he doesn't divulge this to the specialist, then the specialist could get hurt. Or the specialist could then mishandle the order and the broker would get hurt. But as an example, when the market is a quarter bid to a half offer. And say, somebody will walk up on the NYSE with an order to buy 200,000 shares at three-eighths, but they don't want their bid displayed as a public quote. The order "remains in the crowd." So what you see on the screen is not necessarily representative of what the real market is. This puts people not on the floor of the NYSE, whether the regional exchanges, the public, or retail brokerage houses, at a disadvantage because they are not present and don't know the real market. The only way around this for me was to ask floor brokers on the NYSE to find out what the "post" market is, that is, what is the real market at the post of the NYSE specialist and not just what the screen market is quoted. In this hypothetical example, I might see that many trades are taking place at three-eighths when the publicly quoted market is one-quarter bid at one-half offered and not know why three-eighths is trading. The answer is that there is a floor broker willing to pay three-eighths but only divulging this on the floor of the NYSE and not to the public. It's not a displayed market. Is it fair? I don't know. A fair market should be a publicly displayed market, yet it doesn't always work that way.

Do you feel that because you've been a specialist, now that you are trading off the floor to jump ahead a little, that you have any special insight or ways of interpreting trades that you see in listed stocks?

I traded listed stocks as a specialist for 14 years, but since becoming an off-floor trader, especially in the last two years, I trade virtually nothing but NASDAQ stocks. The inherent problem with listed stocks that you don't have with NASDAQ stocks is that you have only one person acting as market maker, that is, the NYSE specialist. He is so busy that I can be certain that my order will get lost in the crowd. More often than not, my order does not get filled even if my order is better than the quoted screen price. And I think the reason is that these guys are just too busy. They have to deal with electronic orders flowing in on Super-Dot, the other regional exchange electronic markets, and a crowd of brokers as well. And they only have one or two clerks to help them. I think this is an incredibly inefficient system. I know the NYSE has undergone a revamping of their technology in the last five years, but I still find that too many orders just get lost in the system and that's why I don't trade listed stocks that often especially on the NYSE.

So going back, you started your own firm Maverick Trading. Tell me about that.

I started Maverick in November of 1995, mostly because my wife and I made a decision to move to Colorado. I had reached a point just before this where most of my trading as a specialist was based on order flow, which means that my trades were dependent on how many brokers were bringing orders to me to fill. This was less action on my part and more reaction. I wasn't making the decision to get long or short, but was reacting to the order that the broker had at the time. This, of course, is what a market maker does much of the time. However, order flow by that time had become extremely expensive, because everyone was paying for it.

This was "payment for order flow"?

Yes. And the competition was incredibly high to get that order flow, to get good order flow, to get the best order flow. It was the most expensive cost of doing business in addition to all the other costs of doing business and probably still is. I know from my own experience on the Chicago Stock Exchange, we were providing to our order sending firms the very best executions with regard to both time and price. It was just expensive.

Were there other personal reasons why you decided to leave the exchange floor?

Yes. It was certainly a quality of life thing. As a specialist, I was burnt out, because I had to trade every day to maintain my order book. There is no day off because if you're not there someone else had to watch your book, and that was a burden for him or her. Of course, I reciprocated, but when I had to watch someone else's order book including my own, that was an additional burden for me. It seemed somebody was always suffering, and it was a lot of pressure. I finally got burned out.

Were you successful at first trading without order flow?

I was. I traded by myself and had extremely low overhead. I was making $10,000 to $15,000 a month. This was off-floor speculative trading and probably the beginnings of this new phenomenon called day-trading. At that point I wasn't trading NASDAQ stocks and I still had a Super-DOT terminal to send my orders directly to the NYSE and that certainly helped.

Wasn't that expensive?

Not really, I had formed an alliance with a firm on the floor of the Chicago Stock Exchange to offer off-floor traders electronic access to the exchanges. We saw then what has only continued to happen since then. I should mention that when I was on the floor I was on the trading technology committee and even chaired it for two years. I was on a number of other committees also. You name it and I was on it. I was very actively involved not only with the exchange but the industry. I saw the changes as they were happening. So when I formed an alliance with this firm, we were going to test our vision: Increased direct access to trading was likely to grow. We decided to open a retail office for this kind of public access trading, and since I had already made the decision to go to Colorado, we decided to open an office there. This was much less expensive to do at that time than it would have been five years previously, given the falling cost of computers and the beginning of the Internet.

The office did very well, but this arrangement began to run into trouble in 1997, because my partners also owned a very large specialist firm on the Chicago Stock Exchange. This meant that because they were making a market in so many stocks, I was restricted in my freedom to trade those stocks. Since they intended to expand further, which would have only restricted my freedom to trade further, we amicably dissolved our association. At that point, I formed an alliance with another broker dealer from New York to run some of their offices because I still wanted to have a part in running a business that offered services to off-floor traders. However, all during this time, I was still trading my own account.

How were you so successful when you first started trading off the floor? What did you do that was so right?

I learned very quickly not to overtrade and at what times of day I traded my best. For me, as probably for most traders, that's always been the morning. My mistakes early on were that I'd have a great morning, but then as the day wore on, I'd over trade and often give back what I had made, or worse. So I became strictly a morning trader, and that's all I will trade, even now.

Why do you think it is so much better to trade only mornings?

Because there's an enormous amount of irrationality that goes on at the opening of trading. Openings are generally overactive one way or the other. People panic on overnight news and they sell, so stocks trade too low on the open. Or people become too optimistic and buy, meaning prices trade too high on the open. There are just a great number of inefficiencies on the open that you can take advantage of. I've found that there are many opportunities available during the first hour of the day.

Do you have any specific examples of these irrationalities?

A stock announces earnings that don't meet the analysts' secret number, what's called the "whisper number." The stock may have already been run up in price the previous day in anticipation of good numbers. Because the numbers either were not met or maybe just met, the stock opens down 15 points. To me that's nothing but a buying opportunity. Someone once said that when "the street" turns crimson, you just have to close your eyes and buy with both hands. Generally, when everyone's selling, that's when you should be buying. A lot of this selling is just the irrationality of people desperate to get out. And conversely, when everyone's buying that's when you should be short selling.

Do you find yourself counter-trend trading in the morning?

Absolutely. I counter-trend trade but I follow momentum.

Tell me what momentum means to you.

Momentum is going with the flow and trend—up or down. I see what's trading right now, what the quotes are, what's being taken. If it's a NASDAQ stock, I look whether bids are filling in and offers are thinning out. Regardless of the quotes, I look at where the stock is trading. Early on I will buy or sell into this momentum. Sometimes you may get a point profit but generally I am a consistent three-eighths to a half-point profit trader. The stock may move another 10 points but that's not my game. I try to catch these smaller moves with 500 to a 1,000 shares or so, and do this as often as I can. By the end of the day, these small profits will add up to a decent profit.

I try to keep my risks nominal. If the stock turns against me, I get out. I don't dilly-dally. I can always get back in. These markets are so fast and so volatile that you could lose 10 points in a matter of minutes. You must keep any losses to an absolute minimum. The key to staying in business is recognizing when you are wrong and taking advantage of when you are right.

How many trades are you making in a day, which for you is the morning?

Twenty or thirty; sometimes more, sometimes less. And most of this is in the first hour or so. I'm holding trades for seconds.

What kind of stocks are you trading mostly?

I trade volatile and expensive stocks. For the last year, like everyone else, I trade technology and Internet stocks. I also trade IPOs. When I first started trading off-floor, I traded Wells Fargo a lot. It was a listed stock, but also a $300 stock. It was not unusual for Wells Fargo to have a 20 or 30 point move in a day. And they were often obvious moves. Because, all of a sudden, you would see a 320 bid come in for 2,000 shares and only 100 shares offered at 321, and I would take those shares. The bid would move up to 321 and I would immediately offer my shares out at 321¾ or 322. Trading that stock was very similar to trading an Internet stock today.

You liked the expensive stocks just because they were more likely to move more points?

Yes. I have no patience to sit with a trade. I'm not a long-term investor and I want instant gratification.

It is sometimes suggested that you should trade your personality. Are you an impatient person?

During market hours, yes. Outside this business I'm not, but in this business, I'm impatient. If I put on a trade, and it doesn't move in my direction, then I'm out. Unless there's some underlying reason, such as overwhelming support that says to stay in. But that's rare. I can always get back in. If I feel the stock should be going up and it isn't, then why isn't it? If I don't know, then I'm going to get out. The risks in this business are too great to sit on something that's not doing anything. This is true for several reasons. One, you're tying up capital. Second, if it's not moving, and I don't know why, then I shouldn't be in the trade. There are too many other trades that I could be making instead.

How many times do you buy on the offer when you initiate a trade on the long side?

I almost always buy on the offer. And that's because I trade the momentum. If you want to get in, you have to ride the wave. I see too many people miss a good trade because they want to buy on the bid, or they try to get filled in between the bid and offer. If the stock is in play and moving, and everyone is buying, you must buy on the offer. From experience, this tells me this stock is going up. If I have to buy on the offer and pay a point above the current displayed offer, then so be it.

Is this true correspondingly when you sell a stock you are already long. Do you usually sell on the bid?

When I get out, about 75 percent of the time I'm selling on the offer. This is because when I go long, I almost always immediately put in a limit order to sell at some higher price. I have a rule I tell my new traders: when you make a long trade, you offer it out at three teenies. You make money and you're out of the trade. It does two things for you: It bolsters your confidence because you did the right thing, and you put money in the bank.

So you usually buy on the offer, sell on the offer?

Usually. The only time I'm selling on the bid is when the stock momentum is turned and I'm just trying to get rid of my position.

And on the short side, how do you trade?

I'm not a real good short trader. If the market is down 300 Dow points, I'm generally making money on the long side. I don't make money on the short side. Shorting stock is a psychologically difficult thing to do because you have to offer the short in an up move because of the short sale rule. (NASD rules require that short sales take place on an up-tick.) It takes a lot more conviction.

How do you do that and make money buying stock during market declines?

Nothing goes straight down. I'm not a hero, but I can make small profits on the small rallies. Don't get me wrong. I do make some money on the short side, but 85 percent of my trades are from the long side.

Do you make as much money on market declines as you would on an up day?

Yes. But I do trade differently when I'm just shorting. I've usually done a little more analysis of the stock and believe it is a weak candidate, so shorting makes sense. I also let my stops run, by which I mean that I will let myself take a larger loss on the trade before I get out or cover. This is in part because if you are shorting you are selling into the momentum and sometimes this carries you a little higher. Sometimes I will let the trade run against me by a point. or point and a half, a loss that I wouldn't let myself take on the long side. But I must be convinced that I am right to make the trade. I also don't want to get out of the short because, as I've said, it is more difficult to initiate, and I can't get back in as easily if I try to cover a small loss.

Do you ever trade stock indexes?

One of the products that came out that cost me a lot of money was the "spiders" (SPDRs). I tended to short them in rising markets. Probably I did it because it was easy. It's a psychological temptation. When the market is rising to very high levels, I can fall into the trap of asking, "How high can this go?" and answer by trying to pick the top. I think that if I'm short 5,000 spiders and the market really does drop, I'll make a killing. But the market hasn't dropped that often in the past several years, and I've been so shook out of spiders that I've stopped doing it.

Do you trade every day?

If there are days I don't feel comfortable about the market, I just won't trade it. I'll just watch it or attend to other business.

What percentages of your trades are profitable?

About 80 percent.

How much do you lose on a losing trade on average?

About a half-point.

What's the largest loss you ever allowed yourself to take?

About 23 points! This was a stock that went from $3 to $20 where I shorted it. I continued to go up to 30 where I got out with a $10 loss. But I reversed my position at that point and went long and watched it go up to 50. I made up all the money I lost. But I then bought more because I thought it was going to 75. And then it turned down suddenly! And there was nothing but air under the bids. There was nothing there and I couldn't get out until 23 points lower. The stock was KTEL.

When was that trade?

This was in March of 1998. This was one of the early Internet stocks that had been trading at a dollar and a half for two years and then it just took off. About this time, other Internet stocks also started to take off. I remember once when eBay opened up 100 points higher. I thought this was so irrational that I shorted the hell out of it. And for about 10 minutes I was nearly ready to puke because the stock just didn't go down and that is usually a bad sign. Well, it finally did drop and I made 10 or 15 points on it. This was all in the first 15 minutes of the day. These stocks can be scary. This can be a dangerous business, there's no question in my mind. Many people do get hurt trading these kinds of stocks. And this type of trading is not for the inexperienced or novice trader.

Yet you had been profitable from the start. Tell me more about why did it work for you and not so many other traders when they first started?

Well, part of this was the discipline I learned as a specialist. As a specialist I had to watch just a dozen or so stocks. If these stocks were not doing much, then you don't do much either. I learned over the 13 years on the floor to have patience to wait for my stocks to move and to take advantage of those times. As a specialist, you may only make a small amount of money on most days, but the days your stocks are in play you will make the majority of your earnings for the month. And this can be true trading off floor also. Also, as a specialist I knew a lot about trading as a business. I understand the emotional roller coaster of trading and these kinds of things.

And people just starting to trade don't understand this?

I think this is true. Most of these people have no real strategy. What I tell new traders is to take a core group of stocks and just trade those. These stocks should be liquid by which I mean you can get out of them when you need to because there are a lot of participants and market makers. On NASDAQ these could be Dell, Cisco, Miscrosoft, and so forth. Don't try to jump around trying to trade many stocks that you don't know well. They might get lucky and make some money, but mostly new traders have no strategy. They've heard somewhere that you can make hundreds of thousands of dollars trading a month and think they can just start off and do this too. None of them even know any successful traders personally who could help them. I met a professional poker player one time from Las Vegas, who, although had never traded a share in his life, knew when to fold them. He would have been a good candidate for day trading. He understood the discipline it required to be a successful card player. Most "newbies" have zero concept of discipline and therefore find themselves on the losing end of this business.

You mentioned handling emotions while trading. Why is that important?

In my experience, most new traders have trouble with the emotions of trading. They can't separate the analytics of the trade from the emotions of the trade. This is often reflected in the fact that they can't be disciplined handling losses. If a stock goes against them for several points, they get upset but then decide they are really long-term investors. This makes them feel better temporarily. But then the stock continues to go down and pretty soon their $15,000 of capital is gone. I should mention that the most important emotion to have about trading is passion. If you are passionate about it and really have fun doing it, you will have a greater chance of being successful.

Do you think it is better to trade in an office with other people or remotely?

I think human beings need other people around them to get the best results. We are social animals. I suspect that many new traders are sitting in remote locations alone. What happens is that they sit there thinking they are focused on what they are doing but really they lose attention doing this by themselves. I think that trading from a trading office with other people is very important, especially for new traders. They need the minor distractions and the camaraderie that goes on. This, at least, is true for me. I learn something new every day being with other people.

You mentioned why you had developed many of the important characteristics of good trading before you started trading off floor. But what has been the most important thing you learned since you came off the floor?

Well, my style has changed somewhat. I traded more listed stocks at first, but now I usually trade only NASDAQ stocks. I felt I was at too much of a disadvantage trading listed stocks since I can't see the depth of the order book, which only the specialist knows. This does not mean that I think seeing all the publicly displayed bids and offers above and below the market on NASDAQ are always an accurate representation of the market. But I know that some of these displayed orders, at least from other day traders on Island, are real orders. I can see what's going on at least a little bit. All I want is a little bit of an edge about knowing what's going on. There is no magic dust that will make you a great trader. But NASDAQ Level II can be a valuable tool of trading.

Do you use other sources of information before trading?

I do no research. I read no papers. I listen to almost no news. I do sometimes go to some chat rooms on the Internet just to see what people are thinking. Some of this is just for my own amusement because many of them are absolutely insane. But occasionally some of them come up with a good idea. Aside from this, though, I don't do much homework. Now, I know other successful traders who do spend hours doing research and I can't discredit what they are doing. What works for me may not work for you and what works for you may not work for me. So everyone has to find his own way.

Do people in your office try to follow how you trade?

People in my office sometimes ask me to tell them when I'm going to buy something so they can put on the same trade. They want to mimic my trades. I don't allow them to do this for two reasons. One, because they don't learn anything by doing this; They have to learn by making their own mistakes. Second, I don't want the pressure if I'm wrong. I will feel responsible for them. Now, there are exceptions to this rule. Sometimes I will suggest people get into a trade if I think it's an obvious winner. For example, several months ago (spring of 1999), Dell reported less than expected earnings and the stock was down about 12 points the next day. I did recommend that people in my office buy and we did. It was a good trade. But for momentum-type trades, no, I don't encourage people to follow my trade. I could just as well be wrong and I don't want to bring people down with me. I talk to the people in my office and mentor them. I continually tell them what to look for in a good trade. I also go as far as questioning their logic as to why they might have put a particular trade on. If they're shooting from the hip and have no strategy, I get them out of the trade. I want people to have longevity in this business.

What time do you usually get into your office in the morning?

I usually get to my office 15 to 20 minutes before the opening, and then carefully watch what's going on at the open. I do keep CNBC on for about an hour, but then turn it off because I can't stand listening to their commentators. After that I listen to music. If there is an important event expected such as Alan Greenspan speaking, I will try to listen to it, although frankly, he often puts me to sleep.

Do you use charts in trading?

I keep a daily chart. Generally I'm looking for things that other people are looking at also. Maybe a price chart is bottoming out, or there is some other recognizable pattern. If I see it, probably so does everyone else. For example, many traders are following a 200-day moving average on the stocks they trade. If a stock retraces to this average, many people are going to look to get long believing this will be a support area. I may try to buy here for a short bounce. I also look at 50-day moving averages for the same reason. I also use Japanese candlesticks. Western bar charts are almost useless to me. Candlesticks provide much more information that can be seen at a glance, particularly whether buyers or sellers are in there. With candlesticks, I look for the obvious reversals such as shooting starts, hammers, engulfing patterns, and so on. I find these patterns very useful. If I'm trading Internet stocks, I will have a one- or two-minute chart of the Internet index up. I find this a very useful tool. If I am trading the semiconductor stocks, then I will have the semiconductor index up. Generally, whatever stocks I am trading, I will follow the index of that industry on a short-term chart. I pay very close attention to short-term charts.

Tell me what your screen actually looks like.

I usually have three or four NASDAQ Level II boxes. I also keep all the stocks in the industry that I am trading on a quote screen. Right now I am trading mostly the Internet stocks so I will have about 30 or 40 stocks up there. I keep the one-minute index chart up and also a one-minute S&P futures chart. I used to pay a lot more attention to the S&P futures but find I don't watch this as much any more. I don't care what the general market is doing such as the Dow unless it affects what I am trading which is rarely the case. The Internet stocks can move as a group with or against the general market so some of these broader stock indices are not going to be helpful.

How much technical analysis do you do?

I don't look at stochastics, relative strength, or any oscillators. Trendlines are sometimes useful, and I use candlestick charting. Generally, I don't look at any advanced charting. Many people use these techniques, I know, but for me, it's a waste of time. The most important piece of information is where the stock is trading now. My old boss use to say, forget everything else, just trade the tape. He was right!

What execution system are you using?

I've used everyone's system at one point. Without naming the current system I use, I use it because it's a fast keyboard drive order-routing system. I'm not a proponent of point and click, which I find too slow. I'm faster at a keyboard than with a mouse. By the time I move that little arrow to the market maker I want to hit, he's already gone. It's too slow for my type of trading.

Do you trade SOES?

No.

Did you ever trade SOES or do you have an opinion about it?

It's a great marketing tool but I'm not sure how practical it is. For example, you can only trade the same stock once every five minutes with it. To me that's too limiting. Also, with all the new ECNs trading, the market is fairly liquid. To be honest, I've never traded SOES, so I can't really say.

What is your average percentage winning days?

I'm not really sure, but it's pretty high. Focus and discipline have been my most helpful tools.

During the last 12 months, how many losing weeks did you have?

Probably none. I consider myself an extremely conservative trader but I am consistently profitable. I don't have the $100,000 winning months, but I don't have the $10,000 losing months either.

Can you trade larger sizes than you do and make more money or have you reached a size constraint or ceiling on how much size you can trade?

I'm completely comfortable trading the sizes I do. I feel I have my risk completely managed. That I don't trade larger is probably a personal decision rather than a market imposed constraint on available liquidity. I may be doing other things during the day that take away my attention so I don't want to have positions that are too large to easily manage or get out of. I do run an office and am available to traders. My door is always open. I am involved in a firm that a friend of mine, Tom Daley, and I started in 1998, that is developing a new execution software system called TradeAnywhere, and this can take up a lot of my time. I'm also a fund raiser for the Leukemia Society and Children's Hospital. For these reasons, I prefer to keep my risks on trades to a minimum by not increasing my size.

What are you looking forward to doing in the future? Are you planning to remain a trader or do you have something else in mind?

I find I'm getting burnt out trading right now. Within a year, I may give it up. I've been trading in one form or another for 17 years. As I mentioned, I've started a software firm building an execution system that I believe will have a chance to become the next E*Trade. Something like that takes up an enormous amount of my time and if it works, I probably will make more that way than I can as a trader. Trading is how I make a living right now and pay my bills.

Are you losing your passion for trading?

I love what I'm doing. It's great to be right and the reward is making money but I feel I'm ready to move on to another level. I want to take my talents somewhere else for a while. I'm very passionate about the new execution system we are developing. It's also great fun and I like working with these people. I'll always love trading, but I'm ready to move on. You know, when I first moved to Denver it probably took me a year to calm down from the intensity of trading on the Chicago Stock Exchange. If I missed a trade when I was home, I would end up yelling at my kids. In Colorado I gradually did calm down and began to take time off and relax for the first time in many years; I'm where I want to be. I take vacations. In most years now, I take the entire month of June off. Now I can walk away from trading and not worry about missing that next good trade.

Do you think you can train someone to become a successful trader or must they have some innate skills that just cannot be taught?

I think people can be taught. But it is not easy. Probably people's emotions are the most difficult thing to deal with. I can't tell you how many keyboards I've smashed or phones I've tossed because my emotions got the best of me. Usually it's because of something I've done that is just stupid or silly. The hard thing to teach people is that they just have to be mechanical when they make a trade. It's really about discipline, especially how to get out of a trade. For me there are three levels of discipline: knowing when not to trade; when to get out of a losing trade; and when to exit a winning trade. The most difficult aspect of discipline, for me at least, is knowing when not to trade.

How do you know when not to trade?

When I start trading in the morning and find myself profitable and there comes a point when I just am not making money anymore on trades, I just stop trading. Most people, I think, keep trading and can't stop. This is over-trading. Soon they find that they are down for the day and then they increase the size they are trading just to make back what they've lost. Most of the time they lose more. They don't have the discipline to stop trading earlier in the day when they were profitable.

Do you have any specific rules that prevent you from trading during the day?

If my first five or six trades during the morning are not profitable, then I'm done for the day. Remember, my most profitable time is in the morning, and if I can't make money right from the start, then I'm done. This isn't my day and I'll come back tomorrow. If I come in thinking this is going to be an extremely profitable day for one reason or another, then those are the days I'm going to get hammered. I try to come in completely devoid of any opinions about the market and any emotion.

Do you stop trading during the month if you lose a certain amount or percentage of money?

No.

Do you have a profit target you try to reach during the month?

I have no daily or monthly targets. If I'm up a few hundred or thousand for the day then I may quit at that point. I figure at that rate I'll be making five to ten thousand a week. And that's okay with me.

Is there anything you would like to mention?

I like where I've been in my life and I like where I am now. I love this industry. It's fun, fast moving, and exciting. People should be cautious about trading in the new environment, but that's always been true whenever people strike out in a new venture. New traders are not the only ones who are prone to act emotionally. In my opinion, securities regulators are acting almost irrationally in their charge to save people their money. It is a free country. This is probably no different than the Gold Rush of the 1840s. If people are going to lose their money they will find a way, whether by going to a gambling casino or opening up a restaurant.

Anything else?

One of the things that helped me to succeed was not having family pressures outside of trading. I have a wife who is incredibly supportive. She's allowed me to pursue my career without any conditions set on me. I didn't have pressure from home. Unfortunately, a lot of people don't have that support. Their families may tell them they are just chasing rainbows and this will take its toll on a trader's self-esteem and confidence, sometimes resulting in a trader failing. I do give a lot of credit for my success to my wife for her support.

chapter 12

Jack Rosovsky

Jack Rosovsky is a very successful trader who trades almost exclusively listed stocks. Remarkable for a beginning trader, Jack never lost more than $600 on his original account. But even after three years of consistent profits, without a losing month other than his first, he believes that he is still growing as a trader.

Jack is 25 years old and was born in Kharkov, Ukraine, where his father was an engineer and his mother was trained as a chemist. In 1987 his family migrated to the United States to escape anti-Semitism and find a better life. His family settled in Boston where he finished high school. He then attended Bentley College. He worked full time at night to support himself in college, where he obtained a degree in finance in 1996. Upon graduating from college, he took a job as a financial planner in the tax department of a financial planning firm in Boston. Dissatisfied after five months, he quit this job and began to look for something else to do.

When did you first become interested in stocks?

While still in high school, I discovered the financial shows on CNBC quite by accident. At first I had no clue what they were talking about but enjoyed the way they were juggling numbers and charts. I also realized that the stock market is one powerful thing behind all those numbers and that a lot of people make good money playing it. That was really fascinating. This was the reason I entered Bentley College to study finance. However, even after graduating I was very far from trading yet. My first job at the financial planning firm was brief. After I quit I was looking at job listings through my college service and found one that was looking for stock traders. That ad struck me as something I always wanted to try.

The job was with a firm in New York City, a long way from Boston. But I knew that it could be my chance, so I drove from Boston to New York for an interview. It wasn't a formal interview, but someone went over what they did there and how the firm worked. But what I was able to see there was that the atmosphere of the trading floor was like I used to enjoy seeing so much on CNBC. I also realized that all trading decisions as well as all the risks and rewards would be mine. I had no clue what trading was all about. But I knew immediately that I wanted to work there.

Before I moved to New York, I asked some of my college professors if they heard of something called day trading. One professor had been an options trader in Chicago, and he told me it was a great career but 90 percent of the people didn't make it. He also warned me that firms are looking for young traders like me just to make commissions. That didn't scare me and in September 1997, I moved to New York to trade.

How much did you start with?

$15,000. That was pretty much all my life savings. I borrowed money to live on because all my money went into my account. It was scary. My friends and family were worried for me so I promised them and myself that if I lost $5,000, I would quit.

Did you receive any training before you started?

Not really. I was put in a room with about eight other new traders and I watched how they traded. One trader who later became my friend, told me what to do and what not to do, although he wasn't making any money himself at the time. He advised me not to trade stocks like IBM and CCI, because it took a long time to get filled. I believe he saved me several thousand dollars. He had a great sense of humor and kept everyone smiling and laughing even though most people seemed to be losing money.

My fellow rookie-traders and I shared our limited knowledge and experiences trying to help each other. My friend had some expertise in technical analysis and shared it with us. Our triumphs were very modest at best, but one day when the market dropped 500 points we managed to make about $1,000 each. It was our best day to date and got my account positive. This camaraderie kept me going through that difficult period when I started to trade.

And then I saw a guy sitting not far from me who was trading nonstop from 9:30 to 4:00. That was Lee Hsu. Despite being very busy, Lee let me watch him trade, and took time to give me my first trading lessons. He would go over news stories and tell me which stocks to watch for the day. I was just getting pieces of information, but every single bit of it was priceless for me because I literally knew nothing. From that point forward, Lee became a friend and a mentor to me.

Did you read anything that helped you?

I started studying technical analysis by reading Edwards and Magee's *Technical Analysis of Stock Trends* which was very useful. I also read *Reminiscences of a Stock Operator* by Edward Lefevre.

Also, the trading firm I was at gave out a booklet with trading rules. I pretty much remember all these rules in my head and apply them to different situations. They were great rules. A lot of people found them funny, but I found them useful.

Like what?

When in doubt, get out. Never average down. Feed the ducks when they're quacking.

What does that last one mean?

If you're in a stock with a profit, sell it when people still want to buy it.

How did it go at first?

I traded very rarely. Maybe once or twice a day. Some days I didn't trade at all. I was very hard on myself not to lose money. If I showed a loss, I got out immediately. Sometimes my hand was shaking when I would do a trade. I didn't give a stock a chance to do anything. I often sold too soon and cut my profits. I was scared the stock would reverse. Still, I lost only $500 or $600 while I was starting to trade. My goal at the time was to learn and not to lose money.

Why do you think you were able to cut your losses when so many other people find this hard to do at first?

I was very disciplined. Someone told me that if you get into a stock, and it doesn't do what you expect it to do within 30 seconds, get out. Believe me, very often I was wrong. I would get out and then the stock ran a point! That made me feel a lot worse than losing a quarter of a point. That hurt me the most emotionally when I would get out for a small loss and the stock just ran. This still hurts even today. However, now I realize that in trading getting out of a stock too soon happens many times a day. I call it an occupational hazard.

I think in the beginning most people make the mistake of either trading too much or too little. My mistake was trading too little, but I tried to be very conservative. After four or five months, I was trading four or five times a day with 200 and 300 share positions. I would have traded only 100 share positions, except that part of the commission structure included a fixed cost.

Were commissions high at this firm?

I now think they were. I think that was the reason why I didn't trade more often. I was very unhappy with this and felt I could learn a lot quicker if I paid more per share but no ticket charges. At that time I didn't know whether the commissions were too high or too low because I didn't know about other day trading firms. Honestly, I felt like a blind kitten and didn't know any better than to search for other alternatives.

What kind of strategies were you evolving at that point?

At the beginning, it was very random. For example, for a while I would watch the moves on the S&P futures, and try to buy some stock that ran with it. A little bit later I started looking at technical analysis more. Every day after the market closed, I would use Bloomberg to search for stocks in an uptrend, with RSI greater than 95. I would also rank stocks by how close they were to a 52-week high. The closer the stock was to an annual high, the higher rating it got. I would put these stocks on my screen according to ranking. Selecting stocks that were strong in general, I believe, made my chances for success a lot better. That gave me confidence that the stock was being accumulated. That was the first time I realized that there was such a thing as market sentiment, that some stocks were in favor and some out of favor. It also made me realize that institutions were in a buying mood this day or week because of some economic number and selling mood other times. Before then, I did not consider that. I think it is very important to have a feeling for the market and the sentiment of the crowd.

How long were you in trades?

Minutes. I cut my losses short, but I also cut my profits short. I was probably more scared than I should have been. But I knew that I could not afford to lose money and pay commissions.

What kind of execution system did you use then?

Super-Dot. At this firm you could only trade listed stocks. Trading NASDAQ stocks was discouraged and you would have to call an order desk for unlisted stocks.

Why did you leave this firm?

When I started, the guy who interviewed me said I should give it six months. And that's what I decided to give myself, six months. At the end of that time, I had made about $4,000. I wasn't very happy with this result, but Lee encouraged me by saying that I did well, because most traders lose money in the beginning and I didn't. Another experienced trader said that if a trader breaks even in the first six months of his career he will become successful later on. These words of encouragement kept me going.

Still, I often doubted myself. I wondered whether what I was doing made sense. Was I wasting my time and should I find a real job that pays a salary? I was also pretty homesick for Boston. At the same time, my mentor Lee had become a role model for me, because if I could have become only a quarter as successful as he was, I would have been very happy. That also kept me trading.

After six months, I learned that there was another day trading firm in Boston and they charged a lot less than the firm I was at. They charged much less per share for listed stocks and no ticket charge but they did charge a monthly facilities fee. With their commission structure, I was very confident that I could make it. Besides, I was ecstatic to be able to go home.

The following week I started trading at this firm in Boston. That was in March 1998.

How did that go?

It went pretty well. I still traded only 300 shares but I traded more frequently. Obviously, that was my goal. I started making about $3,000 a month. It wasn't much but that summer my activity picked up and so did my profits. I started making five figures a month. I was very thrilled. There was a period when I couldn't make more than $1,000 on my best days, and then one day I made $3,500. At that point I knew I could make my living as a day trader. What's more, by that time I was already thinking like a trader and feeling like a trader and I knew there was no way back for me. I was the happiest person in the world. All my efforts and sacrifices had finally started paying off.

How do you account for the fact that you started to make more money at this time?

I think because of the better commission structure, I could keep more of the profit in the trade, and I was able to trade more frequently. Anything I liked I bought at this new firm, while at my first firm, I wouldn't do that because I was concerned about the commissions.

We also had the Asian currency crisis about this time. That helped because there was a lot of volatility. I was still very conservative though and didn't trade more than 500 shares.

The day I made $3,500 I traded Capital One Financial and the stock was weak. It opened down and was dropping. I got lucky and was able to sell it short. Most of the $3,500 was made on COF. However, I could have made a lot more. After I covered my position, the stock was halted and opened in a few hours a lot lower. On this day I wasn't upset about not making more because it was my record day, I thought life was great!

Was your style of trading changing, too?

Yes, I was paying more attention to technical analysis. It was very simple. I was identifying trends on a daily chart, like higher highs and higher lows, and believed that if it worked on a daily chart it should work on an intraday chart especially if you know what the general market is doing. In addition, resistance and support levels were very important to me. I concentrated more on resistance or breakout levels since I traded on the long side. The more logical or technical reasons I could think of, the more confident I felt about buying the stock.

What do you mean by breakouts?

If a stock hit a new 52-week high, I bought it. Technicians consider a stock making a new 52-week high very bullish, if it breaks out on strong volume. Or if a stock today is trading higher than the high yesterday, and yesterday was a breakout level, I would buy it. It was very basic technical analysis, I took patterns from long-term charts and incorporated them into intraday charts.

Recently, there's a lot more false breakouts than when I first started to trade. That's probably because there are more day traders. Three years ago, I may have made money on seven out of ten breakouts, and now I may make money only in three out of ten.

I've found that if you do the same thing over and over, eventually it's not going to work. You have to change something. If you are a trend follower on breakouts, you may have to become a contrarian. I'm always looking for different strategies when previous ones no longer work. There are many strategies that I wouldn't consider before that I would now.

Like what?

Before I would never buy a stock that was down on the day. Now I'll do that. I have noticed that stocks that were down a point or two finished up positive on the day. That's a pretty good move if you can catch it. I think this strategy has more risk, but if you can identify the right stocks, the rewards are there as well. Unfortunately these reversals don't happen very often, especially in today's choppy market.

How do you handle losses now?

I am still very hard on myself about this. Sometimes I think it's my own stupidity for getting into a trade when I know I shouldn't. For example, take this summer (2000), it's been a very choppy market. I made $6,000 last month, but it was very hard. The same thing was true last summer. My summer income was only about 5 percent of my yearly income. Next summer I'm going to take a vacation.

The only positive thing about trading a choppy market is that it forces me to look at new things and new strategies. I'm still learning and consider myself a beginner in a trading career.

Do you have a fixed stop loss point?

No. If a stock doesn't do what I expect it to do, I will still hold it. If it holds a support level, I don't see a reason to sell it. If it breaks support, I'd sell it. I used to be a lot more disciplined than I am now. Right now, I'll sometimes let the stock go a quarter to a half against me but only if it's at some kind of support level.

Has this made you more successful?

Overall I think I've made more money over time, but that's because I've increased my size and trade more often and not because

I've let my losses run an extra quarter point against me. I very rarely take a half point loss actually. Losing more than a quarter of a point makes me think I'm not doing my job correctly. Sometimes this happens because there are no bids around. That happens more often than I want during choppy markets.

Because you trade listed stocks, do you pay particular attention to what the specialist is trying to do?

Of course. I look at time and sales and where the trades are taking place relative to the bids and offers. For example if the stock is ¼ bid, offered at ½, and I saw prints taking place at ⁷⁄₁₆, that might mean that the specialist is a seller or there is some other large seller. I would have to enter a market order and see where I would get filled to confirm this. If I got filled at ⁷⁄₁₆ this is probably bearish, but if I got filled at ½, then the seller is not there any longer or stepped back for a while.

Big buyers or sellers will tip their hand. If I see a stock trading sizes of 1,000, 2,000, and 3,000, and then a quarter point higher I see 20,000 and 30,000 size blocks, then there are probably some major buyers. I used to be able to read this more clearly before there were as many day traders trading these stocks. Before, I had a much higher probability that I would be right in understanding these situations.

But the specialists do play games. Yesterday, I had my largest loss ever on a trade when I lost two points on MRX. It dropped this much on only 2,500 traded shares!

Do you use limit orders?

Most of my orders are market orders on both sides. I will only use a limit order if I have a gut feeling that I will get a bad fill.

Why did you come to Lexit Capital?

I was at my previous firm for two years, It's a great company. I don't think I would have ever left them if not for Lee Hsu, who had been my mentor since I began trading. He went to Lexit Capital in San Francisco and I decided to go along because I saw an opportunity to bring my trading skills to a new level. My goals were to increase my volume as well as profitability. I also wanted to learn to trade on NASDAQ. Lexit turned out to be a very good firm to trade at. However, recently I've moved back to Boston to be closer to my family.

How many months have you lost money since you started trading?

Except for the first month when I lost $500 or $600, I've been up every month in the last three years. Consistency has become my number one priority. I value it almost as high as making overall profit. I am very hard on myself when I have a losing day and having a losing month would be totally unacceptable.

What was your largest losing trade?

I don't remember my largest losing trade, but my worst day ever was when I lost $2,600. I just wasn't reading the market right that day. That loss did not make a dent in my account.

It is very difficult to make money when institutional investors aren't active because there is no movement or volatility. This gives the specialist an opportunity to mislead day traders about the real current supply-demand situation. From personal experience, this has lead me to buy the offer and sell on the bid. Obviously, one can't make any money trading this way and in those times I have lost the most.

What kind of strategies are you using now?

I'm using the same strategies, but I do larger size and more trades per day. I don't keep track of the number of trades I do, but my record volume was two million shares in one month. My number one goal is to be consistent and continue trading.

How do you find the stocks you are trading?

In the morning I look at the news for things like buyback announcements, upgrades-downgrades, and earnings surprises. If there is a news story out on a stock I feel more confident trading it. A great benefit to news is it provides liquidity. However, there are exceptions to this. Also I watch stocks I've been trading on the previous day and look to see if there is a follow-through today. I now use software that filters stocks according to the criteria input. There are many sources on the Internet now that are very useful.

Why do you only trade listed stocks?

I think because I started trading them when I began and over the years I've become comfortable with them. I think if everyone at my first firm had been trading NASDAQ stocks, today I would be trading them also.

I have looked at Level II and found it fascinating. I would love to learn to trade NASDAQ stocks and probably will in the near future. Obviously, one of the nice things trading NASDAQ is that you can get a quick execution in as little as one second, whereas on listed stocks, the execution is much longer.

What execution system are you using at Lexit?

Redi-Plus. It's a system from Spear, Leeds, and Kellogg, one of the leading specialist firms on the NYSE as well as a leader in market making on NASDAQ.

How do you determine where you take your profits?

When the stock stops going up I get out. Sometimes I look at a chart, and if it hasn't broken a trendline, I try not to get out right away or I may lighten up.

This is one of the toughest decisions I've had to make while trading. Sometimes the stock doesn't reverse but merely has a small pull back, yet I get out. Over the last year, I have become a lot more disciplined in this area. Another important aspect to note is that when holding several positions, it is difficult to make the best possible judgment on a particular position. That's why more mistakes happen here. When the stock goes against you, it's easy because you are clearly wrong, when you are showing a profit, greed comes into play. Sometimes you don't have enough time to evaluate the situation completely and rationally. One of the early rules I've learned about the market is your first reaction is usually the correct one. Obviously, this is another area I need to work on.

Do you trade more than one position at a time?

Oh, sure. It depends on what I see. If I see something I like I will buy it. The most I ever had was 12 positions on at one time. Some of these stocks are in the same industry.

How much attention do you pay to industry sector analysis?

If a stock in a sector is strong and the sector is strong also, it gives me more confidence to add to my position or to buy other stocks in that sector. Catching the sector rotations can be extremely profitable. This happens on a weekly basis as institutional investors take profits in one sector and enter another. Last year I was trading paper stocks frequently, such as Georgia Pacific and Weyerhauser. This year semi-conductors were very strong, and over the summer brokerage stocks were strong as well.

How long do you stay in your trades?

Not long enough probably. On average 10 minutes, sometimes a few minutes or a few hours.

Do you ever increase the size of your positions in a trade?

I never average down on a losing trade, but I will add to my position on profitable trades. Sometimes when I'm right and have a profit, a position looks a lot better than before. So there is even more reason to add to the position, plus the market might look stronger than before. So once again I have some confidence and reason to add to a position.

Do you take home positions overnight?

I haven't done that. However, I see some potential in using this tactic and currently I'm working on developing strategies to do that. It makes sense to hold positions overnight, either if you are having a good profit in a stock, or you think there is very little risk, and a big upside potential. Otherwise, it's not worth the risk and sleepless nights.

How do emotions come into play while trading?

People who know me say that I'm very impatient. It's not the best quality for a stock trader. In the beginning, I was concerned that lack of patience would impair my ability to trade, but luckily this hasn't had any impact on my trading.

One of the rules that I learned at my first firm was never to stay in a stock long enough to hate it. I really don't have emotions while trading, it's a job. But it's a job I love. There are times Sunday evenings when I can't wait to go to work the next morning. There's nothing else I'd rather do.

Do you ever feel run down as a trader?

Last summer. I was making money but not nearly as much as I usually do. Once again Lee's advice came in handy. He said that in a few months I would recall this debacle as a bad dream and he was right. This summer is no better than last year's but I feel a lot better. I guess that's what you call experience.

How often do you take vacations?

A couple of times a year. In the future, I will probably squeeze my vacation into the summertime and trade throughout the rest of the year.

Why do you think you're successful and so many others aren't?

In my personal experience I've seen many people who did not care about money. While learning they took unnecessary risks and got wiped out as a result. I couldn't afford to lose any money. I knew the statistics were against me. I took it seriously as a future career and a business. Cutting your losses is the key.

Do you think successful trading can be taught?

The principles can definitely be taught. But some people will develop from there and some people won't. I've trained a couple of people. One fellow became extremely successful. He was extremely determined and was very risk averse. He became very successful in a short period of time. I've come to realize, however, that a trader's gut feeling is just as important as knowledge of the basics. Obviously, it cannot be taught, but that's what makes the difference between a mediocre trader and a great one.

What does your trading screen look like?

I have two computers and four screens. On one computer I have market indices, such as the S&P, NASDAQ, futures, and cash, both as numbers and in five-minute chart form. I have two lists of stocks that I am watching that display the bids and offers. I feel very uncomfortable if I don't first look at the chart of the stock that I am going to trade, so I have a setup to bring up a daily and intraday chart for a stock. It gives me more confidence. On my second computer, I have my filter program and my execution software.

Do you look at the S&P futures?

From my early days in New York I know how important it is to watch S&P futures. I usually look at a five-minute futures chart, but I don't think it makes any difference whether it is a five- or ten-minute chart. I also like to watch the NASDAQ futures just to see how the two markets are correlated.

Why don't you trade larger size if you are successful with your strategies?

That's a question I ask myself all the time. I think I should. Last spring when the market was active, I traded 3,000 or 4,000 share blocks, but I'm not doing that size this summer. There are periods when my trading activity goes way down. I attribute that to the choppiness in the market or just the summer like we've had recently.

How often do you go short?

Not often. It is harder to get an up-tick on the stocks I want to short. But when I have shorted stocks recently, it has made a difference in giving me a total profit for the day.

Does that mean you don't make as much money when the market is selling off?

That's true. I still make money on down days though. I think it makes sense to be on the same side as the trend, but there are always many long opportunities. Of course, if the market is really bearish, I would try to find something on the short side.

Where do you want to be in your life in 10 years?

I would like to be married and have children. But aside from that there's very little I would rather do than trade. I think I would be bored doing anything else. I might want to manage money.

chapter 13

lessons of the master traders

The traders interviewed in this book are a remarkable group of people, not only in their profit success and the long-term consistency of that success, but in the mastering of their personalities in the service of success. Many will tell you that this last quality is the real key to their becoming superb traders.

You will search in vain, however, for any single style of trading that is simply "the best." Level II, momentum, scalping, technical analysis, swing trading, fundamental analysis, relative strength, arbitrage, and tape reading, are among the different styles and techniques these traders have used successfully. But not all traders use all methods, some use more than one method, and even traders who use similar methods, often apply them differently in practice. Moreover, traders who have developed distinct and particular techniques of trading are often also evaluating complex market conditions and sentiment before they make a trade. There is no simple "black box" set of rules to be applied mechanically, although there are certainly rules. But in the final analysis, there is a person who must make the decision weighing all factors. Mike McMahon probably put it best when he summarized all the reasons he would do a trade, and then noted that they are not the trigger to the trade, he is. Also, more than one trader noted that a trader should trade his or her personality. What may work for me, may not work for you, and vice versa.

Some traders have noted that their styles of trading have remained fairly constant over time, but many others have seen their styles develop and change as they have grown as traders. For most traders, there is probably both continuity and change in their styles, and some will admit that their styles are still changing. Will styles that have worked in the past always work? A note of caution is introduced by Tony Mariniello who believes that technical analysis, although effective in the past, may increasingly not work as more and more traders come to use it. He and other traders have noted that buying breakouts in particular has worked well in the past, but find increasingly these breakouts are often false and do not work. His response has been to search for new patterns that are just developing and to trade them successfully before too many others notice the same thing. There is always a danger in complacency with success. Nevertheless, successful traders are largely satisfied with their styles of trading and have high degrees of confidence in them although their techniques may sometimes change.

To a remarkable degree, the master traders agree on the core principles of good trading. The number one rule without question is to cut losses quickly. Joe Conti noted that he preferred not to use the term "cut losses," since a trader who has taken a three-point loss has still cut his loss to three points. He prefers to tell new traders always to take small losses. But what is a *small* loss? There is diversity in how this general principle is applied by each trader.

A number of traders believe that as soon as there is any loss in a position, that is the loss they are going to take, which might be called the "zero tolerance" approach to losses. The zero tolerance approach believes that a sixteenth, an eighth, or at most a quarter point loss is the only acceptable loss. If you believe a stock is going up and it doesn't, then get out immediately. The quicker you recognize that you are wrong, the better off you are.

Short sales might be a slight exception to this rule for some, since to initiate a short sale you must sell into some upward momentum because of the up-tick rule, which could carry your position into a slight loss before the market turns in your direction. Also, short sales may be more difficult to initiate since it does require an up-tick, and a trader may not wish to cover the short so quickly if he believes he cannot re-establish the short if the market does start to sell off. Some traders have noticed that they do have more trouble handling losses on short sales for these reasons.

As opposed to the zero tolerance approach to losses, some traders believe loss points should be set in relation to key support or resistance levels or some other reason why the trade was put on. Losses in these cases may be larger than a quarter point in many instances. Michael Reise notes that rather then use any specific fixed loss point, losses should be taken when the reason you made the trade is no longer valid. While this is very sound advice for all manners of taking a loss, it may best be implemented only by experienced traders. It may prove especially troubling for a new trader who has gotten into the trade for ill-defined reasons, and therefore it may not be clear when or why the trade is no longer valid, since the trade may not have been valid to do in the first place. For new traders, the best advice is probably never to take more than a small fixed loss, no matter what the reason you made the trade, and usually try to keep your losses even smaller than this.

Many successful traders also believe that losses should bear some relation to how much profit you expect in a trade. The minimum acceptable ratio here is one to one, but many believe that a profit/loss ratio of two, three, or four is actually what they are looking for. If you expect a trade to make two points, a half-point loss may be acceptable. Many traders recommending the zero tolerance approach to losses are very short-term scalpers or momentum traders, where losses must be kept extremely small since the profit objective on these types of trades is also very small.

Not a single successful trader believes that you should "double up" on a losing position by buying more shares as the position goes against you to lower your average price of entry. This is an insidiously deceptive technique since doubling up on losing positions will likely increase the probability of the trade becoming profitable which is perhaps why unwary traders use the technique. Stocks do jiggle up and down, and by lowering the cost basis of your position, you do make it more likely that the trade will be a winner. Having this happen will psychologically reinforce a trader repeating this technique.

But there is a hidden price to pay for using this technique and it is a steep one indeed. Although your percentage profitable trades may increase, the losses you suffer on the smaller percentage of losing trades will also increase, and much more sharply too. A trader who already has a half point loss on a hundred shares and then buys another hundred shares, only to have the price drop another half point, will experience a total loss of a point and a half. This is three times the amount of his loss had he taken the first loss at a half point. Doubling up on positions with losses always means there is a day of reckoning waiting to happen, which when it does, will produce one staggeringly large loss, sometimes enough to wipe out an entire account. Successful traders are not tempted by this bad practice.

There are various other techniques recommended for new traders to ensure they are able to keep losses small. An almost uniform recommendation is to begin small and start trading with only 100 or 200 share size trades. Since most successful traders believe that new traders will inevitably lose some money when they begin, there is no point in magnifying these losses with larger trade sizes. New traders characteristically believe naively that if a trade is thought to be good, then it makes sense to do as much as possible. Do not be tempted to do this, even if it means paying more per share in commissions, until you are able to show a consistent record of profitability. As noted in the chapter on the statistics of trader profitability, this was probably the most important reason why new traders lost money in the Johnson Report study.

Another recommended technique for new traders is to begin by only trading relatively stable and safe stocks that have great liquidity and do not wildly move in price. You may not make much, but you probably won't lose much either. Microsoft is considered the prime example of a safe stock to trade. Avoid high-flying Internet stocks, IPOs, and stocks over a hundred dollars, until you know what you are doing with much greater experience. There is usually a temptation for new traders to trade these stocks since the lure of high profits is strong. Avoid the temptation and follow the suggestions of experienced traders.

Money management for many of the successful traders interviewed seemed to consist in what investment vehicle outside the market they should put their profits into. For traders who rarely have a losing month, this is perhaps not surprising. Several, however, did use some simple money management techniques on a short-term basis. Several traders noted that if they are experiencing a series of losing trades during the time of day they should be making money they will stop trading for the day. Mike McMahon provided the most explicit rule in stopping trading for the day if he lost 1 percent of his trading capital. Several traders will also stop trading for at least a short while, or will cut back on the number or size of their trades, if they experience a series of losing days. Other techniques for avoiding losses are recommended in some of the interviews and should be read carefully.

Closely following the rule to keep losses small is the universal recommendation to have discipline. Over and over again, successful traders mention that following discipline is the absolute key to their success. Discipline means following the rules. It will not help you if you know the rules, but cannot follow them. Most successful traders believe that there are people who cannot learn to trade successfully, and the primary reason is that they do not have discipline. But how can discipline be achieved and how can it be maintained?

There are apparently some people who just do not have discipline, and if they do not already have it, they are, unfortunately, unlikely to acquire it trading. Having discipline in trading, means you have shown at least some discipline elsewhere in you life. But if you have some discipline, then you probably can improve it.

Joe Conti believes the best way to get discipline is to suffer a large and very painful loss early in trading. After that point, you either get it or you don't, and that will determine the course of your trading career. Although we may not wish to admit it, there is probably much truth in this school-of-hard-knocks observation.

Two personal characteristics are closely related to discipline and if you can achieve them, you probably will be disciplined. A number of traders describe discipline as having no ego while trading or being able to trade mechanically without emotion. This approach, although difficult to achieve, is undoubtedly correct, for trading is an emotionally buffeting experiences. A trader's emotions can range from uncertainty, greed, hope, happiness, ecstasy, surprise, anxiety, fear, frustration, anger, stubbornness, apathy, self-loathing, revenge, regret, insecurity, and then back to uncertainty. All in two minutes. In the face of this emotional rollercoaster, discipline is likely to be thrown out the window somewhere along the way. Being ego-less certainly helps.

Related to this is being humble and having the ability to admit you are wrong without difficulty. If you have something to prove to yourself about how correct, perfect, or worthy you are, you are going to be drawn into an emotional war with the market that you will probably not win. The stock market can be a very expensive therapist. Tony Mariniello notes that he's been 100 percent *wrong* in his opinions about the market for the last three years, yet he hasn't had a losing week in that period either.

Related to controlling your emotions and maintaining equilibrium is having an untroubled family or personal life outside trading. If your family does not support what you are doing or if you are worried about paying the bills to support your family, these concerns will enter into your trading, and put great pressure on you to break discipline. Several successful traders have noted that their family's support has been very important to them in being in the proper frame of mind to trade well. Unfortunately, if a new trader has such outside concerns, there may not be much he or she can do about it, except perhaps recognize that he is prone to some outside emotional pressures and consciously attempt to neutralize them.

Self-confidence and a belief in themselves is a theme that runs through many trader interviews about how they were able to persevere in the face of early adversity and maintain discipline. As they became more successful, self-confidence becomes a self-perpetuating feeling. But how can new traders have self-confidence if they haven't yet been tested by the market? Many successful traders seem to bring this characteristic with them from their life outside the market. Some successful traders found a mentor or role model who could lend needed support at times. Mike McMahon believes some degree of self-confidence can be built for new traders using a modest but strict goal-setting program.

Emotions and discipline are extremely important for a new trader and may well spell the difference between success and failure. One universally shared feeling about trading was held by all successful traders interviewed, and that was that trading is fun. All show a passion about their work, which somehow makes it seem not like work. They enjoy trading immensely and are doing exactly what they want in life. More than a few traders noted that they cannot wait for the weekend to be over so they can start trading again on Monday. New traders should early on be able to see whether they have some of these feelings, and if they do, this should bolster their self-confidence. If you feel miserable and perpetually anxious while trading, you may wish to reconsider whether trading is something for you.

Feeling passionate about trading and enjoying it, however, does not mean that successful traders do not feel some tendency toward burnout after trading for many years. Most believe regular vacations are important, but many have not taken vacations for fear that they will miss good trading opportunities, or if they have taken them, find themselves watching the market anyway. Many traders report that they are compulsive people, and there is a point beyond which fun and passion can subtly shade into an addictive quality.

About half of the successful traders interviewed said that they so fully enjoyed trading that they intended to be trading 10 years from now. But many others said that while they would likely stay in the financial industry, they did not want to be trading so actively and might like to do more investing in stocks rather than trading. Some said they didn't know what they wanted to do that far in the future and some wanted to retire.

Traders commonly report that they believe they give something back to society by their work, and economists would agree with them in the liquidity and price discovery services they give to the market. Also, belying the image often portrayed in the media about day traders as ruthless and self-absorbed people, the successful traders interviewed here show a great deal of concern for other people, both in their willingness to help other traders succeed, but also in the many charitable activities that they are involved with. These traders are not only successful, they are productive members of society and have great compassion for others. There can be little doubt that master traders are truly outstanding people in many dimensions.

The master traders all show the hallmarks of good trading. Taking small losses, having discipline, and controlling emotions are perhaps the most important virtues of a good trader, but there are many other similarities and differences among successful traders. The lessons of the master traders are best learned by reading their own words.

glossary

bid   A price at which someone is willing to buy a stock.

bid-offer spread   The absolute difference between the best bid and lowest offer.

call   An option contract that gives the owner (long holder) of the call the right but not the obligation to buy a stock at a specified price, known as the strike price, within a specified period of time. The person who sold the call is short the call and known as the writer.

down-tick   A stock transaction that occurs at a price that is lower than the immediately preceding price.

ECN   Electronic Communications Network. An electronic posting system for bids and offers on NASDAQ.

fill   An executed stock order.

futures   A standardized forward contract that specifies a future settlement date for delivery of a commodity, or the cash settlement of the contract in lieu of delivery for a stock index.

INCA   The Instinet ECN on Level II.

inside market   The highest bid and lowest offer for a stock. Also known as the best bid and offer (BBO).

island   The Island ECN.

Level II   The electronic display of bids and offers on a NASDAQ stock showing bids and offers on the inside and outside markets. Level I shows only the best bid and offer. Level III is the screen available only to market makers.

listed stock   Stocks that are on the New York Stock Exchange, the American Stock Exchange, or one of the regional stock exchanges, such as Philadelphia, Chicago, or Pacific Coast. Listed stocks must satisfy minimum requirements, set by the exchange.

market maker   A broker-dealer who posts bids and offers on NASDAQ.

margin   Money that is borrowed from a broker to purchase a stock. Margin requirements are set by the Federal Reserve Bank, and currently require that retail customers borrow no more than 50 percent in margin to purchase or short a stock.

NASD   National Association of Securities Dealers. The regulatory body for broker-dealers, and the owner of NASDAQ.

NASDAQ   National Association of Securities Dealers Automated Quotation System. The electronic market place for unlisted stocks, sometimes known as the over-the-counter (OTC) market. There are approximately 4,000 stocks on NASDAQ.

NYSE   New York Stock Exchange.

offer   A price at which someone is willing to sell a stock.

outside market   Bids and offers outside the best bid and offer.

over-the-counter market (OTC)   The stock exchange for unlisted stocks.

points   A point is one dollar per share and is used as a measure of profit or movement in a stock.

put   An option contact that gives the owner (long holder) of the put the right but not the obligation to sell a stock at a specified price, known as the strike price, within a specified period of time. The person who sold the put is short the put and known as the writer.

refreshes   Market maker who is filled for his shown quantity and then bids for or offers more shares at the same price.

SEC   The U.S. Securities and Exchange Commission. The regulatory body overseeing the securities markets and trading in all its aspect.

SelectNet   An electronic routing of orders on NASDAQ by broadcasting to market makers as a group or preferencing a market maker individually.

Series 7   The SEC registration license for registered representatives, or retail stock brokers. Also a requirement for members of proprietary trading firms that are members of listed stock exchanges, even though they may have no contact with public customers.

short sale   The sale of a stock that the seller does not own, but must borrow to delivery to the purchaser. Stocks must be sold according to the up-tick rule.

SOES   Small Order Execution System. The order execution route for retail investors on NASDAQ Level II that requires market makers to electronically fill an order received by SOES if certain requirements are met.

SPDR   Standard and Poor's Drawing Rights, also known as the "Spiders." The basket of stocks in the Standard and Poor's 500 stock index which can be traded as a single instrument.

specialist   On listed exchanges such as the New York Stock Exchange, there is only one official market maker known as the specialist.

super-DOT   Super Designated Order Turnaround. The electronic transmission and report of retail orders to and from the floor of the New York Stock Exchange. Super-DOT is not an electronic automatic execution system.

teenie   A sixteenth of a dollar (six and a quarter cents).

time and sales   The scrolling list of sequentially executed trades by price and quantity.

unlisted stock   Stock traded on the over-the-counter or NAS-DAQ market.

up-tick   A stock transaction that is at a price higher than the immediately preceding price.

up-tick rule   The SEC rule that requires that a short sales take place on a up-tick, or a zero-plus tick.